Lecture Notes of the Institute for Computer Sciences, Social Informatics and Telecommunications Engineering 368

More information about this series at http://www.springer.com/series/8197

Hongbo Jiang · Hongyi Wu ·
Fanzi Zeng (Eds.)

Edge Computing and IoT: Systems, Management and Security

First EAI International Conference, ICECI 2020
Virtual Event, November 6, 2020
Proceedings

 Springer

Editors
Hongbo Jiang 🆔
Hunan University
Hunan, China

Hongyi Wu
Old Dominion University
Norfolk, VA, USA

Fanzi Zeng
Hunan University
Changsha, China

ISSN 1867-8211   ISSN 1867-822X   (electronic)
Lecture Notes of the Institute for Computer Sciences, Social Informatics
and Telecommunications Engineering
ISBN 978-3-030-73428-2   ISBN 978-3-030-73429-9   (eBook)
https://doi.org/10.1007/978-3-030-73429-9

This Springer imprint is published by the registered company Springer Nature Switzerland AG
The registered company address is: Gewerbestrasse 11, 6330 Cham, Switzerland

Preface

We are delighted to introduce the proceedings of the 1st edition of the European Alliance for Innovation (EAI) International Conference on Edge Computing and IoT: Systems, Management and Security (ICECI 2020). This new conference, which we hope will become part of a prestigious and long-running series, aims to bring together technical experts and researchers from academia and industry from all around the world to discuss the emerging technologies of edge computing and the Internet of Things (IoT). ICECI 2020 was scheduled to take place in Changsha, China, but due to the ongoing COVID-19 pandemic the organizers instead opted for a virtual conference, which was held via a live stream on November 6, 2020.

The technical program of ICECI 2020 consisted of 18 full papers. All of the selected papers were presented during online sessions as part of the main conference. Aside from the high-quality technical paper presentations, the technical program also featured two keynote speeches: Prof. Xuemin (Sherman) Shen from the University of Waterloo, Canada, discussed the use of reinforcement learning for resource management in Space-Air-Ground (SAG) Integrated Vehicular Networks, whilst Prof. Schahram Dustdar from the Vienna University of Technology provided insights into the emerging field of edge intelligence.

ICECI 2020 would not have been possible without the engagement of the Steering Chair, Imrich Chlamtac, and the General Chair, Dr. Hongbo Jiang, which was essential for the success of the conference. We sincerely appreciate their constant support and guidance. It was also a great pleasure to work with such an excellent Organizing Committee; we are grateful for their hard work in coordinating and supporting the conference. We would like to thank the Technical Program Committee for all their efforts in completing the peer reviews of the technical papers and putting together such a high-quality technical program. We are also grateful to the Conference Managers for their support and to all the authors who submitted their papers to ICECI 2020.

We strongly believe that this conference provides a good forum for all researcher, developers and practitioners to discuss all aspects of science and technology that are relevant to edge computing and IoT. We also expect that the future editions of ICECI will be as successful and stimulating as the inaugural conference, as indicated by the contributions presented in this volume.

April 2021

Hongyi Wu
Fanzi Zeng
Sheng Xiao

Conference Organization

Steering Committee

Imrich Chlamtac   University of Trento, Italy

Organizing Committee

General Chair

Hongbo Jiang   Hunan University, China

Technical Program Committee Co-chairs

Hongyi Wu   Old Dominion University, USA
Fanzi Zeng   Hunan University, China
Sheng Xiao   Hunan University, China

Sponsorship and Exhibit Chair

Siwang Zhou   Hunan University, China

Local Chairs

Huigui Rong   Hunan University, China
Hanling Zhang   Hunan University, China
Wenjuan Tang   Hunan University, China

Workshops Chair

Zhibo Wang   Wuhan University, China

Publicity and Social Media Chair

Zhu Xiao   Hunan University, China

Publications Chair

Daibo Liu   Hunan University, China

Web Chairs

Ping Zhao   Donghua University, China
Yang Xu   Hunan University, China

Technical Program Committee

Zhufang Kuang	Central South University of Forestry and Technology, China
Weijin Jiang	Hunan Unversity of Technology and Business, China
Rongyang Zhao	Beibu Gulf University, China
Lang Li	Hengyang Normal University, China
Luda Wang	Xiangnan University, China
Hai Wang	Northwest University, China
Nan Jiang	East China Jiaotong University, China
Xiao Hui Yang	Hebei University, China
Kun Xie	Hunan University, China
Min He	Yunnan University, China
Jumin Zhao	Taiyuan University of Technology, China
Yuan Wu	Zhejiang University of Technology, China
Peidong Zhu	National University of Defense Technology, China
Jun Wu	Yangzhou University, China
Huan Zhou	China Three Gorges University, China
Jie Ren	Shaanxi Normal University, China
Jianhang Liu	China University of Petroleum, China
Na Fan	Chang'an University, China
Xiaonan Wang	Nanjing University of Science and Technology, China

Contents

Internet of Things

Cloud-Edge Computing

Energy Efficient Service Composition with Delay Guarantee in a Cloud-Edge System

Quan Fang[1](✉), Menghan Xu[1], Hao Li[2], Jun Yu[3], Xin Li[2],
and Zhuzhong Qian[4]

[1] Infomation and Telecommunication Branch,
State Grid Jiangsu Electric Power Co., Ltd., Nanjing, China
[2] College of Computer Science and Technology,
Nanjing University of Aeronautics and Astronautics, Nanjing, China
{lh97,lics}@nuaa.edu.cn
[3] Nari Group Corporation, Nanjing, China
yujun@sgepri.sgcc.com.cn
[4] Department of Computer Science and Technology,
Nanjing University, Nanjing, China
qzz@nju.edu.cn

Abstract. In a cloud-edge system, mobile users submit comprehensive service requests, on-the-fly service composition to orchestrate service components from different edge nodes is a promising way to achieve a quick response to these requests. Since several mobile applications consume large amount of energy during waiting for the responses, it is critical to achieve less service delay for energy saving as well as improve QoE (Quality of Experience). However, the service completion time in an edge is quite unstable, which increases the overall response time of the composite service. This paper argues that we may accelerate services through service clone via different edges, so that we can guarantee the overall response time of the composite service. And since the data fetch is also time consuming, we propose an effective data-aware service composition algorithm via service cloning to minimize the overall response time. We implement the algorithm and evaluate the performance with extensive simulations. The simulation results show that the proposed algorithm has a good performance improvement on service delay and energy consumption reduction, compared to the traditional algorithms.

Keywords: Cloud-edge system · Edge computing · Energy efficient · Service composition · QoS

1 Introduction

With the rapid development of the Internet of Things (IoT) and wireless communication technology, the intelligent era of the Internet of Everything is accelerating, with which the data volume grows quickly [1]. This situation poses a huge challenge to the currently widely used cloud computing models [2–4]. Although

H. Jiang et al. (Eds.): ICECI 2020, LNICST 368, pp. 3–14, 2021.
https://doi.org/10.1007/978-3-030-73429-9_1

the traditional cloud data center can provide powerful data analysis capability, the large volume of data transmission from mobile users to far away data center results in long service delay. In the meantime, mobile devices are energy-aware, and long service delay actually significantly increases the energy consumption, since most applications consume energy during waiting for the response [5]. Deploying services on the edges nearby is a promising way to reduce the service delay, and it also reduces the waiting time of applications on mobile devices. Thus, edge computing actually reduces the energy consumption via shorten the service delay.

In a cloud-edge system, many edges are resource-limited and only suitable for running certain service components. To achieve a comprehensive requirement, several service components need to be composed into a composite service. When a user's request is submitted to an edge via a mobile device, the edge will be in charge of this request and generate a composite service based on the predefined business logic to achieve the composite service [6]. In the running time, the edge orchestrates the composite service and coordinates involved edges to correctly proceed the data and return the final results to mobile users.

Since the resource limitation, edges are usually unstable. When the workload grows, the response time of edge increases, or even could not get response [7]. Thus, cloning service requests to more than one edge and could get response with the earliest one, through which we may guarantee the service response time in an uncertain environment. On the other hand, several services are data-intensive, thus, the service response time is also closely related to data transmission delay. The data transmission includes both data transfer among service components and the other required data that needed during the processing. How to choose suitable service components to construct an effective service path on-the-fly is a non-trivial resource scheduling problem.

With the rise of cloud-edge system, researchers have proposed a variety of service selection methods to support on-demand service composition. However, they assume that the network resources are over-provisioned and do not consider the use of these resources when making quality-aware service composition decisions [8,9]. In [10], the authors proposed a collaborative filtering-based service recommendation method applied in the mobile edge computing environment and performing QoS prediction based on user mobility. This method first calculates the similarity of users or edge servers and selects the k-nearest neighbours to predict service QoS, and then performs service recommendation. Reference [11] studied the task allocation problem of reducing service delay in cloud edge systems. The authors used W-DAG (Weighted Directed Acyclic Graph) to model data-intensive services or business logic, and analyzed the tasks that constitute integrated services.

In this paper, we investigate on-line service composition problem in a cloud-edge system. We try to minimize the overall composite service response time to reduce the energy consumption of mobile devices. Our main idea is to clone some key service components and construct more than one service path to guarantee the response time, with limited clone budget. And since the data fetch is also time and resource consuming, we also design a data-aware service selection strategy to further accelerate the composite service.

The main contributions are as follows:

- Model and formalize the service composition problem in a cloud-edge system.
- An energy efficient data-aware service composition algorithm is proposed to minimize the overall response time via service components cloning.
- Extensive simulations show that the proposed service composition algorithm can achieve a good performance in reducing response time, compared with the stochastic algorithm and the greedy algorithm.

This paper is organized as follows. Section 2 presents the system model and formalizes the service composition problem and Sect. 3 is the energy efficient service composition algorithm. We evaluate the performance of the algorithm in Sect. 4. Finally, Sect. 5 concludes this paper.

2   Problem Statement

For a typical cloud-edge system, it consists of terminal layer, edge computing layer and cloud computing layer [12–14], as shown in Fig. 1. There always be one cloud data center (DC) and multiple edge nodes (EN) in the cloud-edge system. Also, it is feasible to perform inter-layer and cross-layer communication through the network for each layer.

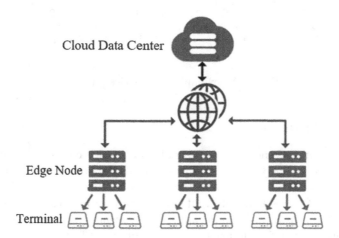

Fig. 1. Cloud-edge system.

To accelerate the service response and reduce energy consumption, some service component should be deployed on the edge, since the edge is close to the mobile users who submit the service requests. However, the edge nodes have limited resource and many service components must be placed on cloud data center due to the security issues.

To achieve a comprehensive service request, it is necessary to select some service components to construct a composite service. The classical method is to select some of the best service components with minimized service delay. However, it is challenging to construct the service path due to the uncertainty of edges, which may get unexpected long service delay.

In this paper, we aim to accelerate the service response by selecting more service components, which can generate more service paths. Thus, we can get the quick service response with high probability since any service path could response the service request. But select more service components means more computing and communication resources, hence, we need to investigate how to select the service components in a cloud-edge system with quantitative limitation due to budget constraint.

2.1   Service Path

We use the service path to represent the construction of a composite service, represented by F_i. An example of a service path is shown in Fig. 2. This composite service requires 4 service components. For each service component, several duplicated instances may be deployed in different edges in a cloud-edge system. Actually, what we need to do is to select a set of service component instances to achieve the service response. In the Fig. 2, the number above the service component indicates the number instance of the service component.

Fig. 2. An example of a service path.

2.2   Service Instance

The service instance is the service entity of each service component, represented by $s = <pos, ra, o, e>$, which is described by 4 attributes: *pos* represents the location of the service instance, and there are two options (DC/EN); *ra* represents the ratio of the amount of input and output data of the service instance, that is, $ra = amount_{output}/amount_{intput}$; *o* represents the time that the service instance spends processing unit data; *e* represents the effectiveness of the service (0/1), whether it is available or not. The relationship between the settings of *o* and *e* and the location of this instance is shown in Table 1. $mEN(s)$ in the table indicates the maximum number of service instances that can be selected on the node where service instance *s* is located. $pEN(s)$ represents the number of selected services currently owned by the node where the service instance *s* is located.

Table 1. Setting of o and e

	DC	EN
o	C_0	$N_o\left(\mu, \sigma_o^2\right)$
e	1	If $pEN(pos) + 1 \leq mEN(pos)e = 1$
e	1	If $pEN(pos)+ > mEN(pos)e = 0$

2.3 Service Graph

The service (instance) is labeled as $SG = < S, E, s_0 >$. s_0 is the location of the initial data required to complete the composite service. When the composite service is requested, a corresponding SG will be generated according to the service path of the composite service. S represents the set of all service instances of the service components involved in the path; E represents the set of directed edges between service instances in S. Note that s_0 is added to S as a starting point.

2.4 Service (Instance) Chain ω

ω represents a service instance chain of the service path. For example, for a service path, $s_0 \rightarrow s_1^x \rightarrow s_2^x \rightarrow s_3^x \rightarrow s_4^x(1 \leq x \leq N(F_i))$ is an ω. The total number of service chains of a service path $path$ is denoted as $L(path)$, and the calculation method is shown in Eq. 1.

$$L(path) = \prod_{F_i \in path} N(F_i) \tag{1}$$

3 Service Composition Algorithm

The problem is to select some instances to form a composite service in the cloud-edge system. The most noteworthy problem is that the edges (servers) have limited resources, and the performance is unstable, which is different from the cloud data center with stable performance. Meanwhile, the network status between edge nodes and cloud data center is unstable. If only one instance chain is selected for a composite service, we can not guarantee the response time. If an edge is unable to respond due to limited resources or network communication terminals, etc., it will increase both service delay and energy consumption. Because service execution is very energy-intensive, for this problem, the first thing is to ensure that multiple chains are selected to complete a certain composition of tasks to prevent the above situation. For the selected multiple chains, their structures may have intersections (there are common service instances) or completely independent from each other (there are no common service instances), and they can be executed simultaneously at the same time.

3.1   The Delay of a Service Chain

In this paper, the delay of the instance chain set is used as the indicator to evaluate different service composition algorithms, and define the delay of the instance chain in the set that completes the composite task most quickly as the delay of the instance chain set. Therefore, we need to consider a calculation method of instance chain delay as shown in Fig. 3 (blue circle indicates that the service instance is deployed in the cloud data center).

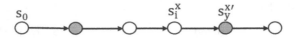

Fig. 3. Instance chain ω. (Color figure online)

$D(\omega)$ represents an ω delay, which consists of processing data time and transmitting data time. In order to calculate the delay of the whole chain, we first analyze the delay between two adjacent instances in the chain, as shown in Fig. 4.

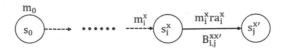

Fig. 4. Schematic diagram of data transmission and processing.

In Fig. 4, m_0 represents the initial amount of data at s_0, x represents the sequence number of the corresponding instance in its service class, $1 \leqslant x \leqslant N(F_i)$. m_i^x is the amount of data getting into the current service s_i^x, $m_i^x ra_i^x$ indicates the amount of data to be transferred to the subsequent service $m_j^{x'}$ after the current instance s_i^x has processed the data. $B_{i,j}^{xx'}$ indicates the bandwidth of data transmission. The setting of $B_{i,j}^{xx'}$ is related to the location of s_i^x and $s_j^{x'}$.

When both s_i^x and $s_j^{x'}$ are in the cloud data center or the same edge node, set $B_{i,j}^{xx'}$ to a larger value. If both s_i^x and $s_j^{x'}$ are in two different edges, or one is in the cloud center, the other is in the edge, then $B_{i,j}^{xx'}$ is regarded as a random variable, let it follow the Gaussian distribution of the mean and variance as the corresponding values.

Therefore, the part of processing data in the delay between s_i^x and $s_j^{x'}$ (recorded as $D_{i,j}$) is described by attribute o in Table. 1, and the part of transmitting data is described by $B_{i,j}^{xx'}$. Therefore, the calculation method of $D_{i,j}$ is shown in Eq. 2.

$$D_{i,j} = \frac{m_i^x ra_i^x}{B_{i,j}^{xx'}} + m_i^x ra_i^x * o_j^{x'}$$

$$= m_i^x ra_i^x \left(\frac{1}{B_{i,j}^{xx'}} + o_j^{x'} \right) \tag{2}$$

In Eq. 2, $o_j^{x'}$ represents the time taken by $s_j^{x'}$ to process unit data. $D_{i,j}$ is actually the sum of the time of data transmission between s_i^x and $s_j^{x'}$ and the time of data processing in $s_j^{x'}$. At the same time, the $m_i^x ra_i^x$ in Eq. 2 can be determined by the initial data amount m_0, and the ra attribute of all service instances passing from s_0 to s_i^x on the current ω, this paper assumes that all service instances ra of an abstract service are the same, but their service processing time and network environment are different, so another expression of $m_i^x ra_i^x$ is shown in Eq. 3.

$$m_i^x ra_i^x = m_0 * \left(\prod_{s_j^x \in \omega_{s_0, s_i^x}}^{\cdot} ra\left(s_j^x\right) \right) \tag{3}$$

In Eq. 3, $ra\left(s_i^x\right)$ represents the ra attribute value of s_i^x. Therefore, $D_{i,j}$ can be expressed in the form of formula 4.

$$D_{i,j} = m_0 \left(\prod_{s_j^x \in \omega_{s_0, s_i^x}} ra\left(s_j^x\right) \right) * \left(\frac{1}{B_{i,j}^{xx'}} + o_j^{x'} \right) \tag{4}$$

For Eq. 4, let $\eta_{i\omega} = \prod_{s_j^x \in \omega_{s_0, s_i^x}} ra\left(s_j^x\right)$, according to the previous settings, for a certain s_i^x on a given chain ω, $\eta_{i\omega}$ is a fixed constant. Set $\omega_{i,j} = \frac{1}{B_{i,j}^{xx'}} + o_j^{x'}$, note that except for the case that s_i^x and $s_j^{x'}$ are in the center of the cloud, other cases $\omega_{i,j}$ are random variables subject to a certain distribution. And $\omega_{i,j}$ represents the comprehensive performance of the network environment where a service is located and the data processing capability of the service. The smaller the $\omega_{i,j}$, the better. Thus, the form of $D_{i,j}$ can be reduced to Eq. 5.

$$D_{i,j} = m_0 \eta_{i\omega} * \omega_{i,j} \tag{5}$$

It should also be noted that s_0 only represents the location of the initial data, that is, only the data is transmitted and not processed. Based on the above, the total delay $D(\omega)$ of a service instance chain ω can be described in the form shown in Eq. 6.

$$D(\omega) = \sum_{e_{ij} \in \omega} D_{i,j} = \sum_{e_{ij} \in \omega} m_0 * \left(\eta_{i\omega} * \omega_{i,j} \right)$$
$$= m_0 \sum_{e_{ij} \in \omega} \left(\eta_{i\omega} * \omega_{i,j} \right) \tag{6}$$

According to Eq. 6, it is also mentioned above that for each service instance of a specific chain, $\eta_{i\omega}$ is a constant value, and m_0 and o_0 are known constants. Therefore, in the intuitive form, to make the total delay of the selected instance chain as small as possible, it is necessary to make $\omega_{i,j}$ as small as possible.

3.2   Data-Aware Service Composition Algorithm

Algorithm 1: locAwareSelect(chainNum, preNode, Ii, pEN)

Input: the number of the current chain *chainNum* , the previous instance *preNode* , the candidate instance set I_i, the array pEN []

Output: Feasible service instance number

1 $I_i \leftarrow rank(l_i)$;

2 prePos = preNode.getPos();

3 samePosNum = findSamePos(I_i);

4 **if** *(samePosNum != -1)* **then**

5   **if** *(I_i.get(samePosNum).getPos() == 0 ||*
    I_i.get(samePosNum).getRunFlag() == 1) **then**

6   **return** samePosNum;

7   **else**

8   **while** *(pEN[I_i.get(samePosNum).getPos()] + 1 > MAX_INS)* **do**

9   samePosNum = random.nextInt(I_i.size() * 50%);

10   **if** *(I_i.get(samePosNum).getPos() == 0 ||*
            I_i.get(samePosNum).getRunFlag() == 1) **then**

11   **break**;

12   **end**

13   **end**

14   **return** samePosNum;

15   **end**

16 **else**

17   choice = random.nextInt(I_i.size() * 50%);

18   **if** *(I_i.get(choice).getPos() == 0 || I_i.get(choice).getRunFlag() == 1)* **then**

19   **return** choice;

20   **else**

21   **while** *(pEN[I_i.get(choice).getPos()] + 1 > MAX_INS)* **do**

22   choice = random.nextInt(I_i.size() * 50%);

23   **if** *(I_i.get(choice).getPos() == 0 || I_i.get(choice).getRunFlag() ==*
            1) **then**

24   **break**;

25   **end**

26   **end**

27   **return** choice;

28   **end**

29 **end**

We propose an energy efficient data-aware service composition algorithm. In fact, from the perspective of the algorithm execution process, there are also greedy algorithms and random ideas: when you want to select the next service instance, first check whether there is one in the same place as the previous instance (both in DC or the same EN) from the candidate set. If there is one, it is preferred; if there is no such instance in the current candidate set, or because of some limiting factors, there is the same location as the previous instance, but the instance cannot be selected, the greedy algorithm is used to select the better one from the remaining instances. The pseudo code is shown in Algorithm 1.

$Rank(I_i)$ in the first line of Algorithm 1 means that the current candidate instance set is sorted from small to large according to its $\omega_{i,j}$; $prePos$ is the location of the previous instance; $findSamePos(I_i)$ is to find the same instance sequence number in the candidate set as the $preNode$ position, and return the instance number if there is one, or -1 if it is not; line 9 means that the current candidate set has the same instance as the $preNode$ position, However, due to conditional constraints, it is not possible to select an instance. Then randomly select the first 50% of the set of instances in the instance set that have already sorted the $\omega_{i,j}$ according to the number of candidate instances, which combines the stochastic algorithm and the greedy algorithm.

4   Evaluation

4.1   Simulation Settings

In the simulation environment, we set up one cloud data center (DC), and 5 edges (1–5). Therefore, the value of *pos* for all service instances is 0~5, where 0 represents the cloud data center; and $1 \sim 5$ represents the corresponding edge nodes. Service path $path{:}F_1 \rightarrow F_2 \rightarrow F_3 \rightarrow F_4$, and its $N(F_i)$ is $3, 4, 2, 5, 3$, which means that the number of service instances is $3, 4, 2, 5, 3$.

Besides, the parameters that need to be set for each instance in this experiment are: location (*pos*), ratio of output to input data (*ra*), unit data processing time (*o*); meanwhile, according to the previous delay analysis, in order to simplify the programming model, the network environment of the instance (that is, the bandwidth allocated to an instance) is also incorporated into the parameters of the instance. Since the edges are closer to users, while the computing capacity of a cloud is better, the general principle of parameter setting is that when the service instance is deployed at the edge: the unit data processing time is longer, the network bandwidth may be better; when the service instance is deployed at the cloud center: the unit data processing time is short, the network bandwidth may be poor.

4.2   Results Analysis

This section mainly introduces comparative experimental methods, processes, and corresponding results display and analysis instructions. The purpose of the experiment is to compare the performance of three service composition algorithms including a stochastic algorithm, a greedy algorithm, and a data-aware service composition algorithm under the same constraints and experimental scenario settings. We investigate the performance of the algorithms by the delay of service instance chain, which actually indicates the energy consumption of the mobile devices. The comparison method is to simulate the running of the instance chain set selected by different methods more than 10,000 times, and the parameters are randomly generated according to the respective obedience distribution, and the delay is plotted into a CDF (distribution function diagram). Generally, the curve, that is closer to the y-axis, means less service delay and less energy consumption.

The main factors that affect the delay of the instance chain set generated by a service instance selection algorithm, includes the number of optional service instance chains, and the total number of optional service instances. Two factors are adjusted and the effects of these factors on the instance chain delay are compared.

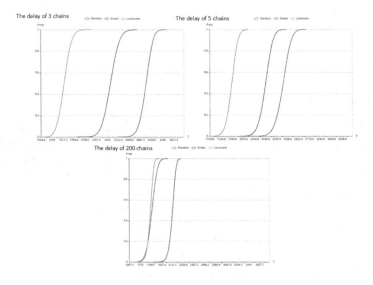

Fig. 5. The first set of experiments.

1# Experiments. For the first set of experiments, according to Fig. 5, intuitively, when the number of instance chains is 3 and 5, the performance of the data-aware service composition algorithm is obviously better than the stochastic algorithm and the greedy algorithm. The service delay of the proposed algorithm is shorter, thus reducing the energy consumption of mobile devices. As the number of instance chains increases, the differences between algorithms become more stable, and the performance of each algorithm become better and closer. However, in a real cloud-edge system, it is impossible to allow a service composition algorithm to select a large number of instance chains because the resources at the edge are limited. Therefore, the proposed algorithm still has a good performance improvement on service delay and energy consumption reduction.

2# Experiments. As the total number of instances changes, according to Fig. 6, the proposed algorithm is always better than the traditional algorithms in reducing service delay, which means that the proposed algorithm reduced the energy

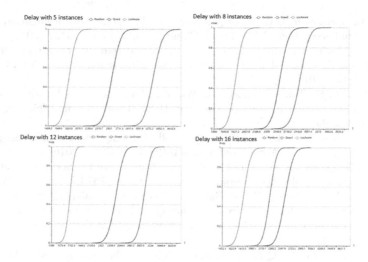

Fig. 6. The second set of experiments.

consumption of mobile devices. At the same time, the performance difference between the three selection algorithms does not change significantly as the number of optional instances increases, because in most cases, the three selection algorithms do not require many chains to select the specified number of instances. Therefore, the proposed algorithm reduces service delay, and it also reduces the waiting time of applications on mobile devices and the energy consumption of mobile devices.

5   Conclusion

In this paper, we investigate service composition problem and propose an energy efficient data-aware service composition algorithm, which is a new extension of service composition in a cloud-edge system. To handle the uncertainty of a single service, we propose an effective service instances selection mechanism to generate multiple service paths to reduce service delay and energy consumption of mobile devices. Extensive simulations show the effectiveness and stability of this method in reducing service delay and energy consumption.

Acknowledgments. This work was supported by science and technology project of State Grid Corporation of China in 2020, Research and Application of Key Technologies of Multiple Data Centers Cooperative Operation and Intelligent Operation and Maintenance for Multi-stite integration, project No. 5210ED200027.

References

1. Hu, Y.C., Patel, M., Sabella, D., Sprecher, N., Young, V.: Mobile edge computing: a key technology towards 5G. ETSI White Paper **11**(11), 1–16 (2015)

2. Paya, A., Marinescu, D.C.: Energy-aware load balancing and application scaling for the cloud ecosystem. IEEE Trans. Cloud Comput. **5**(1), 15–27 (2017)
3. Li, K.: Improving multicore server performance and reducing energy consumption by workload dependent dynamic power management. IEEE Trans. Cloud Comput. **4**(2), 122–137 (2016)
4. Deng, S., Wu, H., Tan, W., Xiang, Z., Wu, Z.: Mobile service selection for composition: an energy consumption perspective. IEEE Trans. Autom. Sci. Eng. **14**(3), 1478–1490 (2017)
5. Gabry, F., Bioglio, V., Land, I.: On energy-efficient edge caching in heterogeneous networks. IEEE J. Sel. Areas Commun. **34**(12), 3288–3298 (2016)
6. Wu, H., Deng, S., Li, W., Fu, M., Yin, J., Zomaya, A.Y.: Service selection for composition in mobile edge computing systems. In: 2018 IEEE International Conference on Web Services (ICWS), San Francisco, CA, pp. 355–358 (2018)
7. Sun, H., Zhou, F., Hu, R.Q.: Joint offloading and computation energy efficiency maximization in a mobile edge computing system. IEEE Trans. Veh. Technol. **68**(3), 3052–3056 (2019)
8. Li, X., Wu, J., Lu, S.: QoS-aware service selection in geographically distributed clouds. In: 2013 22nd International Conference on Computer Communication and Networks (ICCCN), Nassau, pp. 1–5 (2013)
9. Wang, S., Zhou, A., Yang, F., Chang, R.N.: Towards network-aware service composition in the cloud. In: IEEE Transactions on Cloud Computing
10. Wang, S., Zhao, Y., Huang, L., Jinliang, X., Hsu, C.-H.: QoS prediction for service recommendations in mobile edge computing. J. Parallel Distrib. Comput. **127**, 134–144 (2019)
11. Li, X., Lian, Z., Qin, X., Abawajyz, J.: Delay-aware resource allocation for data analysis in cloud-edge system. In: IEEE International Conference on Parallel & Distributed Processing with Applications, Ubiquitous Computing & Communications, Big Data & Cloud Computing, Social Computing & Networking, Sustainable Computing & Communications (ISPA/IUCC/BDCloud/SocialCom/SustainCom). Melbourne, Australia, vol. 2018, pp. 816–823 (2018)
12. Ren, J., Guo, H., Xu, C., Zhang, Y.: Serving at the edge: a scalable IoT architecture based on transparent computing. IEEE Netw. **31**(5), 96–105 (2017)
13. Taleb, T., Samdanis, K., Mada, B., Flinck, H., Dutta, S., Sabella, D.: On multi-access edge computing: a survey of the emerging 5G network edge cloud architecture and orchestration. In: IEEE Communications Surveys & Tutorials, vol. 19, no. 3, pp. 1657–1681 (2017)
14. Lopez, P.G., et al.: Edge-centric computing: vision and challenges. SIGCOMM Comput. Commun. Rev. **45**(5), 37–42 (2015)

SmartDis: Near-Optimal Task Scheduling in Multi-edge Networks

Weiwei Miao[1], Zeng Zeng[1], Chuanjun Wang[1], and Zhuzhong Qian[2(✉)]

[1] State Grid Jiangsu Electric Power Co., Ltd. Information and Telecommunication Branch, Nanjing, China
[2] State Key Laboratory for Novel Software Technology, Nanjing University, Nanjing, China
qzz@nju.edu.cn

Abstract. In multi-edge networks, as the bandwidth and computing resources of edge servers are limited, transmission and processing of large amounts of data could bring significant pressure, leading to violations of service agreements. Thus, it is very important to schedule tasks in edge network efficiently for better performance. In this paper, we formulate the problem as minimizing the overall completion time of tasks in edge networks. Since the problem can be proved to be NP-hard, we propose a novelty algorithm, SmartDis, for scheduling tasks accross multiple edges. The main idea of SmartDis is to select offload slots of tasks based on the principle of choosing the smallest sum of added value of the overall completion time. We show theoretically that the system transmission time of SmartDis is within a constant times of the optimal result, as long as the data upload is scheduled according to the transmission order. The evaluation results illustrate that SmartDis is superior to other cross-domain job scheduling algorithms at this stage, achieving a performance improvement of at least 25%.

Keywords: Multi-edge network · Edge bandwidth · Task schedule

1 Introduction

Multi-edge computing is a distributed computing framework that brings applications closer to data sources. It has become one of the most promising ways to improve response times and bandwidth availability for IoT devices. In a typical multi-job scenario, raw data is first collected from different devices and gathered in an edge server for processing. Edge computing improves the efficiency by dispatching data close to each edge server for distributed execution. Recent research results show that under the distributed execution mode, 90% of the

Supported by the Science and Technology Project of State Grid Corporation of China, Research on Key Technologies of Edge Intelligent Computing for Smart IoT System (Grand No. 5210ED209Q3U).

H. Jiang et al. (Eds.): ICECI 2020, LNICST 368, pp. 15–34, 2021.
https://doi.org/10.1007/978-3-030-73429-9_2

job completion time is shortened to 33% [10], and wide area network bandwidth usage is reduced by a factor of 250 [23,24]. Furthermore, for jobs like query, the speed can be increased by 3–19 times, and the transmission cost of the WAN can be reduced by 15–64% [16]. This framework can bring significant advantage for delay-sensitive tasks and data-privacy tasks, such as automatic driving [14], public security [1,6], customized healthcare [4,15], and unmanned retail [21].

However, since the bandwidth and computing resources in edge networks are limited, it is a critical issue to efficiently schedule and offload tasks. Figure 1 describes an edge network environment, which is composed of a terminal access point (Access Point, AP) and several edge computing slots. Terminals upload the data to the edge servers through the AP. In this scenario, the bottleneck is the upload link bandwidth of the AP, which is less studied in previous researches. The classic multi-machine scheduling problem [2,5,8,12] and the Current Open Shop problem [9,13,18] mainly deal with jobs that can be executed after release, and hence can't cope with such challenges.

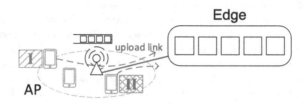

Fig. 1. Edge network environment.

In edge computing, due to the wide distribution of the edge regions and the uneven density of users in different locations, the data processing requirements naturally vary alongside the locations and time. The deviation also exists in the service capability of the edge. Therefore, completing tasks as quickly as possible on a single edge does not necessarily shorten the job completion time. Even providing services for certain subtasks is "wasting" resources, because the sibling tasks of these subtasks on other edges are being delayed due to the imbalance in execution caused by the above deviations. Therefore, to get a better average job completion time, it is more important to give priority to other tasks, such as the task that can dominate the completion time of the job.

In this paper, we propose a novel polynomial-time algorithm SmartDis, for efficient scheduling and offloading tasks in multi-edge computing. Considering the bandwidth constraints, the problem is compounded as a joint scheduling problem of network and computing resources. We first theoretically prove the NP-hardness of the problem. Since the offloading occurs after the data upload is completed, this paper naturally dismantles the problem into two sub-problems of optimizing data upload time and optimizing offload calculation time. The main idea of SmartDis is to arrange the order for the data upload request at each edge AP based on the primal dual method, to minimize the global data upload delay: When the data upload of a certain task is completed, SmartDis immediately selects the offload slot for the task based on the principle of the smallest value added of the sum of the completion time, and arranges the scheduling timing for tasks on the slot.

We rigorously prove the theoretical performance guarantee of SmartDis. If the upload sequence of tasks is arranged according to SmartDis's sequencing strategy, the global data upload delay can be guaranteed to be within a constant times of the optimal value. Finally, we conduct extensive experiments via both implementation and simulation to validate the practical performance of Smart-Dis. We simulate job specifications in an real commercial cluster environment and compare with several scheduling mechanisms, including traditional scheduling mechanisms (FCFS and SRPT), recent scheduling mechanisms designed for concurrent execution of multiple data centers (Reordering and SWAG). Then we conduct evaluations on execution performance, fairness, sensitivity, and scheduling execution cost. Compared with the heuristic scheduling algorithm based on the SRPT class, SmartDis can improve the average job completion time by up to 33%, while keeping the additional calculation and communication overhead low.

2   Related Work

Since the WAN is a key bottleneck in cross-domain analysis, existing work is aimed at coordinating data distribution and task scheduling among multiple data-centers to reduce the WAN transmission time. Literature [16] emphasizes the difference between the upstream and downstream bandwidth of each cluster. If the low bandwidth carries high data volume, the receive/send operation will often become the bottleneck of the job. Literature [16] therefore optimizes the placement of two stages' data and tasks to avoid higher bottlenecks in the data transmission process, thereby reducing job completion time. Literature [23] aimed at minimizing WAN bandwidth consumption, and adjusted the query-execution plan and data backup scheme of SQL jobs. This move uses the cheap storage resources in a single data-center to cache the intermediate results of queries, aiming at avoiding redundant data transmission. The above research work aims to reduce the WAN data transmission delay. However, purely optimizing WAN transmission delay will cause uneven load on clusters, so the task will be backlogged in some "hot spots" clusters, causing execution bottlenecks.

Literature [11] proposed that the task execution sequence within a data center may still extend the completion time of the entire job. The reason is that the completion of the job depends on the most lagging subtask, so the subtasks completed in advance can be postponed appropriately.It is closest to the research work of this paper. It points out that if the subtasks' sibling tasks have a higher delay in other data centers, reducing the subtask's completion time does not speed up job completion. Therefore, it is appropriate to postpone this subtask and give resources to other competitors with "faster" sibling tasks, which may have a better average delay globally. The literature first proposed an auxiliary Reordering mechanism to adjust the existing scheduling order for the imbalance of delay between sibling tasks. The basic idea behind it is to try to delay the tasks in the queue, as long as the delay does not increase the overall completion time of the job, but provides opportunities for other jobs to shorten the completion time. The specific operation is (1) Find the end task of the queue with the longest completion time in each data center. (2) The job to which the task belongs is inferior to other jobs. (3) Extract the task of the job from each queue and update the queue completion time. Repeat the above steps until all jobs are reordered. Since Reordering is a conservative method (used to adjust the existing scheduling), its result depends on the original algorithm's room for improvement. Literature [11] further proposes a complete scheduling algorithm SWAG, and it does not need Reordering assistance. The scheduling principle is to give priority to the jobs that make the longest queue with a least value added. The specific operation is (1) Calculate the increment of the completion time of each queue when executing each job. (2) Select the job that makes the longest queue with a least value added,and schedule it first (3) Update the length of each queue after executing the job. Repeat the above steps to sort all jobs.

However, the above work is based on several assumptions: first, data centers have the same number of computing slots; second, all slots have the same configuration and computing performance. While, in a multi-edge system, the scale of each edge cluster and the configuration of computing slots are heterogeneous (note that the processing time of a task on different edge servers is independent and different in this paper). This will lead to the coupling of scheduling and offloading, that is, the competition and imbalance when tasks are offloaded to different slots are different. The above scheduling algorithm that ignores heterogeneity is therefore not applicable.

3   Model and Problem Formulation

3.1   System Model

During execution, the multi-edge system requires a logically centralized coordinator, which is deployed either in the cloud or on a strong edge. According to the constraints of specific scenarios, the coordinator formulates corresponding decisions and delivers them to the edge for execution. In Fig. 2, a job is submitted to the coordinator. Due to the massive, redundant, and low-quality raw data produced by terminal. The tasks of the job are usually dispatched to the edge near the raw data.

In a wide area network environment, there are several edge APs, forming a set $\mathcal{P}$. Each AP is connected to an edge cluster $p \in \mathcal{P}$ deployed nearby, and let $\mathcal{S}_p$ be the set of computing slots at edge p. Set the uplink bandwidth of the AP to $\mathcal{B}_p$. A batch of analysis jobs $\mathcal{J} = \{1, 2, ..., n\}$ continuously arrives at the system, r_j is the arrival time of job $j \in \mathcal{J}$. The initial stage of each job consists of several tasks, which are responsible for processing the geographically distributed raw data. v_j^p is the amount of data that job j needs to process at edge p. Job j assigns a task u_j^p to edge p to perform data processing, and $d_s^{p,j}$ is the processing time of the task on slot $s \in \mathcal{S}_p$.

Before the task u_j^p performs data processing, data needs to be uploaded from the terminal device to the edge cluster. Let $\mathcal{T}_j^p$ be the data upload completion time,

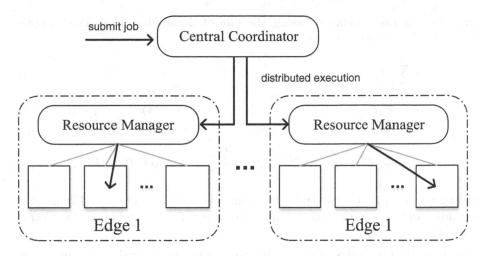

Fig. 2. Data analysis jobs run in the multi-edge system.

$$T_j^p = r_j + wn_j^p + \frac{v_j^p}{B_p}, \tag{1}$$

Among them, wn_j^p is the time that the data of the task is queued up at the access point p to be uploaded. After the data upload is completed, the edge cluster scheduler plans the slots used for offloading and scheduling timing for the task. Considering the limited computing power of the edge server, this paper sets the server to only handle one task at a time. If the task is offloaded to the server $s \in \mathcal{S}_p$ to perform data processing, let $\mathcal{C}_j^p$ be the completion time of the task u_j^p, then

$$\mathcal{C}_j^p = T_j^p + wc_s^{p,j} + d_s^{p,j}, \tag{2}$$

Among them, $wc_s^{p,j}$ is the queuing delay of the task on the server s. Let $\mathcal{C}_j = \max_{p \in \mathcal{P}} \mathcal{C}_j^p$ represent the completion time of job j. For these jobs executed on multiple edges, this paper coordinates the data upload order of tasks(wn_j^p) , the decision of the slot where the task is offloaded (the slot s that executes the task), and the scheduling timing on the slot ($wc_s^{p,j}$), to minimize the sum of the completion time $\sum_j \mathcal{C}_j$. Geo-TORS (Task Offloading and Resource Scheduling for Geo-distributed Jobs) refers to this problem.

3.2   Problem Formulation

Since the offload occurs after the data upload is completed, this paper naturally disassembles the Geo-TORS problem into two problems, which are the optimization of job data upload time (problem I) and the optimization of job offload and calculation time (problem II).

Problem I: Optimize the Upload Time of Jobs' Data. This sub-question determines the data upload completion time T pj for each task of the job. By arranging the task upload sequence, the sum of these job upload times is optimized. Its formal definition is as follows:

$$\min \sum_{j=1}^{n} \mathcal{T}_j \tag{3}$$

$$\text{s.t. } \mathcal{T}_j \geq \mathcal{T}_j^p, \qquad\qquad\qquad\qquad \forall p \in \mathcal{P}, \forall j \in \mathcal{J} \tag{4}$$

$$\mathcal{T}_j^p \geq r_j, \qquad\qquad\qquad\qquad \forall p \in \mathcal{P}, \forall j \in \mathcal{J} \tag{5}$$

$$\mathcal{T}_k^p \geq \mathcal{T}_j^p + \frac{v_k^p}{B_p} \text{ or } \mathcal{T}_j^p \geq \mathcal{T}_k^p + \frac{v_j^p}{B_p}, \qquad \forall p \in \mathcal{P}, \forall j, k \in \mathcal{J} \tag{6}$$

Among them, $\mathcal{T}_j$ is the data uploading completion time of job j, and constraint (6) indicates that the task data is uploaded in strict order and no preemption is allowed.

Problem II: Optimize Jobs' Offloading and Calculation Time. After the data upload is complete, the task u_j^p waits for offload and processing. Let $r_j^p = \mathcal{T}_j^p$ be the time when the task u_j^p can start execution. At time r_j^p, select a computing slot $s \in \mathcal{S}_p$ to offload the task u_j^p, and use variables $x_s^{p,j} \in \{0,1\}$ to represent the task's offloading decision. Then arrange the processing order of this task on slot s, and finally optimize the sum of the completion time of the whole job. Its formal definition is as follows:

$$\min \sum_{j=1}^{n} \mathcal{C}_j \tag{7}$$

$$\text{s.t. } \sum_{s \in \mathcal{S}_p} x_s^{p,j} = 1, \qquad\qquad\qquad \forall p \in \mathcal{P}, \forall j \in \mathcal{J} \tag{8}$$

$$\mathcal{C}_j \geq \mathcal{C}_j^p, \qquad\qquad\qquad\qquad \forall p \in \mathcal{P}, \forall j \in \mathcal{J} \tag{9}$$

$$\mathcal{C}_j^p \geq r_j^p, \qquad\qquad\qquad\qquad \forall p \in \mathcal{P}, \forall j \in \mathcal{J} \tag{10}$$

$$\mathcal{C}_k^p \geq \mathcal{C}_j^p + \sum_{s \in \mathcal{S}_p} x_s^{p,j} d_s^{p,k} \text{ or } \mathcal{C}_j^p \geq \mathcal{C}_k^p + \sum_{s \in \mathcal{S}_p} x_s^{p,j} d_s^{p,j}, \quad \forall p \in \mathcal{P}, \forall j, k \in \mathcal{J} \tag{11}$$

Among them, the constrained formula (8) ensures that a task can and must be offloaded to a slot. Constraint (11) shows that task execution strictly follows the determined scheduling sequence, and preemption is not allowed.

Theorem 1. *The Geo-TORS problem is NP-hard.*

Proof. If the coupling between tasks in this problem is neglected(I.e. tasks belonging to the same job jointly determine the completion time of this job), the problem can be simplified to the problem of offloading and resource scheduling of independent tasks in literature [22]. It has been proved that the offloading and resource scheduling of independent tasks are NP-hard. Therefore, the Geo-TORS problem is at least NP-hard.

4   The SmartDis Algorithm

This paper designs tasks offloading and scheduling algorithm SmartDis. The algorithm's brief overview is that when a distributed execution job is released, SmartDis first arranges the transmission order for the data upload request of the job at each edge AP based on the primary dual method, to minimize the global data transmission delay (GeoOrder component). When the data transmission of a certain task is completed, SmartDis immediately selects the offload slot for the task based on the principle of the smallest value added of the sum of the completion time, and arranges the scheduling timing for tasks on the slot (GeoSRPT+LeastDelta component).

Offloading the task immediately is due to the following two considerations. First, the main scheduler has limited memory. If a large number of tasks are cached in the task pool and only the resources are idle, the scheduling will be performed. During this process, the data in the memory may be frequently switched, which will cause extra time. The second is that in a heterogeneous server cluster, the execution time of tasks on each server is independent. In the face of different idle slots, the priority of tasks changes. If the task pool model is adopted, no matter whether the scheduling is performed regularly or the scheduling is performed after idle resources are available, the scheduling algorithm needs to be executed once for the entire task pool. This is time-consuming.

4.1   Determining Upload Orders

Based on the primary-dual method, when a new job is released, the SmartDis algorithm performs job sequencing for each edge AP's data upload requests, and each edge AP should transmit data according to the ordered job sequence. The transmission ordering strategy GeoOrder proposed in this paper is near optimal, which ensures that the data transmission delay does not exceed 3 times the optimal value.

The main challenge of GeoOrder design is how to capture the impact of the data transmission between jobs in the system under the constraints of upload bandwidth at each edge. This paper achieves this goal based on the job weight scaling step derived from the primary-dual design framework. The execution steps of GeoOrder are summarized as follows in Algorithm 3. Later, this paper introduces the design process of GeoOrder based on the primary-dual framework and the performance analysis of GeoOrder in detail.

Algorithm 1: GeoOrder-simplified version

Input: $\mathcal{J}$ (unordered job set)
$\tilde{v}_j^p$ (Amount of data not uploaded by job j at edge p)
w_j (The weight of job j)
Output: σ (Assignment of jobs)

1 **for** $k = n$ *to* 1 **do**
2 $\quad b \leftarrow \arg\max_p \sum_{j \in \mathcal{J}} \tilde{v}_j^p$ (Find bottleneck AP)
3 $\quad \sigma(k) \leftarrow \arg\min_{j \in \mathcal{J}} \frac{w_j}{\tilde{v}_j^p}$ (Select the job with the largest amount of unuploaded data after weighting)
4 $\quad w_j \leftarrow w_j - w_{\sigma(k)} \times \frac{\tilde{v}_j^p}{\tilde{v}_{\sigma(k)}^p}$ (Job weight scaling)
5 $\quad \mathcal{J} \leftarrow \mathcal{J} \backslash \sigma(k)$ (Update job collections that have not been scheduled)
6 **return** σ

GeoOrder (1) finds the bottleneck AP, that is, the edge AP with the largest amount of unuploaded data (Algorithm 4.1, line 2) (2) Selects the job with the largest amount of unuploaded data among all upload requests of the bottleneck AP. And place the job at the end of all out-of-order jobs (Algorithm 4.1 line 3) (3) scale the weight of all out-of-order jobs to capture the impact of the job sequencing operation in step (2) on the data transmission delay of the remaining jobs (Algorithm 4.1 line 4). Repeat the above steps to sequence all jobs.

The design process of the primary dual algorithm and GeoOrder performance analysis. Let the variable $T_j^p = r_j + wn_j^p + \frac{v_j^p}{B_p}$ be the time when the data transfer of job j is completed at the edge p, and the variable T_j be the time when the data transfer of job j is completed. w_j is the weight of job j, and the default value is 1. With the goal of minimizing the weighted data transmission time, the formal data flow scheduling problem is as follows:

$$\min \sum_{j=1}^{n} w_j T_j \tag{12}$$

$$\text{s.t. } T_j \geq T_j^p, \qquad\qquad \forall p \in \mathcal{P}, \forall j \in \mathcal{J} \tag{13}$$

$$T_j^p \geq r_j, \qquad\qquad \forall p \in \mathcal{P}, \forall j \in \mathcal{J} \tag{14}$$

$$T_k^p \geq T_j^p + v_k^p \text{ or } T_j^p \geq T_k^p + v_j^p, \qquad \forall p \in \mathcal{P}, \forall j, k \in \mathcal{J} \tag{15}$$

In this paper, the nonlinear Primal problem (Eq. (15) is a nonlinear constraint) is further rewritten as the linear programming LP-Primal. Equation (20) is similar to the linear constraints introduced by Wolsye [25] and Queyranne [17] for the One-Machine-N-Job scheduling problem:

$$\sum_{j \in \mathcal{S}} p_j \mathcal{C}_j \geq \frac{1}{2}\left[\left(\sum_{j \in \mathcal{S}} p_j\right)^2 + \sum_{j \in \mathcal{S}} p_j^2\right], \forall \mathcal{S} \subseteq [n] \tag{16}$$

The variable $\mathcal{C}_j$ is the completion time of job j, p_j is the processing time of job j, $[n] = \{1, 2, ..., n\}$. Queyranne [17] shows that the convex hull of a feasible solution to a completion time vector in a scheduling problem can be fully described by this linear constraint.

$$\min \sum_{j=1}^{n} w_j T_j \tag{17}$$

$$\text{s.t. } T_j \geq T_j^p \qquad\qquad\qquad\qquad \forall p \in \mathcal{P}, \forall j \in \mathcal{J} \tag{18}$$

$$T_j^p \geq r_j, \qquad\qquad\qquad\qquad \forall p \in \mathcal{P}, \forall j \in \mathcal{J} \tag{19}$$

$$\sum_{j \in \mathcal{S}} v_j^p T_j^p \geq \frac{1}{2} \left| \left[\sum_{j \in \mathcal{S}} v_j^p \right]^2 + \sum_{j \in \mathcal{S}} (v_j^p)^2 \right. \qquad \forall p \in \mathcal{P}, \forall \mathcal{S} \subseteq [n] \tag{20}$$

This paper considers the duality problem of the LP-Primal problem and analyzes the performance of the data flow scheduling algorithm proposed next in this paper. This paper introduces the dual variable α_j^p for the constrained expression (18), the dual variable γ_j^p for the constrained expression (19), and the dual variable $\beta_{\mathcal{S}}^p$ for the constrained expression (20). The LP-Dual problem is as follows:

$$\max \sum_p \sum_j \gamma_j^p r_j + \frac{1}{2} \sum_{\mathcal{S}} \sum_p \beta_{\mathcal{S}}^p \left[\left(\sum_{j \in \mathcal{S}} v_j^p \right)^2 + \sum_{j \in \mathcal{S}} (v_{\mathcal{S}}^p)^2 \right] \tag{21}$$

$$\text{s.t. } \sum_p \alpha_j^p \leq w_j \qquad\qquad\qquad\qquad \forall j \in [n] \tag{22}$$

$$\sum_{\mathcal{S} \ni j} \beta_{\mathcal{S}}^p v_j^p \leq \alpha_j^p - \gamma_j^p, \qquad\qquad\qquad \forall p \in \mathcal{P}, \forall j \in [n] \tag{23}$$

$$\alpha_j^p \geq 0, \gamma_j^p \geq 0, \qquad\qquad\qquad\qquad \forall p \in \mathcal{P}, \forall j \in [n] \tag{24}$$

$$\beta_{\mathcal{S}}^p \geq 0, \qquad\qquad\qquad\qquad \forall p \in \mathcal{P}, \forall \mathcal{S} \subseteq [n] \tag{25}$$

Primal-Dual algorithm GeoOrder full version description see Algorithm 4.2 for details. Algorithm 4.1 has the following simplifications in Algorithm 4.2, so that it can run at a certain time (specifically the time when a new job is released) to sequence all jobs that have not uploaded data in the current system: (1) Ignore the job release time r_j (2) The input is the amount of data that the job has not uploaded at each moment on each edge.

For the convenience of analysis, after GeoOrder calculates the job arrangement σ, this paper renumbers the job so that $\sigma(k) = k, \forall k \in [n]$. Next, this paper transfers data according to the sequence of jobs generated by Geo-Order. The approximate ratio of the weighted data transmission completion time ($\sum_{j=1}^{n} w_j T_j$) to the optimal transmission completion time ($\sum_{j=1}^{n} w_j T_j^{OPT}$) is less than or equal to 3.

Algorithm 2: GeoOrder

Input: $\mathcal{J}$ (unordered job set)
v_j^p (Amount of data not uploaded by job j at edge p)
w_j (The weight of job j)
Output: σ (Assignment of jobs)

1   **for** $k = n$ *to* 1 **do**

2     $b_k \leftarrow \arg\max_p \sum_{j \in \mathcal{J}} v_j^p$ (Find bottleneck AP)

3     $r_{max} \leftarrow \max_{j \in \mathcal{J}} r_j$ (Find the latest release time)

4   **if** $r_{max} \leq \frac{1}{2} \sum_{j \in \mathcal{J}} v_j^{b_k}$ **then**

5       $\sigma(k) \leftarrow \arg\min_{j \in \mathcal{J}} \frac{w_j - \sum_{l > k} \beta_l v_j^{b_l}}{v_j^{b_k}}$ (Select the job with the largest amount of unuploaded data after weighting)

6       $\beta(k) \leftarrow \frac{w_{\sigma(k)} - \sum_{l > k} \beta_l v_j^{b_l}}{v_{\sigma(k)}^{b_k}}$ (Update related parameters)

7   **else**

8       $\sigma(k) \leftarrow \arg\max_{j \in \mathcal{J}} r_j$ (Select the job with the closest arrival time)

9       $\gamma_{\sigma(k)} \leftarrow w_{\sigma(k)} - \sum_{l > k} \beta_l v_{\sigma(k)}^{b_l}$ (Update related parameters)

10     $\mathcal{J} \leftarrow \mathcal{J} \backslash \sigma(k)$ (Update job collections that have not been scheduled)

11   **return** σ

Theorem 2. *If the order generated by the GeoOrder algorithm is used,*

$$\sum_{j=1}^{n} w_j T_j \leq 3 \sum_{j=1}^{n} w_j T_j^{OPT}$$

Proof. We first construct a feasible solution for the LP-Dual problem and compare the performance between SOL_{Dual} of the feasible solution with SOL_{Primal} of the LP-Primal solution. Since SOL_{Primal} equals $\sum_{k=1}^{n} w_k T_k$, we can get the following equation according to weak duality theorem,

$$SOL_{Dual} \leq OPT_{Dual} \leq OPT_{Primal}$$

Thus, we can show that the primal solution of SOL_{Primal} is within a constant times of the optimal solution.

4.2   Computing Slot Selection and Task Scheduling

After the data transfer is completed, the task is ready to perform data processing. Let $r_j^p = T_j^p$ be the time at which the data processing task u_j^p of job j at edge p can start execution. Let $\mathcal{S}_p = 1, 2, ..., m$ be the server cluster of edge p. At time r_j^p, select a computing slot $s \in \mathcal{S}_p$ to offload the data processing task u_j^p, and arrange the scheduling timing of tasks on slot s.

With the goal of minimizing the sum of the completion delays, this paper proposes a compute slot selection strategy (LeastDelta) and a task scheduling strategy on the slot (GeoSRPT). Each edge cluster executes the same slot selection strategy. When the data transmission of a task is completed, it selects the computing slot for the task; each computing slot executes the same task scheduling strategy and sequentially processes the offloaded computing tasks.

Algorithm 3: LeastDelta&GeoSRPT

1　Node Selection (LeastDelta): When the data transmission of task μ_j^p is completed (that is $t = r_j^p$), we offload the task to the node
$$s^* = \arg\min_{s \in S_p} Q_{sj}^p(t)$$
2　Tasks scheduling on a node (GeoSRPT): At any time t', the node s performs task μ_{j*}^p, $j^* = \arg\min_{j \in \mathcal{A}_f t^*} u_s^{p,j}(t')$

Computing Task Scheduling Strategy (GeoSRPT). For single-task jobs (or in more detail, for One-Server-One-Queue scheduling problems and preemption is allowed). The SRPT (Shortest Remaining Processing Time) scheduling strategy is optimal [20] (with the goal of minimizing the completion time of weighted jobs). Based on SRPT and considering the multi-task job distributed execution mode (Geo-execution), this paper designs GeoSRPT scheduling strategy.

Use $d_s^{p,j}(t)$ to denote the remaining execution time at time t after the task u_j^p is offloaded to slot s. Let $u_s^{p,j}(t) = \max_{(i \in \mathcal{P})} d_j^i(t)$ denote at least the remaining execution time of the job to which the task belongs at time t. $d_j^i(t)$ is defined as:

$$d_j^i(t) = \begin{cases} d_{s'}^{i,j}(t), & \text{If the task } \mu_j^i \text{ has been offloaded to the node } s' \in \mathcal{S}_i. \\ t - r_j^i + d_{s'}^{i,j} s'' = \arg\min_{s \in \mathcal{S}_i} d_s^{i,j}, & \text{If the task } \mu_j^i \text{ has not been offloaded.} \end{cases}$$

At time t, for tasks that have not been completed on slot s (denoted by the set $\mathcal{A}_s(t)$), and the task u_j^p with the smallest $u_s^{p,j}(t)$ value is executed.

Slot Selection Strategy (LeastDelta). When $t = r_j^p$, the data transmission of a task is completed, and an execution slot needs to be selected for the task. LeastDelta's slot selection principle is to offload the task to a certain slot, so that the increase in the sum of the delays in the completion of the job is minimal. When the task u_j^p is offloaded to a slot s, and it is assumed that no new task will be offloaded to the slot s after time t, the increase in the overall job completion time is composed of three parts:

1. Because there are some other tasks (Type-I tasks) with a smaller $u_s^{p,j}$ value than task u_j^p on slot s, the waiting time of task u_j^p increases.
2. The processing time of the task itself.
3. Other tasks (Type-II tasks) that have a larger $u_s^{p,j}$ value than task u_j^p existing on slot s have an additional waiting time due to the execution of task u_j^p.

When no new task is offloaded to slot s after time t, the completion time of task u_j^p can be calculated and expressed as $t_{j,s}^p$ (available by simulating task scheduling on slot s, the scheduling strategy is GeoSRPT). Let $c_j(t)$ record the time t, which is the maximum estimated completion time in the offloaded tasks of job j. The maintenance of the $c_j(t)$ value will be described in detail after each offloading decision.

Let $\mathcal{A}^p_{sj}$ be the set of tasks that reach slot s at time t and have not been completed. The definition is as follows,

$$\mathcal{A}^p_{sj} = \left\{ j' \mid s^p_{j'} = s, r^p_{j'} \leq t, d^p_{j'}(t) > 0 \right\} \tag{26}$$

Among them, $s^p_{j'}$ is the slot selected for the task $u^p_{j'}$. $\mathcal{A}^p_{sj}(t)$ contains Type-I and Type-II tasks affected by task u^p_j.

Let $mathcal{B}1^p_{j,s}(t)$ denote the type-I task set affected by the task u^p_j, defined as follows,

$$\mathcal{B}1^p_{j,s}(t) = \left\{ j' \mid j' \in \mathcal{A}^p_{sj} : u^{p,j'}_s(t') \leq u^{p,j}_s(t') \right\} \tag{27}$$

Let $mathcal{B}2^p_{j,s}(t)$ denote the type-II task set affected by the task u^p_j, defined as follows,

$$\mathcal{B}2^p_{j,s}(t) = \left\{ j' \mid j' \in \mathcal{A}^p_{sj} : u^{p,j'}_s(t') \leq u^{p,j}_s(t') \right\} \tag{28}$$

Based on the above symbols, when the task u^p_j is offloaded to the slot s at $t = r^p_j$, the calculation value of the increase in the completion time of the overall job $\mathcal{Q}^p_{sj}(t)$ is as follows,

$$\mathcal{Q}^p_{sj}(t) = \max \left\{ \sum_{j' \in \mathcal{B}1^p_{j,s}(t)} d^p_{j'}(t) + d^p_j - c_j(t), 0 \right\} \tag{29}$$

$$+ \sum_{j' \in \mathcal{B}2^p_,(t)} \max \left\{ d^p_j - c_{j'}(t), 0 \right\} \tag{30}$$

Among them, the formula (29) is the increase of the completion time of the task u^p_j caused by the Type-I task, and the formula (30) is the increase of the completion time of the Type-II task caused by the task u^p_j. LeastDelta selects the slot $s^* = \arg\min_{s \in \mathcal{S}_p} \mathcal{Q}^p_{\mathcal{S}j}(t)$ for the task u^p_j to perform the calculation. After offloading, update the c_j value of the job to which the related task belongs. Update the c_j value for the job to which the task u^p_j belongs, as follows,

$$c_j = \max \left\{ c_j, t + \sum_{j' \in \mathcal{B}1^p_{j,s*}(t)} d^p_{j'}(t) + d^p_j \right\}. \tag{31}$$

Update the c_j value for the job of Type-II tasks $u^p_{j'} \mid j' \in \mathcal{B}2^p_{j,s*}(t)$ on slot s^*, as follows,

$$c_j = \max \left\{ c_{j'}, t + t^p_{j',s*} + d^p_j \right\}. \tag{32}$$

5   Experiments

In this section, we simulate job specifications in an actual commercial cluster environment and compared to several other scheduling mechanisms, including traditional scheduling mechanisms (FCFS and SRPT), recent scheduling mechanisms designed for concurrent execution of multiple data centers (Reordering and SWAG), and SmartDis mechanism in this paper. Then we conduct evaluations on execution performance (Sect. 5.2), fairness (Sect. 5.3), sensitivity (Sect. 5.4), and scheduling execution cost (Sect. 5.5).

5.1   Experimental Setup

System Scale: This paper expands the CloudSim simulator to simulate the multi-edge system, with the number of edges ranging from 20 to 500. The main evaluation experiment of this paper was run in a system environment with 100 edges and 3000 servers. The number of servers is scaled according to the ratio of the number of servers to the number of edges (for example, a system with 50 edges deployed has $3000/100 \times 50 = 1500$ servers).

Server Distribution: In order to evaluate the impact of the difference in edge size, this paper models the skewness of the server distribution between edges based on the Zipf distribution. When there is no skew, the server is evenly distributed to each edge. As the skew parameter of the Zipf distribution is higher, the degree of skew of the server's distribution between the edges is greater . The default setting of the skew parameter is 2.

Job Specifications: This paper synthesizes simulated experimental loads based on the job size specifications in Facebook's commercial Hadoop cluster and Google's working cluster [11]. Both types of workloads are dominated by small jobs. This paper is also based on high-performance computing clusters to synthesize large-scale jobs. Refer to Table 1 for details of the three types of loads. This paper adjusts the job release interval based on the Poisson process to keep the utilization rate of each load system consistent.

Table 1. Load specifications

Composition ratio	Small job (1–150)	Medium job (151–500)	Large job (501+)	Average job size (task numbers)
Facebook-like	89%	8%	3%	241
Google-like	96%	3%	2%	94
HPC-like	18%	29%	53%	582

Data Distribution: To evaluate the impact of job data distribution on scheduling algorithms, this paper uses Zipf distribution to model the skewness of job data distribution between edges. As the skew parameter of the Zipf distribution is higher, the distribution of data between edges is more skewed. There are two extreme cases. One is that the job data is evenly distributed on the relevant edges, and the other is that the job data is concentrated on a single edge. The default setting of the skew parameter is 2.

Task Duration: This paper models job duration based on Pareto distribution with $\beta = 1.259$, and the average task duration is $2\,s$. This model is consistent with the fitting of the task duration in Facebook cluster in [3].In the simulation experiment, the server performance was randomly sampled from the normal distribution. In order to show the heterogeneity of server performance between edges, this paper sets different mean and variance parameters for the normal distribution model based on the edge scale. For parameter setting, refer to the results of virtual machine performance measurement in the Amazon cloud [7,19].

Evaluation Criteria: The main performance indicator that this paper focuses on is the average completion time of the job. In addition, this paper focuses on the degree of delay in the execution of the job, that is, the ideal execution time without waiting divided by the actual execution time, as an indicator to measure the fairness between the jobs.

The SmartDis in this paper is compared with the First Come First Schedule strategy(FCFS),Global Shortest Remaining Processing Time (GlobalSRPT), Independent Shortest Remaining Processing Time(IndependentSRPT), and these two types of SRPT scheduling strategies adjusted by Reordering, and SWAG Scheduling strategies. In this paper,the results of FCFS are used to standardize the results of the remaining scheduling algorithms under the same experimental environment setting.

5.2   Execution Performance

Figure 3 shows the average completion time of each scheduling algorithm under different workload specifications (Facebook-like see Fig. 3(a), Google-like see Fig. 3(b), HPC-like see Fig. 3(c)). The experimental results show that SmartDis performs better than other scheduling strategies. Compared with the heuristic scheduling strategy based on SRPT, SmartDis performance is improved by 33% (Facebook-like), 25% (Google-like) and 27% (HPC-like) at high utilization rate (82%). At low utilization (26%), the performance improvement is at least 15% more. SmartDis chooses to execute the job that minimizes the increase in the overall execution delay by sensing the imbalance between the upload and calculation requirements of each subtask of the job. Compared with the Reordering and SWAG strategies, SmartDis's performance improvement is better at the meticulous processing of the edge scale and server performance heterogeneity. Under various load conditions, SmartDis's performance improvement advantage remains above 10%.

5.3   Fairness

Figure 4 shows the degree of delay of jobs of different size categories under each scheduling algorithm, in order to show the degree of fairness between jobs. Since the job delay in FCFS is too large compared to other algorithms, it is ignored

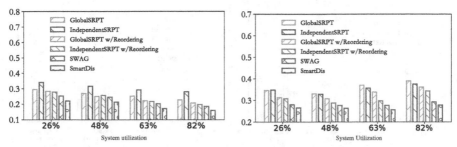

(a) Simulate Facebook business Hadoop clus- (b) Simulate Google cluster job specifications
ter job specifications

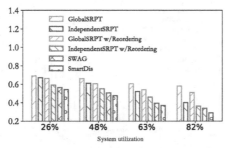

(c) Simulation of high-performance computing cluster job specifications

Fig. 3. Comparison of execution performance of various scheduling algorithms under different job specifications

in the results. Overall, the delay of small jobs is the smallest and the delay of large jobs is the largest under all scheduling methods.Because all algorithms essentially reduce the average job completion time by prioritizing the small jobs.

The difference in fairness is mainly reflected in the difference in the degree of delay in large jobs. First, it is observed that GlobalSRPT and IndependentSRPT are almost identical in maintaining fairness, so the following will only analyze the gap between IndependentSRPT and other scheduling algorithms. From the perspective of load type, the gap between the delay of large jobs in the Google-like load and the overall job delay is more significant. This is because almost all jobs in the Google-like are small jobs, resulting in a small number of large jobs being queued for too long due to the preference for small jobs. Even so, the big jobs in the SmartDis still maintain relatively low latency compared to others. In Facebook-like and HPC-like, the delay of large jobs under the IndependentSRPT is at least 38% higher than the delay of their overall jobs. While, IndependentSRPT's large job delay adjusted by Reordering is controlled to not exceed 28%. SWAG can control this gap to not exceed 23%, and SmartDis further controls this gap to within 20%. Therefore, it can be concluded that SmartDis does not significantly sacrifice the performance of large jobs when improving performance.

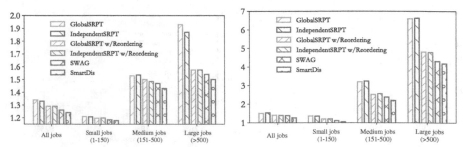

(a) Simulate Facebook business Hadoop cluster job specifications (b) Simulate Google cluster job specifications

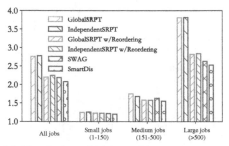

(c) Simulation of high-performance computing cluster job specifications

Fig. 4. Fairness comparison of scheduling algorithms under different job specifications

5.4 Sensitivity

The Impact of the Degree of Data Dispersion: Figure 5 presents the general trend that as the data skewness increases, the performance of the algorithm increases first and then decreases. When the job data is evenly distributed on the relevant edges, there is less room for optimization. When the data distribution starts to be unbalanced, multi-edge job scheduling collaboration can reduce job completion time. However, when the skewness exceeds a certain level, the imbalance of data distribution becomes so severe that most of the data of the same job is only distributed on a few edges. In this case, too much collaborative work is not required.

The Impact of Edge Scale Differences: Figure 6 shows that with the increase in edge scale heterogeneity, SmartDis performance has always maintained an advantage, and compared with other algorithms, SmartDis is more sensitive to edge scale differences. This is because SmartDis's scheduling proactively senses the imbalance in the execution delay between sibling tasks due to the difference in the overall service capabilities of the edge caused by the difference in the number of servers on the edge, and is committed to reducing the increase in global completion time caused by the imbalance.

The Effect of the Number of Edges: In Fig. 7, as the number of edges increases, the performance improvement of Reordering, SWAG, and SmartDis all show an increasing trend, because more edges provide more coordination opportunities for execution.

The Effect of Task Duration Estimation Accuracy: In the experiment, the estimation error is introduced based on the uniform distribution with the original task duration as the mean. The results in Fig. 8 show that with the increase in the accuracy of task duration estimation, the performance of each algorithm will be slightly improved, but it is not obvious. This is because due to the existence of various interference factors in the execution process, the original set time of the task is originally quite different, so the estimation error is not enough to seriously affect the scheduling decision. SmartDis maintains the best performance under different estimation accuracy, and it is robust to the estimation error of task duration.

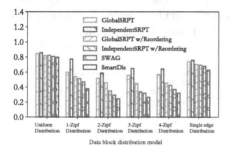

Fig. 5. The influence of the degree of data dispersion on each scheduling algorithm

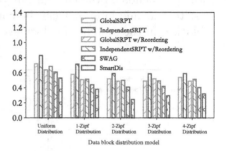

Fig. 6. Influence of the difference in size between edges on each scheduling algorithm

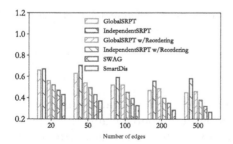

Fig. 7. Influence of the number of edges on each scheduling algorithm

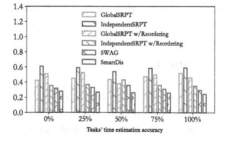

Fig. 8. Influence of the accuracy of task time estimation on each scheduling algorithm

5.5   Scheduling Execution Cost

Comparison of Running Time: The experiment measures the length of time to run the algorithm at each scheduling decision point. Figure 9(a) shows the running time of the algorithm under different system utilization rates. FCFS, GlobalSRPT, and IndependentSRPT are not shown in the results due to their minimal running time compared to others. The results show that even at high utilization rates (82%), Smart's scheduled runtime (4.61 ms) is much smaller than the average task duration (2 s).

Comparison of Extra Traffic: Extra traffic is defined as the information required by the scheduling algorithm to be transmitted from each edge to the global scheduler. Note that this does not include the basic and necessary information required for jobs. Figure 9(b) shows the traffic of each scheduling algorithm. FCFS and IndependentSRPT do not require the edge to provide any other information to the global scheduler, so their traffic is zero. The amount of traffic essentially depends on the current number of jobs in the system. SmartDis does its best to schedule jobs that can be completed quickly, keeping the number of jobs blocked in the system at a low level, so its traffic is acceptable.

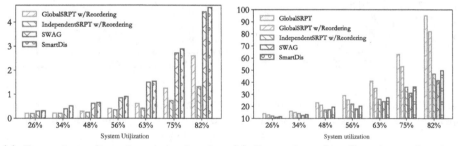

(a) Comparison of running time of various scheduling algorithms (b) Comparison of traffic volume of various scheduling algorithms

Fig. 9. Fairness comparison of scheduling algorithms under different job specifications

6   Conclusion

In the era of big data, the amount of data continues to grow at an alarming rate. This paper emphasizes the network and computing resource competition problems encountered by cross-domain big data analysis jobs in the edge environment. A resource coordination algorithm SmartDis is proposed to schedule subtasks across regions on multiple edges. SmartDis can achieve a near-optimal average completion time. Furthermore, the time-consuming transmission can prove the efficient approximate ratio. This paper conducts extensive experiments based on job execution specifications in real clusters to evaluate the performance of SmartDis in a wide range of scenarios. Compared with the heuristic scheduling algorithm based on the SRPT class, SmartDis improves the average completion time up to 33%, and keeps the additional calculation and communication overhead low.

References

1. Aazam, M., Huh, E.N.: E-HAMC: Leveraging fog computing for emergency alert service. In: 2015 IEEE International Conference on Pervasive Computing and Communication Workshops (PerCom Workshops), pp. 518–523. IEEE (2015)
2. Anand, S., Garg, N., Kumar, A.: Resource augmentation for weighted flow-time explained by dual fitting. In: Proceedings of the twenty-third annual ACM-SIAM symposium on Discrete Algorithms, pp. 1228–1241. SIAM (2012)
3. Ananthanarayanan, G., Hung, M.C.C., Ren, X., Stoica, I., Wierman, A., Yu, M.: GRASS: trimming stragglers in approximation analytics. In: 11th USENIX Symposium on Networked Systems Design and Implementation (NSDI 2014), pp. 289–302 (2014)
4. Asif-Ur-Rahman, M., et al.: Toward a heterogeneous mist, fog, and cloud-based framework for the internet of healthcare things. IEEE Internet Things J. **6**(3), 4049–4062 (2018)
5. Chadha, J.S., Garg, N., Kumar, A., Muralidhara, V.: A competitive algorithm for minimizing weighted flow time on unrelated machines with speed augmentation. In: Proceedings of the Forty-First Annual ACM Symposium on Theory of Computing, pp. 679–684 (2009)
6. Chen, N., Chen, Y., Song, S., Huang, C.T., Ye, X.: Smart urban surveillance using fog computing. In: 2016 IEEE/ACM Symposium on Edge Computing (SEC), pp. 95–96. IEEE (2016)
7. Dejun, J., Pierre, G., Chi, C.-H.: EC2 performance analysis for resource provisioning of service-oriented applications. In: Dan, A., Gittler, F., Toumani, F. (eds.) ICSOC/ServiceWave-2009. LNCS, vol. 6275, pp. 197–207. Springer, Heidelberg (2010). https://doi.org/10.1007/978-3-642-16132-2_19
8. Garg, N., Kumar, A.: Minimizing average flow-time: Upper and lower bounds. In: 48th Annual IEEE Symposium on Foundations of Computer Science (FOCS 2007), pp. 603–613. IEEE (2007)
9. Garg, N., Kumar, A., Pandit, V.: Order scheduling models: hardness and algorithms. In: Arvind, V., Prasad, S. (eds.) FSTTCS 2007. LNCS, vol. 4855, pp. 96–107. Springer, Heidelberg (2007). https://doi.org/10.1007/978-3-540-77050-3_8
10. Hajjat, M., Maltz, D., Rao, S., Sripanidkulchai, K.: Dealer: application-aware request splitting for interactive cloud applications. In: Proceedings of the 8th International Conference on Emerging Networking Experiments and Technologies, pp. 157–168 (2012)
11. Hung, C.C., Golubchik, L., Yu, M.: Scheduling jobs across geo-distributed datacenters. In: Proceedings of the Sixth ACM Symposium on Cloud Computing, pp. 111–124 (2015)
12. Im, S., Moseley, B.: An online scalable algorithm for minimizing lk-norms of weighted flow time on unrelated machines. In: Proceedings of the Twenty-sScond Annual ACM-SIAM Symposium on Discrete Algorithms, pp. 95–108. SIAM (2011)
13. Mastrolilli, M., Queyranne, M., Schulz, A.S., Svensson, O., Uhan, N.A.: Minimizing the sum of weighted completion times in a concurrent open shop. Oper. Res. Lett. **38**(5), 390–395 (2010)

14. Mohan, P., Thakurta, A., Shi, E., Song, D., Culler, D.: GUPT: privacy preserving data analysis made easy. In: Proceedings of the 2012 ACM SIGMOD International Conference on Management of Data, pp. 349–360 (2012)
15. Mutlag, A.A., Abd Ghani, M.K., Arunkumar, N.A., Mohammed, M.A., Mohd, O.: Enabling technologies for fog computing in healthcare IoT systems. Future Gener. Comput. Syst. **90**, 62–78 (2019)
16. Pu, Q., Ananthanarayanan, G., Bodik, P., Kandula, S., Akella, A., Bahl, P., Stoica, I.: Low latency geo-distributed data analytics. ACM SIGCOMM Comput. Commun. Rev. **45**(4), 421–434 (2015)
17. Queyranne, M.: Structure of a simple scheduling polyhedron. Math. Program. **58**(1–3), 263–285 (1993). https://doi.org/10.1007/BF01581271
18. Roemer, T.A.: A note on the complexity of the concurrent open shop problem. J. Sched. **9**(4), 389–396 (2006). https://doi.org/10.1007/s10951-006-7042-y
19. Schad, J., Dittrich, J., Quiané-Ruiz, J.A.: Runtime measurements in the cloud: observing, analyzing, and reducing variance. Proc. VLDB Endow. **3**(1–2), 460–471 (2010)
20. Schrage, L.: Letter to the editor-a proof of the optimality of the shortest remaining processing time discipline. Oper. Res. **16**(3), 687–690 (1968)
21. Singh, S., Singh, N.: Internet of things (ToT: Security challenges, business opportunities and reference architecture for e-commerce. In: 2015 International Conference on Green Computing and Internet of Things (ICGCIoT), pp. 1577–1581. IEEE (2015)
22. Tan, H., Han, Z., Li, X.Y., Lau, F.C.: Online job dispatching and scheduling in edge-clouds. In: IEEE INFOCOM 2017-IEEE Conference on Computer Communications, pp. 1–9. IEEE (2017)
23. Vulimiri, A., Curino, C., Godfrey, P.B., Jungblut, T., Padhye, J., Varghese, G.: Global analytics in the face of bandwidth and regulatory constraints. In: 12th USENIX Symposium on Networked Systems Design and Implementation (NSDI 2015), pp. 323–336 (2015)
24. Vulimiri, A., Curino, C., Godfrey, P.B., Jungblut, T., Karanasos, K., Padhye, J., Varghese, G.: Wanalytics: Geo-distributed analytics for a data intensive world. In: Proceedings of the 2015 ACM SIGMOD International Conference on Management of Data, pp. 1087–1092 (2015)
25. Wolsey, L., et al.: Formulating single machine scheduling problems with precedence constraints. Université catholique de Louvain, Center for Operations Research, Technical report (1989)

Low-Carbon Emission Driven Traffic Speed Optimization for Internet of Vehicles

Wenjie Chen[1][(✉)], Zhende Xiao[2], and Zou Siming[1]

[1] Business College, Central South University of Forestry and Technology,
Changsha 410004, China
T20142193@csuft.edu.cn
[2] College of Computer Science and Electronic Engineering, Hunan University,
Changsha 410082, China
xiaozhende@hnu.edu.cn

Abstract. Climate change has become a worldwide concern. Reducing CO2 emission is a major challenge for road transportation sector and is of critical importance. This paper, after studying and analyzing the influence of speed on vehicle CO_2 emission, proposes a recommended speed calculation scheme based on IoV to obtain vehicle speed and traffic signal phase information. In the recommended speed scenario, the vehicle is informed of the traffic phase information before arriving at the intersection and can set and optimize the current speed. This paper analyzes the three different status of traffic lights and studies the speed that should be adopted in each status. Under the proposed scheme, the recommended speed helps the driver to reach the destination with higher driving efficiency. The average wait time at red traffic lights is shorter than at speeds that are not recommended, resulting in reduced total travel time, higher uninterrupted pass rates, and decreased vehicle fuel consumption and CO_2 emissions.

Keywords: Internet of Vehicles · Speed optimization · CO_2 emissions mitigation · Traffic management

1 Introduction

Climate change and global warming has become a worldwide challenge. Climate change, as a result of human activities, can be mainly attributed to emissions of carbon dioxide (CO_2) and other greenhouse gases (GHGs) from fossil fuel utilization (Javid et al. 2014).

The transportation system is one of the causes that are largely responsible for the depletion of fossil fuels, the environmental contamination and the climate warming in recent decades (Gasparatos et al. 2009; Lim and Lee 2012). At present, fossil fuels take nearly 80% of the primary energy consumed in the world, of which up to 58% alone are consumed by the transport sector (Salvi et al. 2013). Trucks and passenger vehicles largely contribute to the bulk of GHGs emissions (Chapman 2007; Hensher 2008; Javid et al. 2014; Ong et al. 2012). As for China, there has been a rapid increase annually and it is expected to keep growing, particularly in road transport sector (Lin

H. Jiang et al. (Eds.): ICECI 2020, LNICST 368, pp. 35–50, 2021.
https://doi.org/10.1007/978-3-030-73429-9_3

and Xie 2013), which reflects the importance of traffic management and optimization in achieving long-term CO_2 mitigation.

New technologies for speed optimization control and traffic management are critical to lower transport emissions. Apart from the widely discussed low carbon vehicle technology, driving patterns and driving speed, including daily driving distance and driving condition would influence the emissions of vehicles (Karabasoglu and Michalek 2013; Kelly et al. 2012; Neubauer et al. 2012; Raykin et al. 2012; Traut et al. 2012). It is of interest to transportation planners, environmentalist, economists and government officials whether there are possible means that could ease the burden of emissions reductions in the transportation sector, particularly those emissions generated by road transportation.

Internet-of-Vehicles (IoV) based low carbon transportation management system is a crucial path to lower CO2 emissions. IoV arises from Internet-of-Things (IoT), in which a great many devices on the Internet are different protocols and standards (Gubbi et al. 2012). It is called IoV when every interconnected devices are recognized as vehicles. IoV can be applied to data communication for healthcare, safe driving, infotainment, energy saving and pollution reduction services (Kumar et al. 2015). Recent studies have shown that IoV technology can be applied to driving speed optimization, enhance energy efficiency and reduce CO_2 emissions (Bodenheimer et al. 2014).When IoV becomes integrated with the transport sector, intelligent low carbon traffic management systems aiming at emission mitigation is quite probable. Using dynamic and ubiquitous connectivity, IoV is capable of detecting traffic movement, process incoming information, relay information to drivers or traffic managers, make their decision and behavior more eco-sustainable, optimize their vehicles' speed for energy efficiency, encourage drivers to avoid aggressive and precarious driving behavior, such as sudden stop and go, and arbitrary speeding and idling, so as to reduce GHG emissions, enhance energy efficiency, and prompt a lower carbon path (Barkenbus 2010; Black and Geenhuizen 2006; Grant-Muller and Usher 2014). Therefore, by means of IoV we will be able to address issues such as energy deficiency, millions of tons of CO_2 emissions, and smooth road traffic (Guerrero-Ibanez et al. 2015).

Rapid acceleration, stop-and-go and traffic jams will cause massive carbon dioxide emissions. There are a large number of signal intersections in urban roads. Due to the periodic interference of their control signals, vehicle speed fluctuations will occur, leading to the decrease of vehicle traffic efficiency and the increase of pollutant discharge. Therefore, in order to avoid sudden acceleration, deceleration, idling and other driving behaviors, so as to improve the traffic efficiency at signalized intersections and the energy-saving and emission reduction effect of vehicles, we proposes a solution to calculate the recommended speed in IoV environment.

Actually, many research efforts have been exerted on IoV based technology aiming at reducing vehicles energy consumption and CO_2 emissions. Systems that uses IoV based traffic signal or mobile system were designed to guide drivers' decisions for the CO_2 emissions reduction, as well as the stop-starts and the accelerations frequency minimization (Dobre et al. 2012). Likewise, a scheme shortening traveling time to destinations and reducing CO_2 emission was proposed to reckon the recommended speed. (Li et al.

2013). An architecture was designed to provide alternative vehicular routes, aiming at lowering of energy consumption and journey time (Stolfi and Alba 2014).

As for exploring algorithms that apply traffic signal data to lessen CO_2 release. Critical aspects considered involve intelligent traffic management with the major challenge of CO_2 emissions mitigation. A function helping lowering emissions was proposed to calculate the optimal cycle length and green time segmentation (Ma and Nakamura 2010). In recent years, an intelligent traffic signal management approach was developed for urban traffic emission reduction (Li et al. 2015). A method was developed to minimize the stops frequency and waiting time for private vehicles (Dujardin et al. 2015). Moreover, a methodology was presented in which signal timings Pareto Fronts containing mobility, safety, and environment, are optimized (Stevanovic et al. 2015).

In this paper, we propose a low-carbon emission driven traffic speed optimization scheme, which is based on IoV to obtain vehicle speed and phase information of traffic signals. So as to reduce CO_2 emissions and increase energy efficiency of vehicles.

The remainder of this article is organized as follows. Section 2 illustrates the interaction between vehicles and traffic signals within IoV. Section 3 introduces the simulation framework of traffic flow-CO_2 emission. Next, Sect. 4 elaborates on the impact of speed on vehicle CO_2 emission. Then, Sect. 5 proposes the recommended speed calculation scheme. Finally, simulation results are presented and discussed in Sect. 6, and conclusions are arrived at in the Sect. 7.

2 Interaction Between Vehicles and Traffic Signals Within IoV

It is predicted that more than 24 billion "things" are expected to be interconnected by 2020, with vehicles occupying an important place (Dua et al. 2014). As more and more vehicles are connected to the IoT, IoV is in the boom (Yang et al. 2014). IoV, consisting of integrated users, vehicles, things, environment and networks, is a dynamic mobile communication system characterized by the collection, sharing, handling, calculating and secure delivery of data, and can be developed into the innovative intelligent transportation system (ITSs) (Lu et al. 2014).

There are two main technical areas of IoV: networking and intelligentization (Yang et al. 2014). Based on interaction between vehicles and traffic control infrastructure, vehicles stop frequency can be minimized and waiting queue at traffic lights can be optimized thereby reducing GHG emissions and improving energy efficiency.

This paper presumes that all the signal controllers are geared with roadside units (RSU). Each vehicle is provided with an on-board unit (OBU). OBU regularly transfer vehicle ID, GPS location, travelling speed, direction and status as well as other related vehicle information. RSU, coordinating with the neighboring RSU, gathers the real-time traffic information through integrating the OBUs information to determine the green segmentation and circular length, thus reducing fuel consumptions and CO_2 emissions. As shown in Fig. 1, based on Dedicated Short Range Communications (DSRC) technology, which is a set of standards at the core of automobile safety information exchange (Morgan 2010), OBU and RSU are capable of mutual communication. Each RSU can communicate with the vehicle if it is within the coverage of IoV communication. RSUs can communicate directly to their adjacent RSUs with one-hop connection. Besides,

RSUs can also communicate with each other under IoV. By building up a regional traffic control center that enables two-way communication with each individual RSU, the RSUs are able to communicate with others even these RSUs are far apart. In most cases, the vehicle is associated with a RSU when it is within the coverage area of this RSU. Due to the massive deployment of RSUs, IoV is able to provide nearly seamless coverage for the vehicles that are driving on the road. To this end, IoV can implement handover between adjacent RSUs that hence guarantees the continuous connection for the moving vehicles (Dua et al. 2014; Yang et al. 2014).

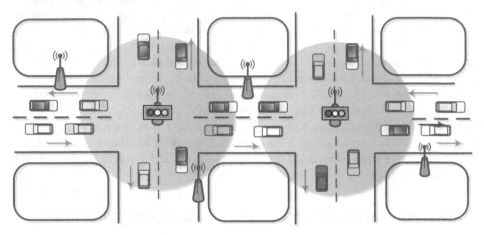

Fig. 1. Interaction between vehicles and traffic signal

As shown in Fig. 1, the RSU at an intersection, while sending packets periodically, corresponds with vehicles in all directions. Once the vehicle enters this range, it receives information from the intersection RSU broadcast, and sends its position, speed, and direction information to the RSU via a packet. After receiving the packet, the RSU sends the data to the traffic control center via the physical device. After receiving related information, the OBU will analyze and provide a recommended driving speed. This speed helps the driver to reach the destination with higher driving efficiency, thus enhancing the traffic efficiency at the signal intersection and the vehicle's energy conservation and emission reduction effect.

The IoV architecture is used for sharing road traffic flow data with adjacent intersections and for the whole city's traffic management as well. One intersection will send its road traffic data to its neighbor, and in turn these data will help the neighbor generate a better traffic signal cycles for vehicles. Through the communication module, adjacent intersections will cooperate with one another to smooth vehicle flow and alleviate traffic congestion.

3   Simulation Framework of Traffic Flow-CO$_2$ Emission

The simulation framework of traffic flow-CO$_2$ emission (Fig. 2) has the following features.

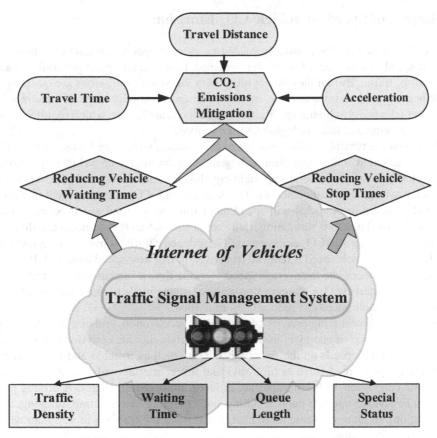

Fig. 2. Simulation framework of traffic flow-CO_2 emission

This paper introduces a CO_2 emission-estimation model, as shown in Eq. (1) and (2) to illustrate the relationship between CO_2 emissions and vehicle motion status(Suzuki and Horiuchi 2005).

$$E = 0.3K_C T + 0.028K_C D + 0.056K_C A \tag{1}$$

$$A = \sum_{k=1}^{n} \delta_k \left(v_k^2 - v_{k-1}^2 \right) \tag{2}$$

In Eq. (1) and (2), E signifies the CO_2 emissions [g]. T and D indicate the travel distance [m] and travel time [sec], respectively. K_c describes the coefficient. A and V_k are the accelerated speed value and the velocity in time k [m/sec], respectively. δ_k would be 1 when a vehicle is accelerating at time k, otherwise it would be 0. In a word, when the travel distance is constant, vehicles CO_2 emissions largely rest on the driving time and accelerated speed value.

4 Impact of Speed on Vehicle CO_2 Emission

CO_2 emission of vehicles is usually related to average speed. Researchers often use average speed as a measure of traffic performance. Low average speed generally means stop-and-go traffic. Even if they do not travel very far, vehicle emissions are quite high;

When the vehicle stops and the engine turns, emissions can increase indefinitely. When vehicles travel at higher speeds, the engine loads are higher, which requires more fuel consumption and leads to higher CO_2 emissions.

Based on the typical speed-emission curve in reality, which can be used to test the impact of different traffic operation management technologies on vehicle emissions, such as CO_2 emissions. Several important conclusions can be drawn. 1) If congestion causes the average speed of vehicles to be lower than 45, CO_2 emissions will increase, and at the same time, vehicles will spend more time on the road and produce higher CO2 emissions. Therefore, mitigating traffic congestion under this scenario can directly reduce CO2 emissions. 2) CO_2 emissions will be reduced if traffic congestion is alleviated and the average vehicle speed is reduced from over 70 free flow speed to 45–55. If traffic congestion is reduced and the average speed of traffic flow is increased to over 65, CO_2 emissions will increase. 3) Changing stop-and-go driving mode to make the vehicle run at a relatively stable speed can reduce CO_2 emissions.

A representative driving process covers idling, acceleration, cruising and deceleration. The proportion of energy consumption and carbon dioxide emissions at different stages of driving depends on the driver's behavior (such as irritable and mild driving habits), the type of road (such as highways and urban arterial roads, rural and urban) and traffic congestion. CO_2 emissions are different in these four stages. A driving process can be divided into two parts: 1) idling and 2) driving (accelerating, cruising, and deceleration). Engines consume more energy and release more CO_2 at idle than when the vehicle is in motion.

Moreover, reducing waiting time and driving at a constant velocity will result in lower CO_2 emissions, and studies have shown that vehicles have higher emissions when accelerating and decelerating than when idling. Moreover, the most common cause of engine idling is stop-and-go. Because vehicles slow down, stop, and then speed up for a short period. During that time, the vehicle releases more CO_2. Stop-and-go driving styles normally occur when parking or crossing an intersection. in order to reduce energy consumption and exhaust emission, it is better for vehicles to drive within an effective speed to avoid stopping at intersections.

5 Recommended Speed Calculation Scheme

5.1 Road Condition Detection

Road conditions include current vehicle velocity, vehicle spacing, and vehicle distance to destination. Traffic signal information should also be included when vehicles arrive at intersections.

5.2 Information Exchange

RSU and OBU exchange message via V2V and V2R cycles when the vehicle arrives at the intersection. This information exchange process is shown as follows: First, when the vehicle arrives at the intersection, the on-board unit of the vehicle will send the status information of the vehicle to the traffic signal. Then, the traffic signal receives the information from the vehicle and sends the status of the signal back to the vehicle. The vehicle then receives a response message from the traffic lights, which the unit uses to obtain a recommended speed, which will be provided to drivers.

Therefore, the roadside unit RSUS contain the vehicle's current speed and location information, and the on-board unit will receive the current traffic status information. The current traffic signal information contains the following elements: the traffic signal cycle, the current phase of the traffic signal, and the time left of the current phase. In addition, the on-board unit can also get adjacent workshop spacing.

5.3 Recommended Speed Calculation

The more times the car stops, the more carbon dioxide is released throughout the journey. In this regard, consider giving drivers the recommended speed and speeding through intersections within a reasonable range to avoid unnecessary stops. With this in mind, the vehicle USES the information gathered to calculate a recommended speed that maximizes the vehicle's ability to drive through the intersection in a smooth, low-carbon and environmentally friendly manner. If vehicles cannot cross the intersection with current velocity, take the recommended speed to pass through the intersection, thus reducing the number of vehicle stops.

The distance between the vehicle and the traffic light (d) can be easily obtained through the GPS device. As mentioned earlier, the traffic signal will deliver data packets to the vehicle within communication range. The vehicle is able to compute a recommended velocity after receiving the following message to avoid the vehicle waiting at the intersection.

① Current traffic light status (green, yellow or red).

② Current traffic light status remaining time (L_g, L_r, L_y).

③ The current traffic light cycle CL, the duration of the three stages (T_g, T_y, T_r), among which $C_L = T_g + T_y + T_r$.

In the scheme studied, the duration of red, green and yellow lights is different in each cycle, because the scheme dynamically changes the duration of traffic lights according to real-time traffic flow information. On the strength of this information, the vehicle's OBU device calculates the recommended speed. The maximum speed of the driver is marked as S_{max} and the minimum speed is S_{min}.

In general, vehicle spacing can be divided into two categories: the first type of vehicle spacing is relatively large, so that this type of vehicle can travel freely and is not affected by other vehicles. The second type of vehicle has less space and must follow the vehicle in front of it. Therefore, this type of vehicle cannot exceed the speed of the vehicle in front. Since vehicles can communicate with each other, the front vehicle speed (S_P) can also be obtained. In this scheme, this paper only considers the influence of the front vehicle. Among them, P represents the vehicle spacing is relatively large, $\overline{P}$ represents the vehicle spacing is relatively small.

The following three scenarios demonstrate the calculation of the recommended speed:

$t_0 = d/S_C$: represents the time it takes the vehicle to pass through the intersection at the current speed, distance d.

$t_1 = d/S_{\max}$: refers to the time taken for the vehicle to pass through the intersection at the maximum speed distance d.

(1) The current traffic light is green

① If $L_g > t_0$, it means that the vehicle is sufficient to drive at the current speed through the intersection during the remaining green time, and keep a certain distance between the front and rear vehicles. The recommended speed at this time is the current speed, and its formula is as follows:

$$S_R = S_C \tag{3}$$

② If $t_1 < L_g < t_0$, it means that during the remaining green time, the vehicle is not enough to drive through the intersection at the current speed, but the vehicle can pass at the maximum speed, and the two vehicles keep a certain distance. In this case, the driver needs to accelerate to the maximum speed, so the recommended speed is the maximum speed. The calculation formula is as follows:

$$S_R = S_{\max} \tag{4}$$

③ If $t_1 > L_g$ means that the vehicle cannot pass through the intersection with the maximum speed in the remaining time, then the vehicle needs to wait for the next cycle. To do this, the vehicle must slow down and wait for at least one red light and one yellow light, as shown below:

$$S_R = \min\left(\max\left(\frac{d}{(N_g - 1) \cdot C_L + L_g + T_y + T_r + M - T_D}, S_{\min}\right), S_F\right) \tag{5}$$

Where, $N_g = \frac{d/S_F - L_g}{C_L}$ represents the number of traffic signal cycles that vehicles need to wait for during the green light period.

④ If the space between the two cars at this time is relatively small, so the vehicle speed is not greater than the front of the vehicle speed, the calculation is as follows:

$$S_R = \min(S_P, S_{\max}) \tag{6}$$

(2) The current traffic signal is red

① If $L_r < t_0 < L_r + T_g$, means that after the red light turns to green, the vehicle can reach the intersection at the current speed, and keep a certain distance between the front and rear vehicles. Then the recommended speed is set to the current speed, which is calculated as follows:

$$S_R = S_C \tag{7}$$

② If $L_r < t_1 < L_r + T_g < t_0$, it means that during the remaining red light time plus green time, the vehicle cannot reach the intersection at the current speed but can reach the intersection at the maximum speed, and the two vehicles in front and behind keep a certain distance. In this case, it is necessary to accelerate to the maximum speed. The calculation is as follows:

$$S_R = S_{max} \tag{8}$$

③ If $t_1 > T_g + L_r + C_L$, it means that the vehicle still cannot reach the intersection with the maximum speed before the traffic light changes from green to yellow, the vehicle needs to wait for at least one traffic signal cycle, and keep a certain distance between the front and rear vehicles. In this case, the car must slow down. S_R calculation is as follows:

$$S_R = \min\left(\max\left(\frac{d}{N_r \cdot C_L + L_r + M - T_D}, S_{min} \right), S_F \right) \tag{9}$$

Where, $N_r = \frac{d/S_F - L_r - T_g}{C_L}$ represents the number of cycles in which vehicles need to wait for traffic signals during the red light period.

④ If the space between the two cars at this time is relatively small, so the vehicle speed is not greater than the front of the vehicle speed, the calculation is as follows:

$$S_R = \min(S_P, S_{max}) \tag{10}$$

(3) The current traffic lights are yellow

Compared to the case of red light, the vehicle needs one or more yellow light time. The calculation of the recommended speed is similar to that of the current red light scheme. The calculation formula is shown as below:

① If $t_y + T_R < t_0 + T_R + T_G$

$$S_R = S_C \tag{11}$$

② If $L_y + T_r + T_g < t_1 < L_y + C_L$

$$S_R = S_{max} \tag{12}$$

③ If $L_y + C_L < t_1$

$$S_R = \min\left(\max\left(\frac{d}{N_y \cdot C_L + L_r + M - T_D}, S_{min} \right), S_F \right) \tag{13}$$

Where, $N_y = \frac{d/S_F - T_r - L_y - T_g}{C_L}$ represents the number of cycles in which vehicles need to wait for traffic signals during the yellow light period.

④ If the space between the two cars at this time is relatively small, so the vehicle speed is not greater than the front of the vehicle speed, the calculation is as follows:

$$S_R = \min(S_P, S_{max}) \tag{14}$$

In Formula (5), (9), (13), T_D represents the transmission delay between the RSU of traffic signal as well as the OBU of vehicle. M represents the time it takes the vehicle to convert from the current speed to the recommended speed.

6 Simulations and Results

This section, based on MATLAB and VISSIM simulation software, is mainly to carry out experimental simulation of speed optimization control, and compare the experiment with no recommended speed, so as to appraise the effect of the proposed solution.

6.1 Simulation Settings

This paper adopts the scenario in Fig. 3, where Road R1 and R2 are the main roads, with a larger traffic flow than R3 and R4, and the driving route is from S to D. When a vehicle passes through an intersection, the driver receives a recommended speed.

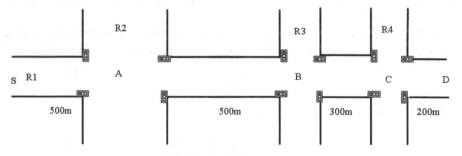

Fig. 3. Simulation scenes

In the experiment, the timing method is used to compare the recommended speed and verify the CO_2 emission of vehicles. The main related parameters are shown in Table 1 below:

Table 1. Simulation parameters

Parameters	Values	Parameters	Values
R1A (green, red, yellow)	(55, 60, 5)	R1B (green, red, yellow)	(55, 50, 5)
R2A (green, red, yellow)	(55, 60, 5)	R3B (green, red, yellow)	(45, 60, 5)

(continued)

Table 1. (*continued*)

Parameters	Values	Parameters	Values
R1C (green, red, yellow)	(55, 30, 5)	R4C (green, red, yellow)	(25, 60, 5)
A area coverage	$12 \times 12 \text{ m}^2$	B area coverage	$12 \times 6 \text{ m}^2$
C area coverage	$12 \times 4 \text{ m}^2$	Maximum speed S_{max}	60 km/h
Minimum speed S_{min}	10 km/h	Mobility models	Car following model
Vehicle speed	10–60 km/h	M	3s
T_D	0 s		
Traffic flow	50, 100, 200, 400, 600, 800, 100 veh/h		

6.2 Simulation Results and Analysis

Figure 4 and 5 show that compared with no recommended speed, vehicles with recommended speed can drive across the intersection with shorter waiting time and less stops. Moreover, vehicles with the recommended speed will have less waiting time than

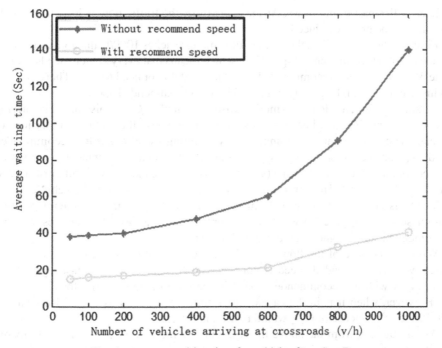

Fig. 4. Average waiting time for vehicles from S to D

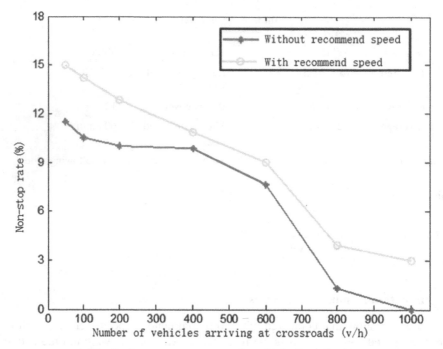

Fig. 5. Average non-stop rate for vehicles from S to D

vehicles with small traffic flows. At the same time, the traffic flow is low; the vehicle stop rate can be greatly reduced.

Figure 4 shows that when the number of vehicles reaches 1000/h, the non-stop rate of vehicles without recommended speed is 0, which means that every vehicle needs to stop, while 3% vehicles with recommended speed method do not need to stop. Therefore, the driving efficiency can be greatly improved by the recommended speed.

As stated before, a calculation model is used to calculate CO_2 emissions. The driving distance, driving time and instantaneous speed of vehicles all affect CO_2 emissions of vehicles. The vehicle can avoid unnecessary stopping by adopting the recommended speed (S_R), such as $S_{min} < S_R < S_{max}$. If the vehicle inevitably comes to a stop at an intersection, it is necessary to adjust the speed to S_R by reducing the number of useless vehicles at high speed. The purpose is to mitigate the acceleration of the vehicle.

The S_R is calculated to achieve the maximum possible speed through the intersection without stopping. Figure 6 shows the amount of CO_2 released by vehicles with no recommended speed higher than those with recommended speed do.

With the increase of the flow of traffic, the amount of CO_2 release growth of the vehicle with recommended speed is not big. The amount of CO_2 released growth of the vehicles with no recommended speed in the case of light traffic flow is also not big. However, when it is in the case of large traffic flow, such as traffic flow reaches 800–1000/h, the release of CO_2 would reach a new peak.

As can be seen from the above figures, with the increase of traffic flow, compared with the speed without recommendation, the average waiting time of vehicles passing the

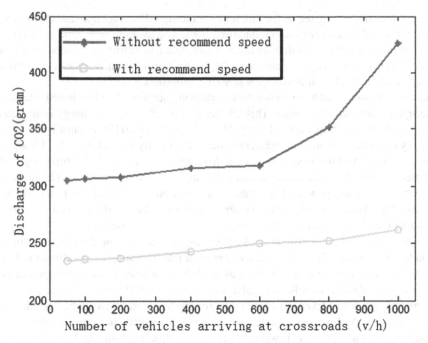

Fig. 6. CO_2 emissions for vehicles from S to D

intersection will be shorter, so the total driving time will be reduced and the uninterrupted pass rate will be higher. At the same time, vehicle energy efficiency will be enhanced, which will cut down CO_2 emissions.

7 Conclusions

Climate change and energy shortage have become a serious problem for many countries. Among the primary GHGs responsible for human-induced climate change, CO2, as the main GHGs component, has the greatest impact on the man-made climatic variation (Javid et al. 2014; Zhi et al. 2013). Therefore, reducing CO_2 emission is a major challenge for road transportation sector and is of vital importance.

There are a large number of signal intersections in urban roads. Due to the periodic interference of their control signals, vehicle velocity fluctuations will occur, leading to the decrease of vehicle's traffic and energy efficiency and pollutant discharge when driving across the intersections.

Based on this, in order to avoid sudden acceleration, deceleration, idling and other driving behaviors, so as to improve the traffic efficiency at signalized intersections and the energy-saving and emission reduction effect of vehicles, this paper proposes a recommended speed calculation scheme, which is based on IoV to obtain vehicle speed and phase information of traffic lights.

Under the recommended scheme, drivers would be notified to drive with the optimized speed. This speed helps the driver to reach the destination with higher driving efficiency, thus improving the traffic efficiency at the signal intersection and the vehicle's energy conservation and emission reduction effect. The average wait time at red traffic lights is shorter than at speeds that are not recommended, resulting in reduced total travel time and higher uninterrupted pass rates. At the same time, vehicle fuel consumption will be reduced, which will make for lesser CO_2 emissions.

The benefits observed have shown the low carbon potential of an IoV based intelligent traffic signal management system. This implies that the climate and energy costs can be reduced without affecting traffic fluidity. However, CO_2 or GHGs cannot be mitigated by simply exploiting traffic management system. This study have shown that for a given conditions there exist the possibility to cut down environment costs by referring to the IoV based intelligent traffic management solution, even at a micro-level. The results of our simulation present powerful arguments for the strategic development and diffusion of the IoV based traffic management systems, which can hardly do without the support and cooperation of the government, other institutions and the public.

Political will and commitment is of critical importance for the development of low carbon traffic system (Yin et al. 2015). Clear local political support combined with the cooperation of related institutions, such as setting up infrastructure development programs and promulgating beneficial regulations, is one channel to provide more consistent assist and planning for developing and popularizing IoV based low carbon traffic management system. As low carbon and sustainable development is interdisciplinary, and IoV based transport system is inseparable from scientific planning and construction of urban infrastructure emphasizing the concerted effort so as to realize desired outcomes (Baltazar et al. 2015).

Although, this paper presents evidence that there are optional paths for achieving the low carbon future without sacrificing the mobility, convenience, comfort and safety. There are still some area worth future work and improvement. The CO_2 emission model used in this research is relatively simple one, which does not take relevant factors into consideration, such as vehicle type, vehicle age, vehicle condition, driving habits and infrastructure features. Cautions need to be taken when the proposed approach is applied to a specific vehicle in a specific infrastructure environment (Li et al. 2014). So, further investigations on how to incorporate more advanced CO_2 emission estimation model is necessary (Rakha et al. 2011).

Acknowledgement. This work was supported by the National Social Sciences Foundation of China (Grants No. 19CGL043).

References

de Andrade, J.B.S.O., Ribeiro, J.M.P., Fernandez, F., Bailey, C., Barbosa, S.B., da Silva Neiva, S.: The adoption of strategies for sustainable cities: A comparative study between Newcastle and Florianópolis focused on urban mobility. J. Clean. Prod. **113**, 681–694 (2016). https://doi.org/10.1016/j.jclepro.2015.07.135. https://www.sciencedirect.com/science/article/pii/S0959652615010665. ISSN 0959-6526

Barkenbus, J.N.: Eco-driving: an overlooked climate change initiative. Energy Policy **38**(2), 762–769 (2010)

Black, W.R., Van Geenhuizen, M.: ICT Innovation and sustainability of the transport sector. Eur. J. Transp. Infrastruct. Res. 6(1) (2006). ISSN 1567-7141

Bodenheimer, R., Brauer, A., Eckhoff, D., German, R.: Enabling GLOSA for adaptive traffic lights. In: Paper Presented at the Vehicular Networking Conference (VNC), 2014. IEEE (2014)

Chapman, L.: Transport and climate change: a review. J. Transp. Geogr. 15(5), 354–367 (2007)

Dobre, C., Szekeres, A., Pop, F., Cristea, V.: Intelligent traffic lights to reduce vehicle emissions. Int. J. Innov. Comput. Inf. Control 8(9), 6283–6302 (2012)

Dua, A., Kumar, N., Bawa, S.: A systematic review on routing protocols for Vehicular Ad Hoc Networks. Veh. Commun. 1(1), 33–52 (2014)

Dujardin, Y., Vanderpooten, D., Boillot, F.: A multi-objective interactive system for adaptive traffic control. Eur. J. Oper. Res. 244(2), 601–610 (2015)

Gasparatos, A., El-Haram, M., Horner, M.: A longitudinal analysis of the UK transport sector, 1970–2010. Energy Policy 37(2), 623–632 (2009)

Grant-Muller, S., Usher, M.: Intelligent transport systems: the propensity for environmental and economic benefits. Technol. Forecast. Soc. Chang. 82(1), 149–166 (2014)

Gubbi, J., Buyya, R., Marusic, S., Palaniswami, M.: Internet of Things (IoT): a vision, architectural elements, and future directions. Futur. Gener. Comput. Syst. 29(7), 1645–1660 (2012)

Guerrero-Ibanez, J.A., Zeadally, S., Contreras-Castillo, J.: Integration challenges of intelligent transportation systems with connected vehicle, cloud computing, and internet of things technologies. IEEE Wirel. Commun. 22(6), 122–128 (2015)

Hensher, D.A.: Climate change, enhanced greenhouse gas emissions and passenger transport – what can we do to make a difference? Transp. Res. Part D Transp. Environ. 13(2), 95–111 (2008)

Javid, R.J., Nejat, A., Hayhoe, K.: Selection of CO_2 mitigation strategies for road transportation in the United States using a multi-criteria approach. Renew. Sustain. Energy Rev. 38(5), 960–972 (2014)

Karabasoglu, O., Michalek, J.: Influence of driving patterns on life cycle cost and emissions of hybrid and plug-in electric vehicle powertrains. Energy Policy 60(5), 445–461 (2013)

Kelly, J.C., Macdonald, J.S., Keoleian, G.A.: Time-dependent plug-in hybrid electric vehicle charging based on national driving patterns and demographics. Appl. Energy 94(2), 395–405 (2012)

Kumar, N., Kaur, K., Jindal, A., Rodrigues, J.J.P.C.: Providing healthcare services on-the-fly using multi-player cooperation game theory in Internet of Vehicles (IoV) environment. Digital Commun. Netw. 29(3), 191–203 (2015)

Li, C., Chen, W., He, D., Hu, X., Shimamoto, S.: A travel-efficient driving assistance scheme in VANETs by providing recommended speed. IEICE Trans. Fundam. Electron. Commun. Comput. Sci. e96.a(10), 2007–2015 (2013)

Li, C., Ni, A., Ding, J.: Eco-driving --- current strategies and issues, a preliminary survey. In: Paper presented at the 2015 Information Technology and Mechatronics Engineering Conference (2015)

Li, X., Cui, J., An, S., Parsafard, M.: Stop-and-go traffic analysis: theoretical properties, environmental impacts and oscillation mitigation. Transp. Res. Part B Methodol. 70(1), 319–339 (2014)

Lim, S., Lee, K.T.: Implementation of biofuels in Malaysian transportation sector towards sustainable development: a case study of international cooperation between Malaysia and Japan. Renew. Sustain. Energy Rev. 16(4), 1790–1800 (2012)

Lin, B., Xie, C.: Estimation on oil demand and oil saving potential of China's road transport sector. Energy Policy 61, 472–482 (2013)

Lu, N., Cheng, N., Zhang, N., Shen, X.: Connected vehicles: solutions and challenges. IEEE Internet Things J. 1(4), 289–299 (2014)

Ma, D., Nakamura, H.: Cycle length optimization at isolated signalized intersections from the viewpoint of emission. In: Paper Presented at the Seventh International Conference on Traffic and Transportation Studies (2010)

Morgan, Y.L.: Notes on DSRC & WAVE standards suite: its architecture, design, and characteristics. IEEE Commun. Surv. Tutorials **12**(4), 504–518 (2010)

Neubauer, J., Brooker, A., Wood, E.: Sensitivity of battery electric vehicle economics to drive patterns, vehicle range, and charge strategies. J. Power Sources **209**(7), 269–277 (2012)

Ong, H.C., Mahlia, T.M.I., Masjuki, H.H.: A review on energy pattern and policy for transportation sector in Malaysia. Renew. Sustain. Energy Rev. **16**(1), 532–542 (2012)

Rakha, H.A., Ahn, K., Moran, K., Saerens, B., Bulck, E.V.D.: Virginia tech comprehensive power-based fuel consumption model: model development and testing. Transp. Res. Part D Transp. Environ. **16**(16), 492–503 (2011)

Raykin, L., Roorda, M.J., Maclean, H.I.: Impacts of driving patterns on tank-to-wheel energy use of plug-in hybrid electric vehicles. Transp. Res. Part D Transp. Environ. **17**(3), 243–250 (2012)

Salvi, B.L., Subramanian, K.A., Panwar, N.L.: Alternative fuels for transportation vehicles: a technical review. Renew. Sustain. Energy Rev. **25**(5), 404–419 (2013)

Stevanovic, A., Stevanovic, J., So, J., Ostojic, M.: Multi-criteria optimization of traffic signals: mobility, safety, and environment. Trans. Res. Part C: Emerg. Technol. **55**, 46–68 (2015)

Stolfi, D.H., Alba, E.: Eco-friendly reduction of travel times in european smart cities. In: Paper Presented at the Proceedings of the 2014 Conference on Genetic and Evolutionary Computation (2014)

Suzuki, S., Horiuchi, N.: A study of the signal control for the minimization of CO_2 emission. In: World Congress on Intelligent Transport Systems, vol. 12, pp. 41–44 (2005)

Traut, E., Hendrickson, C., Klampfl, E., Liu, Y., Michalek, J.J.: Optimal design and allocation of electrified vehicles and dedicated charging infrastructure for minimum life cycle greenhouse gas emissions and cost. Energy Policy **51**(4), 524–534 (2012)

Yang, F., Wang, S., Li, J., Liu, Z., Sun, Q.: An overview of internet of vehicles. China Commun. **11**(10), 1–15 (2014)

Yin, Y., Olsson, A.R., Håkansson, M.: The role of local governance and environmental policy integration in Swedish and Chinese eco-city development. J. Clean. Prod. **134, Part A**, 78–86 (2016). https://doi.org/10.1016/j.jclepro.2015.10.087. https://www.sciencedirect.com/science/article/pii/S0959652615015589. ISSN 0959-6526

Zhi, H.L., Sethupathi, S., Lee, K.T., Bhatia, S., Mohamed, A.R.: An overview on global warming in Southeast Asia: CO_2 emission status, efforts done, and barriers. Renew. Sustain. Energy Rev. **28**(8), 71–81 (2013)

Data Gathering System Based on Multi-layer Edge Computing Nodes

Shuzhen Xiang, Huigui Rong$^{(\boxtimes)}$, and Zhangchi Xu

Hunan University, Changsha, China
{shuzhenxiang,ronghg,zhangchixu}@hnu.edu.cn

Abstract. The development of Internet of Things technology brings new opportunities for the development of edge computing. As an emerging computing model, edge computing makes full use of the equipment resources at the edge of the network and creates a new network computing system at the edge of the network. At the same time, the emergence of edge computing solves the problem of high latency in WAN which cannot be solved for a long time in the field of cloud computing, and brings users with low latency, fast response and good service experience. This article will use the edges computing architecture to construct a multi-layer data collection system. In this system model, sensors upload data to the designated edge nodes for processing, rather than remote cloud computing centers. Data collection and sample training tasks of sensor nodes in different ranges are realized through the design of multi-layer edge nodes. This system reduces the energy consumption of data uploading and the delay in network communication. As a result, it provides a better network experience for the end users. And it tries to solve the problem that the edge node in the edge system cannot satisfy multiple training task requests at the same time.

Keywords: Data gathering · Edge computing · Compress sense

1 Introduction

In general, after collecting the data generated by the terminal devices, the cloud data center uses powerful computing power to train the AI service model, and then stores the trained model on the cloud and the service devices at the edge. However, using cloud data center to collect data will cause two very tricky problems. First, cloud data center is usually far away from the end devices, and the end devices need to be connected through wide area network (WAN), resulting in a large delay. Secondly, when users' data is transmitted in a WAN, data privacy cannot be guaranteed due to the fact that WAN covers a wide range of regions and there may be many intermediate nodes [1]. In the edge of computing architecture, the edge nodes have proximity. That is to say, the geographic distance between the edge node and the end device is very close, which is much smaller than the distance between the end device and the cloud data center. At the same time, using wireless LAN for network connection, the propagation delay is much smaller than in WAN. Based on the wireless local area network to transmit

© ICST Institute for Computer Sciences, Social Informatics and Telecommunications Engineering 2021
Published by Springer Nature Switzerland AG 2021. All Rights Reserved
H. Jiang et al. (Eds.): ICECI 2020, LNICST 368, pp. 51–64, 2021.
https://doi.org/10.1007/978-3-030-73429-9_4

data, there is no need to worry about some relatively confidential data being leaked. So the network system based on edge computing architectures constructing can well solve the two problems. In addition, the analysis engine is close to the data source and only a small amount of condensed information is sent back to the central system, which is more effective.

However, in the edge system, there may be many different AI service models that need to be trained, but the relatively scarce computing resources and storage resources of the edge devices cannot meet the requests of all training tasks at the same time. As a result, this article puts forward a kind of multi-layer edge data collection system, which makes the data can be collected and trained on the edge of the network side, in order to complete the training tasks of the AI service model as much as possible with limited resources.

2 Related Work

With the emergence of new computing models such as IoT, edge computing, and fog computing, some research efforts have attempted to implement distributed machine learning model training in network edge devices with more geographical locations [1–4]. These network edge devices are usually connected to each other through wireless LAN. Moreover, compared with the server cluster in the data center, the computing and storage capacity of a single network edge device is more limited. These factors have brought challenges to the training of distributed machine learning in the edge network. Reference [2] considers a distributed machine learning model training algorithm for parameter aggregation through a central parameter server. This method does not need to transfer the original data to the central server. Instead, it uploads the local model parameters on each distributed node after the aggregation. Based on the theoretical analysis of the convergence rate of distributed gradient descent, a control algorithm is proposed to determine the optimal tradeoff between local update and global parameter aggregation to minimize the loss function under a given resource budget. Reference [3] proposes to divide each layer of the deep neural network model (DNN) into several parts, which are mapped to various hierarchical structures in the edge computing architecture. Through joint training of each part, the network edge can quickly generate small neural network model (that is, a neural network model with fewer parameters) for quick task inference, while generating a larger neural network model (that is, a neural network model with more parameters) on the cloud data center side for more accurate tasks inference. It is inferred that this joint training method minimizes device communication and resource utilization, and improves the practicality of feature extraction in a cloud computing environment. Reference [4] introduces edge computing into IoT applications based on deep learning, and proposes a new scheduling strategy to optimize the performance of deep learning applications in the IoT through the edge computing architecture. However, in the case of training distributed machine learning models to attract edge computing architecture, it is not covered that how to effectively collect data from terminal devices and offload tasks and correctly allocate limited resources for each task. Since machine learning is usually resource-intensive and time-consuming, the data collection mechanism and resource allocation mechanism will have a great impact on the accuracy and training efficiency of the training model. Therefore, it is essential to tailor an effective data collection mechanism and an appropriate resource allocation mechanism for the training of AI service model in the edge.

For data collection in distributed networks, many scholars at home and abroad have also proposed the principle of using compressed sensing to sample and compress data. Reference [5–8] studies the distributed source coding technology of multi-sensor collaboration. The source coding algorithm based on compressed sensing is adopted to reduce the repetitive coding of data, improve the compression ratio and save energy. In recent years, a large number of research achievements have been made on compressed sensing itself and its application in medical detection, radar imaging, image processing and other fields.

3 Theoretical Basis

3.1 Compressed Sensing

With a large amount of information growing now, the compressed sensing method breaks through many limitations of traditional methods in data sampling, storage, and signal bandwidth. Sampling and compression are completed at the same time without losing the original information, which saves a lot of resources. Compressed sensing theory proves that if the signal satisfies the sparse characteristics in an orthogonal transform space, the original signal can be reconstructed accurately or with high probability through fewer sampling points. Suppose there is a signal $f^{(N \times 1)}$, the length is N, and the basis vector is Ψ_i ($i = 1, 2,..., N$) to transform the signal.

$$f = \sum_{i=1}^{N} \chi_i \psi_i \text{ or } f = \Psi X \tag{1}$$

From the above, the current theory of compressed sensing mainly involves three aspects:

(1) Sparse representation of signals;
(2) Design of measurement matrix;
(3) Design of reconstruction algorithm.

3.2 Random Walk

In computer, physics, biology and other fields, random walk has been widely used. More and more attention has been paid to the random walk model. "Random Walk" describes a situation in which a person standing on a straight line in three dimensions has only two directions to choose from, and now he can only choose to go left or right. In probability theory, he takes one step to the left as much as he takes one to the right, and when he takes enough steps he must come back to where he started.

First, the introduction of random walk on the graph: define the graph G (V, E, ω), G (V, E, ω) is a right undirected graph with n vertices and m edges, where V is the vertex set, E is the edge set, and $\omega: V \times V \rightarrow R$ is the connection weight function. As shown in Fig. 1:

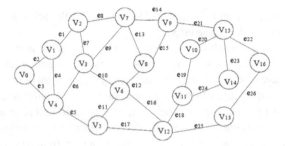

Fig. 1. Undirected graph

Figure 1 an undirected graph with 17 vertices $\{V_0, V_1 \ldots, V_{16}\}$, and 26 edges $\{e_1,$ $e_2, e_3 \ldots e_{26}\}$. Each edge is given a certain weight ω_i..

If particle A goes from vertex V_i to vertex V_j with probability P_{ij}, then the vertices visited by particle A form a random sequence $X_n, n = 0,1,2,\ldots$

4 Multi-layer Edge Data Collection System

This system combines the topology of the network with the compressed sensing and the edge server, and sets the cluster and cluster head in the edge server in a fixed structure. This paper mainly describes how to set up the edge network structure and how to realize data collection on this structure. The logic diagram of the specific framework is shown in Fig. 2.

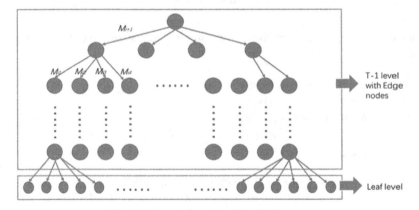

Fig. 2. System framework logic diagram

4.1 System Model and Problem Description

The network architecture in Fig. 2 is adopted in this paper. The first layer is leaf level, where each node is a data source node and corresponds to an area with a geographical area of s. The i ($i >= 2$) layer is the edge computing layer, which is composed of multiple edge computing nodes.

Each edge computing node of the i-th layer can collect and process the data of the n nodes of the specified $I - 1$th layer and upload it to the specified edge node of the $i + 1$th layer.

$C_{i,n}$ represents the nth node in the i-th layer, and $M_{i,n}$ represents the measured number of the nth node in the i-layer ($n = 1, 2, \ldots N_i$, N_i is the number of nodes shared in the i-th layer). $C_{i,n}$ has a data amount of $D_{i,n}$ and generates a training task request $q_{i,n,k}$.

When faced with the assignment of training tasks. Each edge node of the system can regard the upper node in its own cluster as the source node that can send training requests. At the same time, in the training model of AI, for the same model, the greater the amount of input data during training, the higher the accuracy of the training model, and otherwise the effect is very poor. Therefore, our model has the potential to improve the accuracy of the model by actively collecting more data.

4.2 Data Collection Process

Level 1: Source Node Data Collection

Random Walk. We correspond the vertices of the undirected graph to the sensor nodes in the wireless sensor network, and apply the random walk model to the first-level leaf nodes of the system. We can define the starting node of the Random Walk randomly or according to some properties of the signal, set the number of steps to be taken by the Walk, and then generate a random sequence of access paths Xn. In a vector of $1 \times N$ with all zeros, set the position of the path to 1, which means that the information of this node is collected. If the node has been passed in this path, the value in the vector is not changed, indicating that the information of this node is not collected. After a walk, the last node will pass the collected data to the cluster-head node. In this way, a path can be transformed into a 0/1 vector, and the 0/1 vector of M paths can be generated by repeating M random walks. These vectors are combined together to form an $M \times N$ matrix, which is the measurement matrix of compressed sensing, so as to collect and measure information. The logical diagram is shown in Fig. 3:

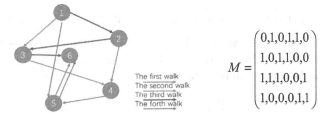

$$M = \begin{pmatrix} 0,1,0,1,1,0 \\ 1,0,1,1,0,0 \\ 1,1,1,0,0,1 \\ 1,0,0,0,1,1 \end{pmatrix}$$

Fig. 3. Random walk roadmap

There are 6 nodes in the figure, and each color represents a node that a walk passes through. A total of 4 walks are made. The resulting measurement matrix is M.

In the measurement matrix formed by Random walk, each row vector is independently generated, and the data collection process is also collected through one by one path. These characteristics make the use of stopping rule to ensure the quality of data with higher efficiency. Increasing the number of samplings at a time can be achieved by simply increasing the number of other walks without re-sampling.

Stopping Rule to Ensure Data Quality. Since the data information of the node is unknown, the sparsity of the information cannot be accurately estimated, which brings certain problems to the setting of the sampling rate. If the sampling rate is set too high, both communication overhead and computational overhead are wasted. And if the sampling rate is set too low, the quality of the reconstructed data cannot be guaranteed.

First, let's look at the sampling rate and the quality of data reconstruction. Figure 4 shows the relationship between the change of sampling rate and the quality of signal reconstruction when sampling a certain signal. As the sampling rate increases, the quality change of signal reconstruction tends to be stable. However, different types of signals tend to stabilize at different sampling rates.

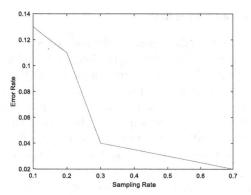

Fig. 4. The relationship between the change of sampling rate and the quality of signal reconstruction when sampling a certain signal.

Stop Rule: compare the reconstructed $x(m)$ and $x(m + 1)$ when the number of measurements is m and the number of measurements is $m + 1$, if $x(m) \overset{\Delta}{\approx} x(m+1)$, stop increasing the number of measurements and upload the measurement results of $m + 1$ to the next layer; if the conditions are not met, increase the number of measurements once, update the value of m, and compare again, until the conditions are met. Then, stop increasing the number of measurements. $x(m) \overset{\Delta}{\approx} x(m + 1)$ is expressed as:

$$\frac{\sqrt{\sum (x'(m - 1)_{ij} - x'(m)_{ij})^2}}{\sqrt{\sum (1/2(x'(m - 1)_{ij} + x'(m)_{ij}))^2}} \leq \varepsilon \tag{2}$$

To judge whether the two matrices have reached the stability of the reconstruction effect, ε is a small constant.

Saliency Influence the Choice of the Starting Point of the First Floor Walk. Saliency is the recognition of local mutations in the relevant overall data. Therefore, we introduce the concept of saliency into the sensor data processing.

Since random walk is a randomly walks in the network structure of nodes, each newly added walk in the above termination criterion is arbitrary, which affects the efficiency of the entire reconstruction to a certain extent. If you can choose a walk with the best improvement in overall reconstruction efficiency in the next walk, you can further save the amount of calculation and upload data consumption. The implementation steps are as follows:

(A) Divide the nodes in a cluster into n blocks on average;
(B) According to the reconstruction results of the previous m measurements, calculate the saliency value S_i of each block separately;
(C) Measure the weight of each block according to the saliency value of each block
$$w_i = \frac{S_i}{\sum\limits_{i=1}^{n} S_i};$$
(D) According to the size of the saliency value, assign the block from which the walk starts to walk, $P_i = w_i$;
(E) Generate a new walk.

Algorithm Design of the First Layer

Input: The sampling rate of pre-sampling is R_{pre}, the initial sampling rate R_c, step t, the number of new walks g each time, the stop condition threshold ε;
Step 1: Randomly select the starting point of the random walk of the leaf nodes with the pre-sampled sampling rate R_{pre}, to obtain the pre-sampled measurement matrix M_{pre};
Step 2: Reconstruct the data according to the pre-sampling and use the reconstruction algorithm to obtain the matrix X_{pre};
Step 3: Divide X_{pre} into n blocks and calculate the saliency value S_i of each block;
Step 4: Assign the weight w_i of each block according to the saliency value, and calculate the starting point probability P_i of each block;
Step 5: Select the starting point of random walk according to P_i, and then generate the measurement matrix M_{add} of $(R_c - R_{pre})$ sampling rate to obtain the final initial measurement matrix $M_c = \begin{pmatrix} M_{pre} \\ M_{add} \end{pmatrix}$;
Step 6: According to the measurement matrix M_c, the reconstructed X_c is obtained, and then g new walks are generated by Step 3 and Step 4, and the new walk is added to the measurement matrix to update the measurement matrix M;
Step 7: Compare the reconstructed $X(m)$ and $X(m + 1)$ when the measurement times are m and the measurement times are $m + g$, if $X(m)$ and $X(m + 1)$ meet the conditions formula 2, then stop increasing the number of measurements, and upload the data to the cluster head of the second layer; if the conditions are not met, update $m = m + g$, convert $Xpre$ in step 3 to $X(m)$ and repeat after generating g walks.

Layer i: Data Collection Edge Layer

Saliency Affect the Sampling rate Distribution of the i (2 < i < N) Layer. In the actual situation, the data uploaded by the sensor node is not known, and it is not smooth, but with mutations. When faced with an unsmooth signal, the number of measurements may exceed the total number of nodes, resulting in an increase in the amount of communication data. Therefore, in the i-th layer $(2 < i < n)$ of the entire system, this paper introduces a weighting factor γ to evaluate the value of the data carried by the edge nodes, and updates the measurement value of each edge node to $M'^{(l)} = \gamma * M^{(l)}$, so that each cluster can be adaptively measured.

Because the fixed sensor node is limited by regional time, within a certain period of time, the data acquired by the sensor has certain similarity. All can calculate γ based on the data obtained last time.

Suppose that the data of four edge nodes in layer i will be transferred to an edge node in layer $i + 1$. The data of these four nodes are represented by vectors $x1$, $x2$, $x3$, and $x4$, respectively, and the corresponding measured values are $M1$, $M2$, $M3$, and $M4$. From $x1$, $x2$, $x3$, and $x4$, using the features of saliency, the saliency values of the four vectors are calculated, and the corresponding saliency values are obtained as $S1$, $S2$, $S3$, and $S4$. The γ value corresponding to the jth value is

$$\gamma_j = \frac{S_j}{S_{avg}} \tag{3}$$

Where S_{avg} is the saliency average of this layer,

$$S_{avg} = \frac{\sum\limits_{n=1}^{k} S_i}{k} \tag{4}$$

Where k is the number of clusters contained in this layer, so that the corresponding weighted value for the next retransmission can be obtained.

Algorithm Design of Layer $i(2 < i < N)$

Input: the original assigned $M_i{}^{(l)}$ of the measured value of each cluster;
Step 1: Calculate the saliency value Si of each cluster in the i-th layer under this cluster head according to the data reconstructed by the cluster head in the $i + 1$th layer;
Step 2: According to the saliency value Si, calculate the weighting factor γi of the value of the data carried by the node;

$$\gamma_i = \frac{k \cdot S_i}{\sum\limits_{n=1}^{k} S_n} \tag{5}$$

Step 3: Update the measured value of each cluster $M_i'^{(l)} = \gamma_i * M_i{}^{(l)}$;
Step 4: Use the updated measurement value to perform compression measurement on the data of each cluster.

4.3 Train the Task Assignment Process

Since the training task does not necessarily have frequent periodicity along with the data collection, in addition to the function of data uploading, edge computing nodes can also make use of idle time and collected data to conduct offline training for existing models. This can improve the real-time performance of the request and reduce network pressure.

Then, when the edge computing node receives the training request, it may not accept and respond immediately. First of all, it is necessary to judge whether the training of the request is feasible by combining the requested data volume with the current computing resources. Training to each edge node C_{in} $(i > 2)$ the maximum storage capacity and computing power of rs_{in} and rc_{in}, respectively, at the same time, under the assumption that each data source node generated training mission need to request a unit of the CPU to calculate, we can get about edge training node storage capacity and computing capacity constraints, the sum of all the tasks of computing power and storage capacity of no more than the sum of node threshold.

After the training task of the edge computing node is completed and the updated model is obtained, the training request information is summarized and uploaded to the designated edge computing node at the next level of the system for model training with a larger area. Therefore, the closer the system is to the source node, the more real-time tasks it may have to face. Therefore, it is very likely that there will be insufficient computing capacity of edge nodes and insufficient resources. Therefore, we need to adjust our thought. In case of insufficient computing and resources, the request should be transferred to the next layer. In order to ensure real-time performance and low latency, the number of layers should not be more than 3. The specific algorithm is as follows (Fig. 5):

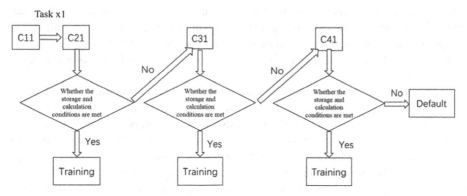

Fig. 5. Train the task assignment process

5 Analysis of Experimental Results

5.1 Performance Measures

(1) Quality of collected data
The collected data quality will directly affect the accuracy of the training model. In this paper, the error rate and SNR are used to represent the data quality.

(2) Communication overhead
Sensors in a small area can generate as much as 8 GB of data a day, and that doesn't include data generated by mobile devices, surveillance cameras, and Web services. Therefore, in modern cities, the amount of data generated in one day will be very large, and the amount of data collected will directly affect the communication cost. The larger the amount of data, the greater the cost. In this paper, the data volume of the first layer is related to walk number. Each walk generates one unit of data. The generation of walk is directly determined by in the stopping rule, so the communication overhead is indirectly expressed as the relationship between walk number and ε.

(3) Training task volume
For each training task request, the system proposed in this paper will determine whether the training task is accepted by the edge node and which edge node should collect the task and its data for training. Depending on the goal of the problem, we should consider the number of tasks the system accepts as a performance measure. Different variables such as the storage capacity of edge nodes and the number of data source nodes will affect the number of training task requests received by the system.

5.2 Experimental Setup

In this paper, the experiments use the experimental data sources (https://tao.ndbc.noaa.gov/tao/datadownload/searchmap.SHTML) of sea surface temperatures. In addition, two groups of signals collected under other conditions are simulated for the experiment. The second group of signals is sparse signal, and the third group of signals are mutated non-sparse signal.

In this paper, a total of 1024 nodes are set, and the total structure is divided into 4 layers. The first layer is divided into 16 clusters, each with 64 nodes. The second layer is divided into 4 clusters, each cluster contains 4 cluster-head nodes. The four cluster-head nodes in the third layer upload the data to the data processing center in the fourth layer. In the first layer, the pre-sampling rate R_{pre} is set to 0.1, the initial sampling rate R_c is set to 0.3, the random walk skip is set to 30, and stopping rule's only selects 1 walk at a time. Measure the m value of the amount of data uploaded to the second layer when the recording stops. In the second layer compression of the algorithm in the paper [9], the same measured value M is used to compress and upload to the third layer, and the sampling rate after the third layer is set at the same sampling rate of 0.9.

We assume that the size if data uploaded by a node is 0.25 MB each time, and the task data collected by a training task is 4 GB, in this paper, data storage capacity of the edge of the tree nodes are assumed to be [10,100] of the GB uniform distribution, the amount of computing power to vCPU decision, to obey [50, 150] vCPU evenly distributed.

5.3 Comparison of Experimental Results

(1) Influence of ε

In the experiment on the influence of ε, we use 1024 data, the predetermined R_{pre} is 0.3, and the corresponding $M_{pre} = 307$.

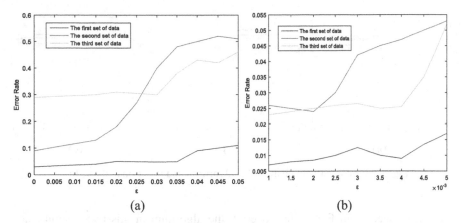

Fig. 6. The effect of ε on the reconstructed data Error Ratio

For different signals, the setting of ε affects them to different degrees, but they all directly affect the quality of the reconstructed data when the algorithm stops. In Fig. 6(a), the setting range of ε is 0.01–0.05, and the error ratio is higher than 0.1. The larger the ε setting, the larger the error ratio, which indicates that the quality of the data increases with ε. In the figure (b), the setting range of ε is 0.0001 to 0.0005, and the error ratio is lower than 0.01, achieving high-quality reconstruction.

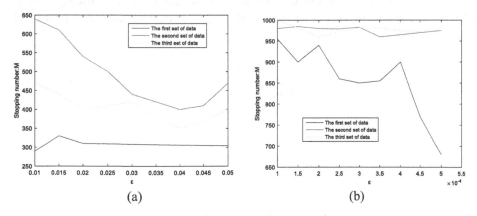

Fig. 7. The effect of ε on the value of M

As ε increases, the value of M at the time of stopping also becomes smaller. The smaller the value of M, that is, the less data need to be uploaded, which directly affects the overall communication overhead. The setting range of ε in Fig. 7(a) is 0.01–0.05, and the range of M value is basically between 300–650, which is equiva-lent to the sampling rate between 0.3–0.6; (b) In the figure, the setting range of ε is 0.0001–0.0005, the M range is basically between 750–1000, which is equivalent to the sampling rate between 0.7–0.9.

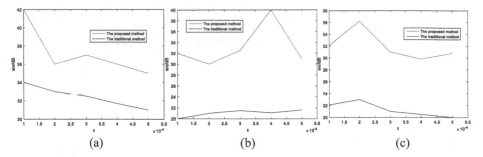

(a)   (b)   (c)

Fig. 8. Snr comparison chart of this algorithm and traditional algorithm

It can be seen from Fig. 8 that, overall, the algorithm in this paper significantly improves the data quality compared to the traditional algorithm. Especially for the two sets of signal data after the mutation, the improvement of the effect is more obvious.

(2) Impact on training business volume

This is mainly for comparison with the most intuitive way of collecting greedy thoughts. According to greedy theory, in order to collect more training task requests, the system should first select those training task requests that provide the least amount of data. Under the greedy strategy, we first select the training task request with the smallest amount of data, and then randomly put this training task request and the data it provides into an edge node. The total number of edge nodes in the greedy thought and the number of all edge nodes in the system.

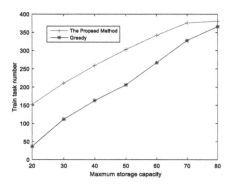

Fig. 9. Impact on training business volume

Figure 9 shows the impact of the storage capacity of the edge training node on the number of training task requests received by the system. As the upper limit of the storage capacity of the edge training node increases, the performance of the system is getting better and better, probably more than the greedy strategy collect about 30% of training mission requests.

6 Summary

This paper proposes a data collection system based on distributed edges, which uses random walk and stopping rule and selects the starting point of walk based on saliency, and applies it to the data collection of the leaf layer structure, so that each cluster can use edge nodes to adapt. To collect data, save the amount of uploaded data while ensuring data quality. In the compressed sampling process of the i-th layer ($2 < i < n$), the sampling rate of each cluster is allocated again according to the reconstructed data obtained in the previous time using saliency, so as to better identify the sudden change area and avoid the situation that the measured value in the abrupt region is greater than the number of cluster nodes, thus wasting the amount of uploaded data. In addition to the cost savings in the data collection process, the system proposed in this paper can better deal with the data collection of edge nodes for AI data training. The data and model of each edge node are closer to the data characteristics within the range of the node. And when the computing power or storage capacity of the edge node is insufficient, the training request can be passed to the edge node of the next layer to process as many training requests as possible. In the future research, the problem of unloading and scheduling of edge training tasks will be analyzed based on more specific scenarios.

Acknowledgments. This research was partly supported by National Natural Science Foundation of China under Grant No. 61672221, and by National Natural Science Foundation of Hunan Province under Grant No. 2020JJ4008.

References

1. Mao, Y., You, C., Zhang, J., et al.: A survey on mobile edge computing: the communication perspective. IEEE Commun. Surv. Tutorials **PP**(99), 1 (2017)
2. Wang, S., Tuor, T., Salonidis, T., et al.: When edge meets learning: adaptive control for resource-constrained distributed machine learning. In: IEEE INFOCOM 2018 IEEE Conference on Computer Communications. IEEE, pp. 63–71 (2018)
3. Teerapittayanon, S., Mcdanel, B., Kung, H.: Distributed deep neural networks over the cloud, the edge and end devices. In: 2017 IEEE 37th International Conference on Distributed Computing Systems (ICDCS), IEEE, pp. 328–339 (2017)
4. Li, H., Ota, K., Dong, M.: Learning IoT in edge: deep learning for the Internet of Things with edge computing. IEEE Netw. **32**(1), 96–101 (2018)
5. Xu, X., Ansari, R., Khokhar, A., Vasilakos, A.V.: Hierarchical data aggregation using compressive sensing (HDACS) in WSNs. ACM Trans. Sens. Netw. **11**(3), 1–25 (2015). Article 45
6. Chong, L., Jun, S., Feng, W.: Compressive network coding for approximate sensor data gathering. In: Global Telecommunications Conference, IEEE Press, pp. 1–6 (2011)

7. Luo, C., Wu, F., Sun, J., Chen, C.W.: Compressive data gathering for large-scale wireless sensor networks. In: Proceedings of MobiCom (2009)

8. Luo, J., Xiang, L., Rosenberg, C.: Does compressed sensing improve the throughput of wireless sensor networks. In: Proceedings of the IEEE International Conference on Communications (2010)

9. Zheng, H., Yang, F., Tian, X., Gan, X., Wang, X., Xiao, S.: Data gathering with compressive sensing in wireless sensor networks: a random walk based approach. IEEE Trans. Parallel Distrib. Syst. **26**(1), 35–44 (2015)

10. Wang, L., et al.: CCS-TA: quality-guaranteed online task allocation in compressive crowd-sensing. In: UBICOMP 2015, Osaka, Japan, 7–11 September 2015

11. Kang, K.D., Chen, L., Yi, H., et al.: Real-time information derivation from big sensor data via edge computing. Big Data Cogn. Comput. **1**(1), 5 (2017)

12. Shi, W., Cao, J., Zhang, Q., et al.: Edge computing: vision and challenges. IEEE Internet Thing J. **3**(5), 637–646 (2016)

13. Sinaeepourfard, A., Garcia, J., Masip-Bruin, X., et al.: Estimating smart city sensors data generation. In: 2016 Mediterranean Ad Hoc Networking Workshop (Med-Hoc-Net). IEEE, pp. 1–8 (2016)

14. Sivakumaean, M, Iacopino, P.: The mobile economy 2018. GSMA Intelligence, pp. 1–60 (2018)

Resource Allocation Method of Edge-Side Server Based on Two Types of Virtual Machines in Cloud and Edge Collaborative Computing Architecture

Junfeng Man, Longqian Zhao, Cheng Peng$^{(\boxtimes)}$, and Qianqian Li

School of Computer Science, Hunnan University of Technology, Zhuzhou 412007, China
chengpeng@csu.edu.cn

Abstract. The process of large-scale manufacturing workshops is complex, and the traditional fixed resource allocation method will cause unbalanced load. Aiming at this problem, an edge-side server resource allocation algorithm based on cloud collaborative architecture has been designed and implemented. By defining the three-dimensional information of each IO-intensive virtual machine in the compute node, the priority of the IO-intensive virtual machine is calculated. Through analyzing the relationship between the CPU-intensive virtual machine and the host physical machine, the number of CPU cores for different tasks of the CPU-intensive virtual machine is obtained, and the hardware resources are uniformly allocated in real time according to the maximum priority list. The experimental results show that the proposed algorithm can significantly satisfy the requirements of high throughput and low latency in large manufacturing workshops, and optimize the resource allocation for actual production.

Keywords: Cloud and edge collaboration · IO-intensive · CPU-intensive · Three dimensional information · Resource allocation

1 Introduction

"Made in China 2025" is China's overall industrial development plan for the next 10 years, marking China's transition from labor-intensive production to technology-intensive, and will make a major breakthrough in cutting-edge advanced technology. In the industrial field, the Internet of Things (IoT) can actively sense and remotely control all physical devices in cloud manufacturing scenario in the existing network infrastructure [1]. By mapping the contents obtained from the physical world (real space) to the data of the information world (cyber space), it can reflect the full life cycle process of corresponding physical equipment and effectively achieve "digital twin" [2, 3].

In industrial-level application scenarios, problems such as single point failure are easy to occur. Therefore, in addition to the unified control of the cloud, certain computing power should be given to the edge terminal nodes to independently judgment and solve

H. Jiang et al. (Eds.): ICECI 2020, LNICST 368, pp. 65–85, 2021.
https://doi.org/10.1007/978-3-030-73429-9_5

problems, so as to improve the factory's capacity and prevent equipment failures. With the continuous research and exploration in the industry, as an important feature of edge computing, cloud and edge collaboration with complementary operation mode has been widely used in many scenarios such as medical, industry and finance [4, 5]. The cloud and edge collaborative computing architecture balances the computing load, reduces the hardware requirements of the edge-side servers, and makes the edge-side servers smaller, lighter, and cheaper while ensuring capacity.

The purpose of this paper is to design corresponding edge-side server resource allocation method, effectively reduce enterprise investment, and fundamentally avoid waste of resources [6]. Due to the difference of the mechanical equipment and business requirements deployed in different factories, the size and meaning of terminal data amount also very from each other. Therefore, the weight of the upload type of the terminal device is important for rational allocation of resources, optimization of operations, and optimization of cluster parameters. The characteristics of time series data generated by mechanical equipment include features such as massive equipment and measuring points, high data acquisition frequency, and large data throughput. In the process of resource allocation, we need to use the available space as a measure to ensure that the edge server can continuously store data [7]. In this background, this paper proposes a resource scheduling scheme and algorithm for cloud and edge collaborative computing architecture for edge-side server clusters in industrial scenarios.

The rest of this paper is arranged as the following sections. In Sect. 2, related works are reviewed. In Sect. 3, a cloud and edge collaborative computing architecture for industrial big data is proposed and the workflow under the architecture is also described. In Sect. 4 and Sect. 5, the system model and problem definitions are introduced, and according resource allocation algorithm is designed. In Sect. 6, the comparative experimental evaluation results are illustrated, and Sect. 7 concludes the paper, and puts forward future work.

2 Related Work

In the edge computing environment, due to the insufficiency of the infrastructure, few studies have focused on the resource allocation of edge-side server. China's 5G technology development in the recent years, focusing on the industrial and manufacturing market, has provoked the interest of the scholars in terms of resource allocation.

A traditional cloud data center is mainly composed of heterogeneous servers that carry multiple virtual machines (VM). The use of these virtual machine resources has potential irregularities and instability, which may result in unbalanced resource usage within the server, resulting in performance degradation. In order to shorten the response time of the system, Rugwiro et al. [8] proposed a task scheduling and resource allocation model based on hybrid ant colony optimization and deep reinforcement learning, based on ant colony algorithm random decision to reduce the chance of falling into local optimum, approximating optimal solution. Devarasetty et al. [9] proposed the improved optimization algorithm for resource allocation by considering the target of minimizing the deployment cost and improving the QoS performance. However, the meta-heuristic algorithm is more slower, and the obtained solution is not always the optimal solution. For this reason, Jangiti et al. [10] proposed a set of hybrid heuristics and an ensemble heuristic to improve the solution quality. This method can effectively allocate and manage virtual resources in the cloud data center. Since cloud computing and fog calculation cannot meet the practical requirements of high response and low latency in large manufacturing workshops, Liu et al. [11] proposed to apply extreme value theory to impose probability and statistical constraints on task queue lengths in order to use a higher rate or visit a nearby server to offload the task. Liao et al. [12] proposed to use machine learning to maximize long-term throughput under the long-term constraints of energy budget and service reliability. However, Liu et al. consider that the data uploaded by an individual unit is much smaller than that collected by mechanical equipment in the actual production workshop, and the uploading protocol is just one type of protocol. This paper studies the impact of the large-scale mechanical equipment data collection on IO-intensive virtual machines [13], and the impact of large-scale manufacturing workshop access on CPU-intensive virtual machines [14].

In view of the above problems, this paper proposes an edge-side server resource allocation method based on the cloud and edge collaborative computing architecture by studying the research results of predecessors. The algorithm is designed on base of the StarlingX virtualization platform. The main contributions are as follows:

Solve the situation that the response delay of the terminal device is high due to the large amount of uploaded data. Solve the case of terminal equipment due to differences in application scenarios lead to the actual deployment difficult. Promote the intelligent and portable products of industrial enterprises, and effectively help traditional industrial enterprises to get rid of backward production capacity.

3 Architecture and Workflow

3.1 Computing Architecture

The classic solution of cloud computing architecture is to upload various types of sensor data on the facilities (vibreation, pressure, temperature, etc.) to the remote cloud server through data acquisition modual (AGV, PLC, RTU, etc.). With the help of big data analysis technologies, mathematical model will be established and the production quality, work efficiency and competitiveness of these facilities can be improved. Taking the coal mining industry as an example, the mine is generally in a remote located in remote areas and network communication is difficult. However, due to the large scale, variety, low value density, and fast update and processing requirements of coal mines, traditional cloud computing architectures cannot be adopted because traditional cloud computing architectures are prone to single-point problems and slow closed-loop response. To this end, this paper proposes a cloud and edge collaborative computing architecture [15] for industrial big data to cope with the problems of fast real-time control response and fast data processing in large manufacturing workshops.

Figure 1 illustrates the proposed architecture, it consists of a cloud component consisting of a remote server cluster and an edge end component consisting of an edge-side server cluster. To gain insight, the cloud component is mainly responsible for model training of the data collected by the terminal data collection device, and the edge component is mainly responsible for providing real-time services for the factory equipment by acquiring the data in the model dictionary. The closed-loop response time and the production quality are improved because of the reduction of the training time. OpenStack and StarlingX are the most widely used open source cloud computing platforms and the latest distributed edge computing platforms, respectively. we use OpenStack [16] and StarlingX [17] to manage and maintain remote server clusters and edge-side server clusters. The cloud and edge collaborative computing architecture shown in Fig. 1 mainly includes a big data analysis application layer, an industrial big data platform service layer, a data resource layer, and a device sensing layer.

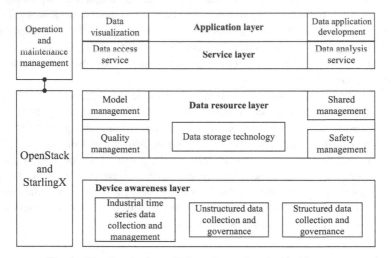

Fig. 1. Cloud and edge collaborative computing architecture.

The industrial big data analysis application layer is mainly responsible for providing corresponding services for data under different application scenarios, such as factory equipment expert knowledge base management system, factory equipment security problem reasoning and interpretation system.

The service platform of the industrial big data platform includes a task scheduling control module, a data dictionary matching module, and a data processing module. The data dictionary matching module monitors and manages the business logic, and returns the data parameters of the corresponding model information to the edge-side server to achieve fast edge-side server data processing. The data processing module specifically processes the data collected by the data acquisition module for different data scales including machine learning, deep learning and traditional data analysis methods.

The data resource layer mainly includes a core database, a business auxiliary database, a file system, etc. The core database is responsible for the cloud data collected by the storage device sensing layer device; the service auxiliary database can use the relational database such as Oracle to assist the rapid processing of the system; the file system adopts the HDFS distributed file system [18].

The device sensing layer mainly includes various sensors installed on industrial equipment, such as temperature, pressure, vibration sensors or smart factory equipment such as controllers and range finder.

3.2 Workflow

Figure 2 shows the workflow of the proposed architecture. The data acquisition device and the request action of the user are collectively referred to as a collector. The intelligent terminal simply pre-processes the information of the collector and sends it to the computing node in the cluster of the edge-side server. The IO-intensive virtual machine in the computing node is responsible for receiving and storing it in the database of the storage node.

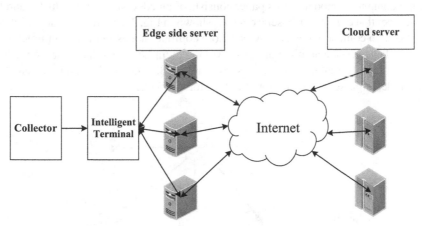

Fig. 2. Schematic diagram of the working process of the cloud and edge collaborative computing architecture.

The following is the detailed communication process:

1) On edge-side server processing
   The intelligent terminal device sends the collected data to the edge data storage module; The data processing module obtains corresponding data from the edge side data storage module according to the requirements of the user; The data processing module performs lightweight big data analysis according to the model parameters provided by the data dictionary module, and synchronizes to the edge side data dictionary module; The decision module feeds back to the intelligent terminal to perform corresponding control according to the result processed by the data processing module.

2) On remote centralized server processing: The edge-side server synchronizes the incremental data to the remote centralized data storage module; The edge-side server synchronizes the incremental data to the remote centralized data storage module; The data processing module performs heavyweight big data analysis according to the model parameters provided by the data dictionary module, and synchronizes to the remote data dictionary module; The remote data dictionary module will synchronize the data and edge data dictionary modules according to specific needs.

The edge-side server and the remote centralized server periodically analyze and mine the stored data to update the data dictionary to ensure the accuracy of the decision message.

4 Resource Allocation for IO-intensive Virtual Machines

4.1 Computing Architecture

The edge computing model of this paper consists of an edge-side server cluster and terminal devices that continuously send data. As shown in Fig. 3, an edge-side server cluster consists of two control nodes and two or more compute nodes in order to implement a highly available service architecture [19]. Among them, different data storage methods are adopted for different data sizes. As shown in Fig. 3, small-scale data is stored in the control node; large-scale data is stored in the storage node.

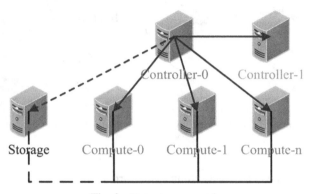

Fig. 3. Data storage mode.

In the industrial scenario, the amount of data sent by the terminal equipment deployed in each factory is different for different factory equipment and actual business needs. Therefore, it is necessary to design a design scheme for the edge-side server equipped with different factories, thereby Scientifically reduce the procurement funds of enterprises and avoid the waste of limited resources. Collaborative computing enables the processing of large-scale manufacturing workshops. Since the important parameters of most mechanical equipment do not change frequently, the mechanical characteristics of the mechanical equipment determine that most of the parameters will remain stable. Taking the piston condition of the fluid equipment as an example, the state and the outlet pressure are strongly correlated in most cases, and the outlet pressure gradually climbs from the safety initial value to the stable value, and changes stably according to the business demand of the mechanical equipment [20]. Therefore, we obtain the dimensionality information from three aspects of IO-intensive virtual machine, namely, the weight W of the data type uploaded by the terminal device, the pre-allocated space S_{pre} corresponding to each IO-intensive virtual machine in the computing node and the actual occupied space S_{post}, and generate the maximum priority list to uniformly allocate hardware resources in real time.

4.2 Resource Allocation Model

In this section, we will obtain the priority P_i of each virtual machine through the dimension information of the three aspects of the IO-intensive virtual machine. Assume that the number of existing terminal devices is N, the data type uploaded by one terminal device is $v_i = \{v_{i1}, v_{i2}, \ldots, v_{in}\}$, and n represents the number of upload types of terminal devices. The data size corresponding to the uploaded data types is $\alpha_i = \{\alpha_{i1}, \alpha_{i2}, \ldots, \alpha_{in}\}$, the corresponding sampling time is $s_i = \{s_{i1}, s_{i2}, \ldots, s_{in}\}$, and the data collection interval is $\sigma_i = \{\sigma_{i1}, \sigma_{i2}, \ldots, \sigma_{in}\}$. The terminal device sends data to the edge-side server cluster, and the data is received by the IO-intensive virtual machine in the computing node. The number of existing virtual machines is Q, the virtual machine in the computing node is $V = \{V_1, V_2, \ldots, V_Q\}$, and the resource of a virtual machine of V_i is configured as $R_i = [x, y, z]$, x is the CPU, y is the memory, and z is the hard disk space. In order to meet the service requirements of the terminal equipment and the edge-side server cluster at the same time, we propose a dynamic resource allocation scheme based on the second-order differential heuristic algorithm. Assuming that the storage rate of the edge-side server cluster is v_i, Then the resources of the host and its internal virtual machine are satisfied:

A V_i virtual machine receives data sent from the terminal device. At the time of sampling t_i, the received data τ_i is as shown in Eq. 1:

$$\tau_i = \sum_{j=1}^{N} \sum_{i=1}^{n} \alpha_{ij} \times 1s + \varepsilon \tag{1}$$

ε represents the error generated by sampling and calculation. The average speed of a V_i virtual machine processing data is v_i, then it takes t_i' time to process all the data sent at time t_i, which satisfies the Eq. 2:

$$t_i' = \frac{\tau_i}{v_i} \tag{2}$$

A V_i virtual machine needs t_i', t_{i+1}', and t_{i+2}' time to store data in the database. The second-order difference of the data received by the virtual machine is used to obtain the data upload rate increment Δv as shown in Eq. 3:

$$\Delta v = \tau_{i+2} - 2\tau_{i+1} + \tau_i \tag{3}$$

It can be known from Eq. 3 that a virtual machine of V_i has six states in the time $t_i \sim t_i + 2\sigma_i$ period, and is represented by a set $status = \{1, 2, 3, 4, 5, 6\}$, where 1 is a no data state; 2 is a reduced state; 3 is a steady state; 4 is an increased state; 5 is an early warning State; 6 is the excess state. When $\Delta v \approx -\tau_i$, it indicates that the virtual machine of the $t_i \sim t_i + 2\sigma_i$ period has not received the data sent by the terminal device. When $-\tau_i < \Delta v < 0$, it indicates that the data uploaded by the terminal device is decreasing during this time period. When $\Delta v \approx 0$, it indicates that the data uploaded by the terminal device remains basically unchanged during this time period. When $\Delta v < M_0$, it indicates that the data uploaded by the terminal device is increasing during the time period. When $M_0 \leq \Delta v < M_1$, it indicates that the data uploaded by the terminal device has exceeded the warning value M_0 during the time period. When $\Delta v \geq M_1$, it indicates that the data uploaded by the terminal device has exceeded the actual physical storage capacity of the storage node during the time period, and the rate of data uploading of the terminal device needs to be solved by increasing the hard disk space or optimizing the data storage solution. M_1 is the actual storage size of the edge-side server storage space.

It is assumed that by collecting a large number of state sets $num_i \subseteq status$ of a V_i virtual machine in a working time period in advance, ξ_i indicates that the previous state of states 4, 5, and 6 is 4, 5, and 6. Then the probability π_i of the previous state of 4, 5, and 6 is 4, 5, and 6 as shown in Eq. 4:

$$\pi_i = \frac{\xi_i}{size(num_i) - 1} \qquad (4)$$

The ith virtual machine in the compute node of the edge-side server soft allocates a pre-storage space of S_{pre}^i, and the data size of a V_i virtual machine that has been stored to the storage node at time t_i is S_{post}^i. When the amount of data received by a V_i virtual machine is τ_i at a time, the priority p_i of the data stored by the virtual machine of the V_i is as shown in Eq. 5:

$$p_i = \frac{S_{pre}^i - S_{post}^i}{\tau_i} \qquad (5)$$

In the industrial application scenario, due to the particularity of the industrial equipment itself, taking the aircraft as an example, there are a large number of key mechanical components such as gears, shafts, bearings, blades, etc. in the power transmission system of the aircraft, and the analysis of the collected data through deep learning is obtained. The weight W [21] of parameter, combined with Eq. 4 and Eq. 5, gives the priority P_i of a V_i virtual machine in response to stored data as shown in Eq. 6:

$$P_i = \frac{\sum w}{\|W\|} \times \frac{1}{p_i} \times \pi_i \qquad (6)$$

w represents the weight of each parameter. N represents the collection of w. It can be known from Eq. 3 that assuming that there are terminal devices transmitting data to the edge-side server, the data type uploaded by one terminal device is $v_i = \{v_{i1}, v_{i2}, \ldots, v_{in}\}$. n indicates the number of terminal device upload types. When the P_i value is larger, the more the virtual machine needs to be allocated to the more memory space in time, thereby increasing the speed of data storage.

4.3 Priority List and Resource Allocation

The edge-side IO-intensive virtual machine in the cloud and edge collaborative computing architecture proposed in this paper is mainly responsible for receiving terminal data. The mathematical model of virtual machine IO performance and hardware resources is established by second-order differential heuristic algorithm, and finally the IO-intensive virtual machine adaptive configuration is realized. Suppose a server at the edge end of V_i receives k tasks $List = \{\tau_1, \tau_2, \ldots, \tau_k\}$ continuously, set the current task waiting queue as $T = \{\tau_i\}$, the weight value of characteristic parameters as W, and the storage space S_{pre} and S_{post} corresponding to IO-intensive virtual machines in the server at the edge end, and the priority is P_i. The priority generation algorithm is shown in Algorithm 1:

Algorithm 1 Priority generation algorithm

Require: T, W, S_{pre}, S_{post}

Ensure: P_i

1: function PriorityGenerate(T, W, S_{pre}, S_{post})

2:   while $\tau_i \in T$ and $i \in \{1, 2, \ldots, k\}$ do

3:     if Data allocation table can view τ_i then

4:       $p_i = \frac{S^i_{pre} - S^i_{post}}{\tau_i}$

5:       $P_i = \frac{\sum w}{\|W\|} \times \frac{1}{p_i} \times \pi_i$

6:     end if

7:   end while

8: end function

Each IO-intensive virtual machine in the edge-side server will have a priority P_i. The control node Controller will obtain this priority P_i and establish the maximum priority queue P. The resource configuration of the IO-intensive virtual machine is updated correspondingly by the change of the priority queue P. The virtual machine resource allocation algorithm is as shown in Algorithm 2:

Algorithm 2 IO-intensive virtual machine resource allocation algorithm

Require: P

Ensure: Max_heap_PList

1: function IOResourceAllocation(P)

2:    InitalGenerate($PList$)

3:    InitalGenerate(Max_heap_PList)

4:    while $P_i \in P$ and $i \in \{1,2,...,k\}$ do

5:       if Data allocation table can view P_i then

6:          size[$PList$] = size[$PList$]+1

7:          PList[size[$PList$]] = 0

8:          if P_i<PList[i] then

9:             Erro

10:          end if

11:          $PList$[i] = P_i

12:          while i>1 && $PList$[PARENT(i)]< $PList$[i] do

13:             exchange PList[i]<-> $PList$[PARENT(i)]

14:             i= PARENT(i)

15:          end while

16:       end if

17:    end while

18:    while $P_i \in P$ and $i \in \{1,2,...,k\}$ do

19:       if size[PList] < 1 then

20:          Error

21:       end if

22:       $\mathbf{max\_}P_i$ = $PList$[1]

23:       $PList$[1] = $PList$[size[$PList$]]

24:       size[PList] = size[$PList$]-1

25:       adjust_max_size($PList$,1)

26:       Max_heap_PList[i] = $\mathbf{max\_}P_i$

27:    end while

28: end function

The Algorithm 2–3 lines initialize the biggest priority queue. Lines 4–7 insert priority P_i into the set in turn. Lines 8–17 new P_i insertion at the end of the priority pair. Then adjust the queue from the rear parent node. Lines 18–27 copy the last element in the *PList* queue to the first location and delete the last node. Put the first element of the *PList* queue into the *Max_heap_PList* queue and delete an element of the *PList* queue. And then adjust the queue.

The time complexity of the algorithm is mainly the process of initializing the *PList* queue and the process of re-establishing the *PList* queue after each selection of the maximum number. The time complexity of initializing the *PList* queue is $O(n)$. The time complexity of changing the queue element to reconstruct the *PList* queue is $O(nlogn)$, and the space complexity of the algorithm is $O(1)$. Based on the original algorithm, the algorithm is applicable to the problem of IO-intensive virtual machine resource allocation caused by large-scale terminal equipment sending data in industrial scenarios, and maximally responds to resource requests of IO-intensive VM.

By using the algorithm of this paper, it is assumed that there are N terminal devices transmitting data to Q virtual machines. The resource allocator unit time average processing capacity is μ, and the average number of requests per unit time is λ [22]. If we need to allocate i virtual machines and can process m requests at the same time, you can get the resource allocator utilization ρ according to multi-queue system, as shown in Eq. 7:

$$\rho = \frac{i}{m\mu}, m \le i \le \lambda \le Q \tag{7}$$

The relationship between the resource allocator utilization ratio ρ and the response time R is as shown in Eq. 8:

$$R \approx \frac{1}{\mu} \times \frac{1}{1 - \rho^m} \tag{8}$$

5   Resource Allocation for CPU-intensive Virtual Machines

The virtual machines in the edge-side server are mainly divided into IO-intensive and CPU-intensive virtual machines. IO-intensive virtual machines are mainly responsible for receiving and storing data. CPU-intensive virtual machines are mainly responsible for lightweight edge calculation of data. At the same time, the IO-intensive virtual machine uses the peer-to-peer mode to receive the data sent by the terminal device, as shown in Fig. 4. Decoupling storage from computing reduces interference between services and helps services become more efficient.

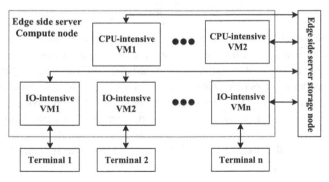

Fig. 4. Storage and computation decoupling, peer-to-peer mode receiving data.

5.1   Resource Allocation Model

In this section we will handle lightweight edge computing tasks with CPU-intensive virtual machines. Suppose the number of existing tasks is b, and the task type $e = \{e_1, e_2, \ldots, e_f\}$ on an edge-side server cluster, f represents the number of task types on an edge-side server cluster. The terminal device sends data to the edge-side server cluster, and the CPU-intensive virtual machine in the compute node processes the data. There are o CPU-intensive virtual machines. CPU-intensive virtual machine $V' = \{V_1', V_2', \ldots, V_o'\}$ in the compute node. The resource configuration of a V_i' virtual machine is $R_i = [x, y, z]$, x is CPU, y is memory, and z is hard disk space. In order to meet the service requirements of terminal equipment and edge side clusters at the same time, we propose a optimal virtual machine performance (OVMP) resource allocation method for CPU-intensive virtual machines. Assuming that T tasks are run in the CPU-intensive virtual machine V_i' in the edge-side server cluster, the execution time of the CPU-intensive application [23] is as shown in Eq. 9:

$$Time = \begin{cases} time, & T \leq C \\ time + \frac{time}{C}(T - C), & T > C \end{cases} \tag{9}$$

Where $time$ is the time when a single task is executed, C is the number of CPU cores, T is the number of simultaneous executions of the application, and $Time$ is the time required for all applications to execute. In industrial scenarios, artificial intelligence algorithms such as machine learning and deep learning are commonly used to implement edge-side data processing, while Hadoop and Spark are useful tools to allow storage and process big data in a distributed environment across computer clusters using a simple programming model [24, 25]. Assuming that the minimum execution time of the CPU-intensive virtual machine in the pseudo-distributed computing environment is R_p, and the minimum execution time in the distributed parallel computing environment is R_n, the acceleration ratio sp obtained by the distributed computing system is as shown in Eq. 10:

$$sp = \frac{R_p}{R_n} \tag{10}$$

Due to the wide variety of tasks in industrial big data, such as filtering for noise data, cleaning and denoising, modeling integration and multi-scale classification, and tasks such as correlation analysis of manufacturing parameters such as process parameters and equipment status parameters [26]. This article uses $time\_com$ to indicate the completion time of task. Considering the communication delay of different tasks, such as cloud computing communication delay is about 100 ms, small data center communication delay is about 10 to 40 ms, router communication delay is about 5 ms, communication delay between terminal devices It is about 1 to 2 ms [27]. The industrial big data task requires completion time as shown in Eq. 11:

$$Req\_Time' \geq time\_com + time\_cor \tag{11}$$

Where Req_Time' indicates the required completion time of the task, $time\_cor$ indicates the communication delay of the task. The virtual machine creates an impact on the performance of the physical machine. When the number of virtual machines is less than the number of CPU cores, the CPU resources occupied by system users increase as the number of virtual machines increases. The execution time of the application is not affected by the number of virtual machines. When the number of virtual machines exceeds the number of host CPU cores C_{phy}, as the number of virtual machines increases, the performance gradually decreases, and the impact rate is θ [28]. Thus, we get the relationship between the number of virtual machines o and the impact rate θ, as shown in Eq. 12:

$$\theta = \frac{o}{C_{phy}} \qquad (12)$$

Assuming b tasks are respectively executed in o CPU-intensive virtual machines of the same configuration and the corresponding execution time $Time = \{Time_1, Time_2, ..., Time_b\}$ is obtained. Combined with Eq. 9 and Eq. 10, the processing time $Time' = \left\{Time'_1, Time'_2, ..., Time'_b\right\}$ is obtained in a distributed parallel environment. For different business needs, the execution time $Time'$ must be less than the required completion time Req_Time', as shown in Eq. 13:

$$\Pi_i = \begin{cases} 0, & Time_i \leq Req\_Time'_i \\ 1, & Time_i > Req\_Time'_i \end{cases} \qquad (13)$$

Suppose there are d in the number of 1 in Π, the task set $b' = \left\{b'_1, b'_2, ..., b'_d\right\}$ is not completed on time, its corresponding sequence $seq = \left\{seq\left(b'_1\right), seq\left(b'_2\right), ..., seq\left(b'_d\right)\right\}$, the corresponding execution time $Time'_{unfinished} = \left\{Time'_{seq\left(b'_1\right)}, Time'_{seq\left(b'_2\right)}, ..., Time'_{seq\left(b'_d\right)}\right\}$, and the corresponding required completion time $Req\_Time'_{unfinished} = \left\{Req\_Time'_{seq\left(b'_1\right)}, Req\_Time'_{seq\left(b'_2\right)}, ..., Req\_Time'_{seq\left(b'_d\right)}\right\}$. Combine Eq. 9 and Eq. 13 to obtain a CPU-intensive virtual machine resource allocation method, as shown in Eq. 14:

$$C_i^{add} = \begin{cases} 1, & \dfrac{Time'_{seq\left(b'_i\right)} \times T}{Req\_Time'_{seq\left(b'_i\right)}} \leq 1 \\[2em] \dfrac{Time'_{seq\left(b'_i\right)} \times T}{Req\_Time'_{seq\left(b'_i\right)}} - \dfrac{1}{2}, & \dfrac{Time'_{seq\left(b'_i\right)} \times T}{Req\_Time'_{seq\left(b'_i\right)}} > 1 \end{cases}, \quad i = 1, 2, ..., d \qquad (14)$$

Through extensive research, CPU-intensive applications mainly consume CPU resources. Combined with Eqs. 12 and 14, it is necessary to increase the number of corresponding C^{add} cores by a maximum priority list of no less than C and no more than d CPU-intensive virtual machines.

5.2 Resource Allocation

The CPU-intensive virtual machine in the edge-side server first allocates the same virtual machine resource. Hadoop sends the task to the corresponding CPU-intensive virtual machine according to the default scheduler. The impact on the resource configuration of the CPU-intensive virtual machine is updated accordingly. The virtual machine resource allocation algorithm is as shown in Algorithm 3:

Algorithm3 CPU-intensive virtual machine resource allocation algorithm

Require: T, C, Req_Time

Ensure: C^{add}

1: function CPUResourceAllocation(T, C, Req_Time)

2:    InitialGenerate(C^{add})

3:    temp $= 0$

4:    while $Time_i \in Time$ and $i \in \{1,2,\dots,b\}$ do

5:        $Time'[i] = \dfrac{Time[i]}{sp}$

6:        if $Time'_i \le Req\_Time'_i$ then

7:            $\Pi_i = 0$

8:        else

9:            $\Pi_i = 1$

10:            temp $=$ temp $+ 1$

11:        end if

12:    end while

13:    while $\Pi_i \in \Pi$ and $i \in \{1,2,\dots,b\}$ do

14:        if $\Pi_i = 1$ then

15:            if $\dfrac{Time'_{seq(b'_i)} \times T}{Req\_Time'_{seq(b'_i)}} \le 1$

16:                $C^{add}[i] = 1$

17:            else

18:                $C^{add}[i] = \left\lceil \dfrac{Time'_{seq(b'_i)} \times T}{Req\_Time'_{seq(b'_i)}} - \dfrac{1}{2} \right\rceil$

19:            end if

20:    end while

21:    while $C_i^{add} \in C^{add}$ and $i \in \{1,2,\dots,C\}$ do

22:        $C[i] = C[i] + C^{add}[i]$

23:    end while

24: end function

Line 2 adds the list of CPU cores for preliminary testing. Lines 4–12 calculate the execution time of each task under a distributed parallel computing system. Lines 13–20 calculate the number of allocated CPU cores for d of the b tasks that do not meet the required completion time. Lines 21–23 assign the corresponding number of C^{add} virtual machine cores to C virtual machines.

6   Experiment and the Results

6.1   Experimental Configuration

In this section, we will get the performance of the modified algorithm through the StarlingX virtualization platform [29].

We created a virtual environment as an edge-side server through the StarlingX virtualization platform, including one Controller node, four IO-intensive virtual machines, and three CPU-intensive virtual machines. For the specific configuration of the above examples, see Table 1, Table 2 and Table 3.

Table 1. Physical host related information.

Parameter	BOGOMIPS	Memory	Disk	Bandwidth	CA	OS
host	3791.22	128 GB	1TB	1000 Mb/s	X86	Linux

Table 2. Information about IO-intensive virtual machines.

Parameter	BOGOMIPS	Memory	Disk	Bandwidth	CA	OS
Controller	3791.22	32 GB	70G	1000 Mb/s	X86	Linux
IO-1	3791.22	12 GB	70G	1000 Mb/s	X86	Linux
IO-2	3791.22	12 GB	70G	1000 Mb/s	X86	Linux
IO-3	3791.22	12 GB	70G	1000 Mb/s	X86	Linux
IO-4	3791.22	12 GB	70G	1000 Mb/s	X86	Linux

Table 3. Information about CPU-intensive virtual machines.

Parameter	BOGOMIPS	Memory	Disk	Bandwidth	CA	OS
CPU-1	3791.22	3	70G	1000 Mb/s	X86	Linux
CPU-2	3791.22	3	70G	1000 Mb/s	X86	Linux
CPU-3	3791.22	3	70G	1000 Mb/s	X86	Linux

6.2   Experimental Results

We run the client service of the resource allocator on four IO-intensive virtual machines, which are responsible for monitoring the IO performance of the virtual machine. The priority is obtained by calculation and sent to the Controller node. The server service of the resource allocator running on the Controller node is responsible for collecting the priority of the IO-intensive virtual machine, and responding to the resource request of

Table 4. Average response time for IO-intensive virtual machines.

Number of IO-intensive virtual machines	Maximum average response time
1	0.017 s
2	0.016 s
3	0.017 s
4	0.014 s

the IO-intensive virtual machine according to the maximum priority list. The average response time of the algorithm is 0.01 s by simulation. As shown in Table 4:

It can be seen from Eq. 5 that the theoretical relationship between the utilization ratio ρ and the response time of the IO-intensive virtual machine is as shown in Fig. 5. It can be seen that when the utilization rate is gradually increased to 1, the response time grows slowly. Explain that our resource utilization rate has little effect on response time when it is close to 90%.

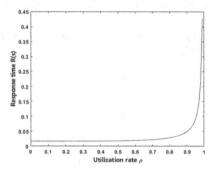

Fig. 5. Relationship between resource utilization and response time under theoretical conditions.

We compare the algorithm with the genetic algorithm and obtain the performance data of the two algorithms in the experimental scene. We can see that the algorithm guarantees the allocation of resources with the optimal response of the IO-intensive virtual machine with a sampling width of 4. However, due to the uncertainty of random number, the genetic algorithm is not reasonable enough to allocate resources. Results are shown in Fig. 6.

We use the dd command to evaluate the hard disk read/write speed of the virtual machine. By setting the memory size of the IO-intensive virtual machine, the bandwidth of the corresponding hard disk data storage in the case of 1 GB data write is obtained, as shown in Table 5. It can be seen from the table that the impact of memory on data storage speed is relatively large. Combined with Fig. 6, we can get the impact of three algorithms on the data written by the hard disk. Using the algorithm IO-intensive virtual machine requires 417.8814 s to store all data to the hard disk, and the genetic algorithm needs 436.9942 s. The specific results are shown in Fig. 7.

Table 5. The effect of different memory on hard disk write data.

Memory (GB)	Bandwidth (MB/s)	Time to write data (s)
16	266	4.0308
20	315	3.4082
24	352	3.05264

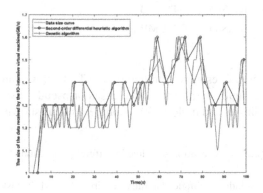

Fig. 6. Resource allocation graph for two algorithms.

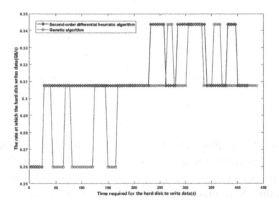

Fig. 7. The effect of two algorithms on the hard disk write data.

We run Hadoop and Spark distributed storage and computing frameworks on three CPU-intensive virtual machines. Common CPU-intensive applications are: WordCount, Sort, TeraSort, RandomWriter [30]. For the above-mentioned types of CPU-intensive applications, we generate different scale test data sets through HiBench and store them in the HDFS file system and submit them to Spark to perform the corresponding tasks [31]. The specific parameters of the tasks are shown in Table 6:

Table 6. CPU-intensive application test case parameters.

Tasks	Task type	Task data set size	Request completion time
Task-1	WordCount	108 MB	20 s
Task-2	WordCount	108 MB	20 s
Task-3	Sort	216 MB	23 s
Task-4	Sort	216 MB	23 s
Task-5	TeraSort	432 MB	25 s
Task-6	TeraSort	432 MB	25 s

According to the initial resource configuration in Table 3, we can get the maximum execution time of the application in the three cases of pseudo-distributed conditions, fully distributed conditions and multi-task co-competition, as shown in Table 7:

Table 7. Application execution schedule in different execution environments.

Tasks	Single task pseudo distributed	Single task fully distributed	Multi-task fully distributed
Task-1	24 s	15 s	24 s
Task-2	24 s	15 s	24 s
Task-3	24 s	15 s	24 s
Task-4	23 s	15 s	23 s
Task-5	27 s	19 s	45 s
Task-6	27 s	19 s	49 s

The OVMP algorithm of this paper is compared with the genetic algorithm and the performance data of the two algorithms under the experimental scene is obtained. We can see that the algorithm does not require a large amount of actual historical data to obtain similar calculation time with other algorithms. The algorithm used in this paper starts from the impact of virtual machine on physical machine performance and the impact of different configured virtual machines on task execution time. The optimal resource allocation method for CPU-intensive virtual machine is given. The experimental results as shown in Table 8 and Fig. 8:

Table 8. CPU core number allocation scheme corresponding to three algorithms.

Parameter	OVMP algorithm	Genetic algorithm
CPU-1	5	5
CPU-2	5	5
CPU-3	6	6

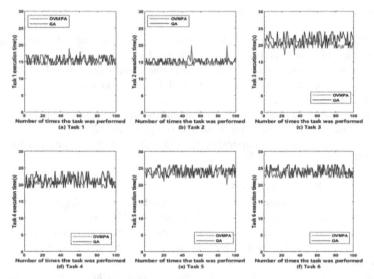

Fig. 8. Algorithm performance comparison chart.

The time complexity for the CPU-intensive resource allocation method used in this paper is $O(n)$, while the time complexity of the genetic algorithm is $O(n^2)$. By adjusting the number of tasks, according to the time complexity, the data of the resource allocation time under the theory can be obtained. By comparison, the algorithm used in this paper is fast and suitable for the actual test lathe inspection environment.

7 Conclusions

In this paper, the cloud and edge collaborative computing architecture and the edge side cluster resource allocation method were proposed. For the IO-intensive virtual machine, the priority of each IO-intensive virtual machine is given in combination with the second-order difference method, and finally the resource allocation algorithm of the dynamic adaptive IO-intensive virtual machine is realized. For the CPU-intensive virtual machine, combined with the application scenario of the test lathe in the actual production environment, the dynamic adaptive CPU-intensive virtual machine resource allocation algorithm is realized. Compared with other heuristic algorithms, the simulation results show that the edge-side server store data and calculation speed of this algorithm were significantly improved, when the number of factory terminal equipment and test tasks are large, the resource consumption is relatively small.

Acknowledgement. This paper is supported by Natural Science Foundation of China (No. 61871432, No. 61702178), The Natural Science Foundation of Hunan Province (No. 2020JJ4275, 2020JJ6086, 2019JJ60008, 2018JJ4063).

References

1. Li, L.: China's manufacturing locus in 2025: with a comparison of "Made-in-China 2025" and "Industry 4.0". Technol. Forecast. Soc. Change **135**, 66–74 (2018)
2. Zhou, J.: Toward New-generation intelligent manufacturing. Engineering **4**(1), 28–47 (2018)
3. Stark, R.: Development and operation of Digital Twins for technical systems and services. CIRP Ann. **68**(1), 129–132 (2019)
4. Shen, W.: Potential applications of 5G communication technologies in collaborative intelligent manufacturing. IET Collab. Intell. Manuf. **1**(4), 109–116 (2019)
5. Xu, L.D.: Big data for cyber physical systems in industry 4.0: a survey. Enterp. Inf. Syst. **13**(2), 148–169 (2019)
6. Jena, M.C.: Application of Industry 4.0 to enhance sustainable manufacturing. Environ. Prog. Sustain. Energy **39**(1), 13360 (2020)
7. Song, T.: Server consolidation energy-saving algorithm based on resource reservation and resource allocation strategy. IEEE Access **7**, 171452–171460 (2019)
8. Rugwiro, U.: Task scheduling and resource allocation based on ant-colony optimization and deep reinforcement learning. J. Internet Technol. **20**(5), 1463–1475 (2019)
9. Devarasetty, P.: Genetic algorithm for quality of service based resource allocation in cloud computing. Evol. Intel. **16**(4), 1–7 (2019). https://doi.org/10.1007/s12065-019-00233-6
10. Jangiti, S.: Scalable hybrid and ensemble heuristics for economic virtual resource allocation in cloud and fog cyber-physical systems. J. Intell. Fuzzy Syst. **36**(5), 4519–4529 (2019)
11. Liu, C.F.: Dynamic task offloading and resource allocation for ultra-reliable low-latency edge computing. IEEE Trans. Commun. **67**(6), 4132–4150 (2019)
12. Liao, H.: Learning-based context-aware resource allocation for edge-computing-empowered industrial IoT. IEEE Internet Things J. **7**(5), 4260–4277 (2019)
13. Hu, A., Xiang, L., Xu, S., Lin, J.: Frequency loss and recovery in rolling bearing fault detection. Chin. J. Mech. Eng. **32**(1), 1–12 (2019). https://doi.org/10.1186/s10033-019-0349-3
14. Shen, G.: A study of the condition monitoring of large mechanical equipment based on a health management theory for mechanical systems. Insight Nondestr. Test. Condition Monit. **61**(8), 448–457 (2019)
15. Zhang, J.X.: Cloud collaborative computing framework for a service robot based on ROS. Comput. Syst. Appl. **25**(9), 85–91 (2016)
16. Merlino, G.: Enabling workload engineering in edge, fog, and cloud computing through OpenStack-based middleware. ACM Trans. Internet Technol. **19**(2), 28–30 (2019)
17. An overview of the StarlingX project. https://www.starlingx.io/learn/. Accessed 15 May 2020
18. Zhu, J.: Research on data mining of electric power system based on Hadoop cloud computing platform. Int. J. Comput. Appl. **41**(4), 289–295 (2019)
19. Yamato, Y.: Fast and reliable restoration method of virtual resources on OpenStack. IEEE Trans. Cloud Comput. **6**(2), 572–576 (2018)

20. Yi, C.: Quaternion singular spectrum analysis using convex optimization and its application to fault diagnosis of rolling bearing. Measurement **103**(6), 321–323 (2017)
21. Chen, F., Fu, Z., Zhen, L.: Thermal power generation fault diagnosis and prediction model based on deep learning and multimedia systems. Multimedia Tools Appl. **78**(4), 4673–4692 (2018). https://doi.org/10.1007/s11042-018-6601-5
22. Huang, Y.: M/M/n/m queuing model under nonpreemptive limited-priority. Chin. J. Appl. Probab. Stat. **34**(4), 364–368 (2018)
23. Peng, J., Chen, J., Kong, S.: Resource optimization strategy for CPU intensive applications in cloud computing environment. In: IEEE 3rd International Conference on Cyber Security and Cloud Computing 2016, CSCloud, Beijing, vol. 10134, pp. 124–128. IEEE (2016)
24. Hu, N.: Power equipment status information parallel fault diagnosis of based on MapReduce. J. Comput. Methods Sci. Eng. **19**(1), 165–170 (2019)
25. Zhi, Y.: Balance resource allocation for spark jobs based on prediction of the optimal resource. Tsinghua Sci. Technol. **25**(04), 487–497 (2020)
26. Zhang, J.: Big data driven intelligent manufacturing. China Mech. Eng. **30**(2), 127–133 (2019)
27. StarlingX Enhancements for Edge Networking, [EB/OL] (2018). https://www.openstack.org/videos/summits/berlin-2018/starlingx-enhancements-for-edge-networknet. Accessed 15 May 2020
28. Guo, W., Kuang, P., Jiang, Y., Xu, X., Tian, W.: SAVE: self-adaptive consolidation of virtual machines for energy efficiency of CPU-intensive applications in the cloud. J. Supercomput. **75**(11), 7076–7100 (2019). https://doi.org/10.1007/s11227-019-02927-1
29. Merlino, G.: Enabling workload engineering in edge, fog, and cloud computing through OpenStack-based middleware. ACM Trans. Internet Technol. (TOIT) **19**(2), 1–22 (2019)
30. Al-Tarazi, M., Chang, J.M.: Network-aware energy saving multi-objective optimization in virtualized data centers. Clust. Comput. **22**(2), 635–647 (2018). https://doi.org/10.1007/s10586-018-2869-5
31. Cao, Y.: Communication optimisation for intermediate data of MapReduce computing model. Int. J. Comput. Sci. Eng. **21**(2), 226–233 (2020)

Few Shot Learning Based on the Street View House Numbers (SVHN) Dataset

Rundong Yang[1], Yancong Deng[2(✉)], Anqi Zhu[3], Xin Tong[4], and Zhihao Chen[5]

[1] Hebei University of Technology, Hebei, China
[2] University of California, San Diego, USA
yad002@eng.ucsd.edu
[3] University of New South Wales, Sydney, Australia
z5141541@unsw.edu.au
[4] University of Illinois at Urbana Champaign, Champaign, IL, USA
xintong2@illinois.edu
[5] Shanghai University, Shanghai, China

Abstract. In recent years, deep learning model has made remarkable achievements in image, voice, text recognition and other fields. However, deep learning model relies heavily on large number of labeled data, which limits its application in the special field of data shortage.

For the practical situation such as lack of data, many scholars carry out research on the few shot learning methods, and there are many typical research directions, among which model-agnostic meta-learning (MAML) is one of them. Aiming at the few shot learning method, this paper systematically expounds the current main research methods on few shot learning, the algorithm of MAML and implements the MAML on the SVHN dataset.

Keywords: Few shot learning · Meta learning · MAML · Digit detection

1 Introduction

Deep learning has made significant progress in areas such as computer vision, but this is based on the fact that they have a large amount of labeled data. However, it is impractical to obtain a large amount of data in real life, for example, in the fields of medicine and security, labeling data is scarce, and the cost of obtaining label data is also very large. For deep learning methods, fitting a more complex model requires more data. Generally speaking, in the case of small amount of data, the training effects of deep learning are not good, and the recognition performance of new kind of samples is also poor.

Since humans can learn from a small number of samples, we believe that deep learning technologies will also get rid of their dependence on the amount of data in the future. Therefore, few shot learning has become a very important research direction in the field of deep learning in recent years.

© ICST Institute for Computer Sciences, Social Informatics and Telecommunications Engineering 2021
Published by Springer Nature Switzerland AG 2021. All Rights Reserved
H. Jiang et al. (Eds.): ICECI 2020, LNICST 368, pp. 86–102, 2021.
https://doi.org/10.1007/978-3-030-73429-9_6

To solve such problems, many methods have been carried out. This paper introduces several current few shot learning methods based on deep neural network with few samples, such as prototype network-based method, optimization-based method, and migration-based learning method.

Among these methods, meta learning is the method with high performance and it was inspired by Human beings. Human beings can not only learn from a small number of samples, but also implement experiences on other kinds of samples. Like human beings, meta learning does not consider new tasks in isolation, but uses previous experience to quickly learn new tasks, so as to achieve the ability to learn how to learn, which can well solve the problem of task-specific categories in few shot learning. In this paper, the model-agnostic meta-learning (MAML) algorithm and the results of experiment on SVHN dataset are described in detail.

2   Related Work

Meta learning, also known as learning to learn, refers to the use of previous experience to quickly learn new tasks without considering new tasks in isolation.

In 2001, Memory based neural network is proved to be useful in meta learning (S. Hochreiter, 2001) [3]. The siamese neural network is composed of two identical convolution neural networks, and the similarity between the two images is calculated by comparing the loss function with the paired samples input(Gregory Koch, 2015) [4]. Prototype network can project each sample of each category into the same space. For each kind of sample, their center point is extracted as the prototype, and the distance between the sample to be classified and the prototype of each category is calculated by Euclidean distance and the distance can be used to classify(Jake Snell, 2017) [10].

A memory enhancement network based on long-term memory network (LSTM) was proposed in 2016 [9]. Memory enhancement network train data as a sequence, and the last label is also used as network input, and external storage is added to store the last input. This enables the labels to establish a relationship with the input when the next input is back propagation, so that the subsequent input can obtain the relevant image through external memory for comparison, so as to achieve better prediction(Adam Santoro, 2016). Other scholars used LSTM as a meta learner, and took the initial parameters, learning rate and loss gradient of the learner as the state of LSTM to learn the initialization parameters and parameter update rules of the learner(Ravi and Larochelle, 2017) [8].

Model agnostic meta learning (MAML) algorithm trains on a large number of different tasks, and can quickly adapt to new tasks through a small number of gradient steps. Compared with the previous meta learning method, this method does not introduce additional parameters and has no restrictions on the structure of the model. Only gradient is used to update the weight of the learner (Chelsea Finn, 2017) [1]. Based on the MAML and neglecting the quadratic differential, Alex Nichol proposed a meta learning method to find the initialization parameters of the neural network, Reptile. Reptile only needs to execute the random gradient descent algorithm on each task, and does not need to compute quadratic differential like the MAML, so it consumes less computation and memory(Alex Nichol, 2018) [6].

3   MAML Algorithm Introduction

MAML directly optimizes the initialization parameters of learners. After updating the parameters by using one or more gradient iterative steps calculated from a small amount of data from the new task, the learner has the maximum generalization performance on the new task, so it has the ability to learn how to learn. MAML can be easily combined with fully connected neural network, convolution neural network or recurrent neural network, and it can also be used in various loss functions, including differential supervised loss and non differential reinforcement learning objectives. For this reason, the MAML is called Model agnostic meta learning.

3.1   Convolution Neural Network

The learner used in this paper is a convolution neural network [5, 13], which consists of four convolution layers and a full connection layer. The convolution kernel sizes are (3 * 3), (3 * 3), (3 * 3), (2 * 2), respectively. After each convolution layer, a RELU activation function layer and a batch normalization layer are applied. The batch normalization layer can prevent over fitting, improve the learning rate, and training speed [7]. The structure of convolution neural network used in this paper is shown in Fig. 1.

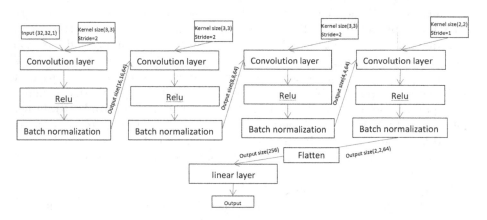

Fig. 1. Convolution neural network

3.2   Pseudo Code

The initial parameter optimization process after one gradient iteration step is shown in Fig. 2. Each task is represented by T_i, $p(T)$ as the distribution function of the task set, $f(\theta)$ as the few shot learner that maps the original pixel characteristic value x of the image to the output value, and θ as the parameter value of the learner. Extract task T_1 from $p(T)$. After a gradient iteration, a new temporary parameter θ_1' that adapts to the specific task is calculated. Then, new samples from task T_1 is taken for testing, and the loss $L_{T_1}f(\theta_1')$ of corresponding task T_1 is calculated. Then, the loss of different tasks will be kept generating until we get the loss of new task T_n. Finally, the sum of test loss in different tasks is used for the parameters optimization of the meta learning process. The parameters of the learner are updated by the gradient descent method, and finally a set of initialization parameters are obtained.

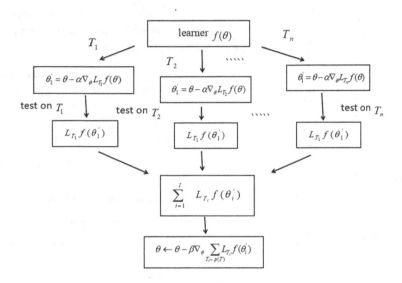

Fig. 2. Flowchart of MAML

To be specific, for the task of N way K shot, first determine the number of tasks in each step, then for each task, select N classes from the dataset, and select $K + Q$ images from each class as the support set and query set(Q is the number of pictures in query set). The support set is input into the convolution neural network, and the cross entropy formula is used to calculate the loss and update the temporary parameters.

$$L_{T_i}(f_\theta) = \sum_{x^{(j)},y^{(j)}\sim T_j} y^{(j)} \log f_\theta\left(x^{(j)}\right) + \left(1 - y^{(j)}\right) \log \left(1 - f_\theta\left(x^{(j)}\right)\right)$$

Then the query set is input into the convolution neural network with temporary parameters, and the loss is calculated. After all the tasks are trained, the average value of all the losses obtained by the query set is calculated, and the value obtained is used to update the initialization parameters of the meta learner through the Adam optimizer.

To sum up, the above can be summarized as the following pseudo codes.

Algorithm 1. Model agnostic meta learning [1]

Require: α, β: learning rate
Require: I: the number of task of per batch
Require: $p(T)$: distribution of tasks
Require: $ADAM(\theta, L)$: using adam optimizer to update
1: Randomly initialize θ
2: **while** not done **do**
3:     sample batch of tasks $T_i \sim p(T)$
4:     **for** all T_i **do**
5:         $S_i = \left\{ x^{(i)}, y^{(j)} \right\}$ # support set
6:         $f_\theta (S_i)$ # train model with parameters θ
7:         $L_{T_i} (f_\theta) = \sum\limits_{x^{(j)}, y^{(j)}} y^{(j)} \log f_\theta \left(x^{(j)} \right) + (1 - y^{(j)}) \log(1 - f_\theta(x^{(j)}))$

                                                        # calculate cross-entropy
8:         $\theta'_i = \theta - \alpha \nabla_\theta L_{S_i} (f_\theta)$ # update parameters of the model temporarily
9:         $Q_i = \left\{ x^{(i)}, y^{(j)} \right\}$ # query set
10:         $f_{\theta'} (Q_i)$ # train model with parameters θ
11:         $L_{T_i} (f_\theta) = \sum\limits_{x^{(j)}, y^{(j)}} y^{(j)} \log f_\theta(x^{(j)}) + (1 - y^{(j)}) \log(1 - f_\theta(x^{(j)}))$

                                                        # calculate cross-entropy
12:     **end for**
13:     $L = \sum\limits_{i=1}^{l} L_{T_i} \left(f_{\theta'_i} \right) / I$ # calculate the total loss of the batch
14:     $ADAM(\theta, L)$ # update parameters of the model
15: **end while**

3.3 Apply to SVHN

In this paper, we use Python to apply MAML to the SVHN dataset to explore how the MAML performs with the digit recognition in natural scene. Firstly, the convolution neural network introduced in Sect. 3.1 is built by using Pytorch. Then we write code to extract tasks from SVHN dataset, each task includes N categories, each category includes $K + Q$ pictures (K is the number of pictures in support set, Q is the number of pictures in query set). An iteration consists of 32 tasks. For each iteration step, we use the support set of each task to update the temporary parameters 5 times. After that, we use the query set to get the loss values, and the average value of the 32 loss values is used to update the parameters.

During the test, we extract one task and update the parameters 10 times using the support set and get the test accuracy using the query set. In addition, we use the Visdom service to visualize the experiment. The hyper parameters used in the program are shown in Table 1.

Table 1. Hyper parameters

Task number	Meta learning rate	Training learning rate	Update step	Test update step
32	0.001	0.4	5	10

4 Experiment

4.1 Preparation

SVHN (street view house number) dataset is the real world data, in order to develop the machine learning and target recognition algorithm [2]. Similar to MNIST, but larger. And they all come from problems that are obviously more difficult and unsolved in the real world. The dataset is from Google Street view pictures.

There are 10 kinds of SVHN. The number 1 is labeled as 1 and the number 9 as 9. There are 73257 training sets and 26032 test sets. There are also 531131 additional, simpler sampling data that can be used as training sets.

Fig. 3. SVHN dataset

Although there are only 10 categories of images in SVHN, the number of images in each category is large, and the selected images will be relabeled in each task. So it can meet the requirements of diverse data types in few shot learning experiments. In addition, the SVHN dataset is shot from the real world. Therefore, compared with the Omniglot dataset commonly used in the few shot learning experiment, few shot learning experiment of SVHN is more challenging. Therefore, in this paper, we use SVHN dataset to do experiments.

Next, we extract the corresponding data from SVHN to complete the few shot learning and one shot learning experiments.

4.2 Two Way One Shot Learning

In order to ensure the accuracy of the test accuracy, the training dataset and the test dataset should be inconsistent [12]. So we divide the ten categories of SVHN dataset into two parts, one includes eight categories of images for training, named training part, the other includes the other two categories of images for testing, named testing part.

For the training tasks of 2-way 1-shot, for each task, we will extract two kinds of images from the eight kinds of images in the training part, and then take one images from the two kinds of images as the support set and 15 images as the query set respectively [11]. For the testing tasks, the two categories images in testing part are all used. And the number of images in the testing tasks is the same as that in the training tasks.

Table 2. Examples of tasks (MAML, SVHN, 2-way 1-shot)

By inputting the above data into the MAML model, we record the training accuracy and loss of each query set in training step. As can be seen from Fig. 4, the growth rate is faster in steps 0–1300, and it starts to rise slowly after steps 1300. Finally, the accuracy of training steps is stable at $89.9\% \pm 5.2\%$ after 3500 steps. It should be noted that the accuracy of training steps is not as reliable as that of testing steps, because there may be over fitting phenomenon due to the small number of datasets. The trend of loss is similar to that of accuracy (Fig. 5).

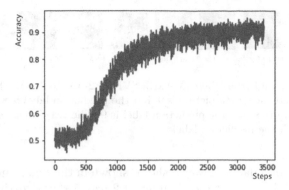

Fig. 4. Accuracy of training steps (MAML, SVHN, 2-way 1-shot)

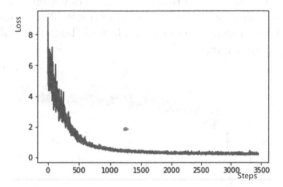

Fig. 5. Loss of training steps (MAML, SVHN, 2-way 1-shot)

Take the parameters obtained in the training steps as the initial parameters of the test step, and carry out one test step every 500 training steps. It can be seen from Table 3 that after 3000 iterations, the test accuracy of the MAML model in this paper can reach 70.3% for 2-way 1-shot. We extract the query set in test step, and compare the predicted value and the true label of the images (Fig. 6). Among the ten images, the predicted values of the first, the fourth and the ninth are not consistent with the true labels, with an accuracy of 70%, which is basically consistent with the test accuracy of the MAML model.

4.3   Two Way Five Shot Learning

Similar to the method of extracting data in 2-way 1-shot, we extract two kinds of images from SVHN dataset for each task. The difference is that five images are extracted from each type of images as the support set. Due to the larger amount of data in few shot learning, theoretically, the accuracy of the test will be higher [12].

Pred:8 True:9 Pred:9 True:9 Pred:9 True:9 Pred:8 True:9 Pred:8 True:8 Pred:9 True:9 Pred:8 True:8 Pred:8 True:8 Pred:9 True:8Pred:9 True:9

Fig. 6. Predictions and true labels (MAML, SVHN, 2-way 1-shot). The true label of the first picture and the fourth picture is 9, but the prediction label is 8. The true label of the ninth picture is 8, and the prediction label is 9. The true labels of other pictures are consistent with the prediction labels.

The experimental data of 2-way 5-shot is shown in the Fig. 7 and Fig. 8. It can be seen from the figures that the accuracy of 2-way 5-shot experiment increases and the loss decreases significantly faster than 2 way 1 shot experiment. Step 0–400 is the fastest range of accuracy and loss. After step 400, accuracy rises slowly and stabilizes at 94.3% ± 0.8%. Compared with Fig. 4 and Fig. 5, it can also be found that the training accuracy and loss of the 2-way 1-shot experiment have a larger fluctuation range.

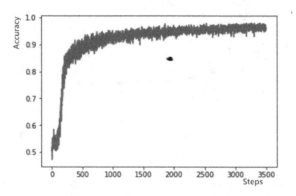

Fig. 7. Accuracy of training steps (MAML, SVHN, 2-way 5-shot)

The results of the test steps are shown in Table 3. After 1500 iterations, the accuracy of the test is 80.1% ± 0.4%. Figure 9 shows ten images extracted from the query set of the test task. From the images, the predicted values of the fifth and seventh images are different from the real labels, and other predicted values are consistent with the real labels, with an accuracy of 80%, consistent with the test results.

4.4 Five Way Five Shot Learning

For the 5-way-5 shot experiment, we have five kinds of images in the training part and the test part of the SVHN dataset respectively. The other algorithms are the same as the two classification experiments. The final experimental results are shown in the figures below.

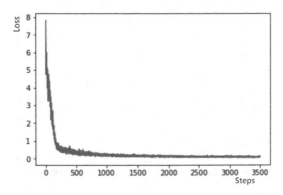

Fig. 8. Loss of training steps (MAML, SVHN, 2-way 5-shot)

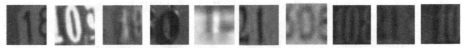

Pred:1True:1 Pred:0True:0 Pred:1True:1 Pred:0True:0 Pred:0True:1 Pred:1True:1 Pred:1True:0 Pred:0True:0 Pred:1True:1 Pred:1True:1

Fig. 9. Predictions and true labels(MAML, SVHN, 2-way 5-shot). There are two false prediction, such as the true label of the fifth picture is 1, but the prediction label is 0. The true label of the seventh picture is 0, and the prediction label is 1. The true labels of other pictures are consistent with the prediction labels.

Based on these figures, the test results can be summarized as follows: after 3000 iterations the training accuracy can be stabilized at $98\% \pm 0.5\%$, the accuracy of the test is $53.6\% \pm 3\%$.

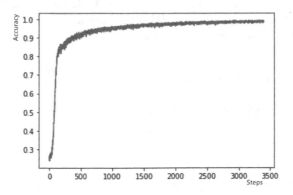

Fig. 10. Accuracy of training steps (MAML, SVHN, 5-way 5-shot)

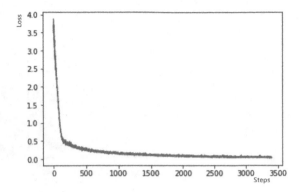

Fig. 11. Loss of training steps (MAML, SVHN, 5-way 5-shot)

Table 3. Test accuracy (MAML, SVHN)

Test accuracy						
Steps	500	1000	1500	2000	2500	3000
Test accuracy (%)	2-way 1-shot learning					
	51.7	58.1	65.9	68.8	70.3	69.6
	2-way 5-shot learning					
	77.1	80.5	80.2	79.7	79.9	80.3
	5-way 5-shot learning					
	56.6	54.6	52.9	52.4	50.5	50.6

In order to show clearly the performance of MAML for few shot learning with SVHN dataset, we refer to the results of MAML for few shot learning with Omniglot and MiniImagenet dataset [1]. In addition, we also apply the MAML model to the MNIST dataset as a reference (Table 4).

Table 4. Test accuracy with different dataset (MAML, 5-way 5-shot)

Dataset	Omniglot	MiniImagenet	SVHN (ours)	MNIST (ours)
Test accuracy	$99.9 \pm 0.1\%$	$63.11 \pm 0.92\%$	$53.6 \pm 3\%$	$72.4 \pm 1.4\%$

Among these results, the experimental accuracy of Omniglot dataset is much higher than that of other datasets. The accuracy of MNIST dataset and MiniImage dataset is the second and third, while the accuracy result of SVHN dataset is the lowest. This proves that the relatively simple and less interference images have a higher experimental accuracy.

5   Comparison with Siamese Network

In order to compare the performance of different few shot learning methods for SVHN dataset, we also use Siamese network to carry out 5-way 5-shot learning for SVHN dataset.

5.1   Siamese Neural Networks

Siamese network [4] is still based on convolutional neural network, but unlike traditional CNN, the input data is paired (x_1 and x_2). In these pairs of data, if the two kinds of data are the same, label the pair of data as 1, if the two kinds of data are different, label the pair of data as 0.

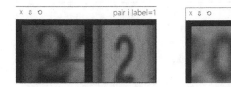

Fig. 12. Examples of pairs (Siamese). The two pictures on the left have the same category, so the label is 1; the two pictures on the right have different categories, so the label is 0.

The two images in a pair of data will be input into the same CNN respectively, and the output data will be merged by Euclidean distance, and the resulting data will be classified into 0 (different categories) or 1 (same category). Correspondingly, the loss function should be binary cross entropy and the optimizer is Adam.

5.2   Experiment

For the experiment of 5-way 5-shot, we extract 5 kinds of images from the SVHN dataset, and extract 5 images from each kind as the support set. Then, with the first category of the support set as the reference, we extract 5 * 5 pictures from the SVHN dataset as the test set. In this way, the first five of these data pairs should have a prediction value of 1 (the same picture type), and the next 20 should have a prediction value of 0 (different picture types).

For the test after each iteration, if the predicted results show that the first five pairs of data have the highest similarity, then the test is regarded as a prediction success. The experimental results are shown in the figures below.

From the figures, the accuracy of Siamese network for 5-way 5-shot learning with SVHN dataset can reach 47.63%. But the range of its accuracy is relatively large. On average, the accuracy of Siamese network is between 40% ± 5%.

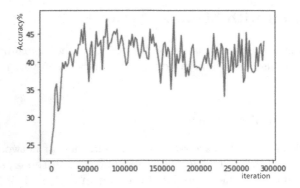

Fig. 13. Test accuracy of Siamese net (SVHN, 5-way 5-shot)

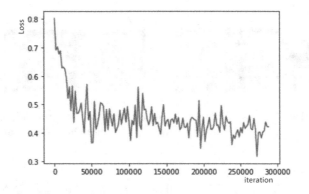

Fig. 14. Loss of Siamese net (SVHN, 5-way 5-shot)

Table 5. Test accuracy of Siamese (SVHN, 5-way 5-shot)

Steps	60000	120000	180000	240000	300000
Test accuracy (%)	45.4	41.8	37.2	38.3	39.2

5.3   Comparison

In our experiment, it took only 6150 s for Siamese network to carry out 300000 iterations, and achieved relatively stable data, while it took 9522 s for MAML method to complete 1500 iterations to achieve stable data., The accuracy of 5-way 5-shot experiment with MAML method is 5 to 10% points higher than that of Siamese network.

In addition, it can be seen from the figures that the test accuracy and loss range of Siamese network is relatively large and from the perspective of percentage error (Table 7), the percentage error of MAML is 5.6% and the percentage error of Siamese network is 12.5%. This means that the generalization performance of MAML network is better, and MAML has better stability when dealing with various types of few shot learning tasks.

In order to further verify the difference between MAML and Siamese network, we apply Siamese network to MNIST dataset, and the experimental results are shown in Table 6, Table 7 and Fig. 15. In MNIST dataset, the advantages of MAML model are more obvious. The accuracy of test is 73%, while the Siamese network is only 59%. Moreover, the percentage error of MAML is lower than that of Siamese network.

In Table 7, we also record the performance of traditional CNN model in 5-way 5-shot learning. For the simple MNIST dataset, CNN has a 48.6% ± 6.1% accuracy rate, but for the complex SVHN dataset, CNN's performance is much worse than the other two methods dedicated to few shot learning. In order to show the performance of the three methods more intuitively, we also summarize the test accuracy of the three methods and draw Figs. 16 and 17.

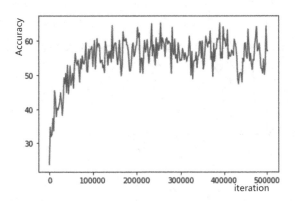

Fig. 15. Test accuracy of Siamese net (MNIST, 5-way 5-shot)

Table 6. Test accuracy of Siamese (MNIST, 5-way 5-shot)

Steps	60000	120000	180000	240000	300000
Test accuracy (%)	54.8	54.3	60.1	64.1	59.8

MAML and Siamese are two different ways to solve the problem of feed shot learning. The goal of MAML is to get the best initial parameters of generalization performance, while Siamese is trying to judge the similarity of two images to

Table 7. Comparison of MAML, SIAMESE and CNN (5-way 5-shot)

Comparison of MAML, SIAMESE and CNN (5-way 5-shot)			
SVHN			
	MAML	SIAMESE	CNN
Steps	1500	300000	500
Time spent(s)	9522	6150	579
Test accuracy	53.6% ± 3%	41.8% ± 5%	20.8% ± 1%
Percentage error of test accuracy	5.6%	12.5%	4.8%
MNIST			
Steps	1500	300000	500
Times spent(s)	8015	4929	554
Test accuracy	72.4% ± 1.4%	57.2% ± 7%	48.6% ± 6.1%
Percentage error of test accuracy	1.9%	12.2%	12.5%

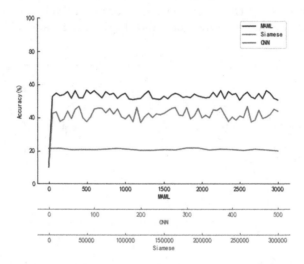

Fig. 16. Test accuracy of 5-way 5-shot of different methods (SVHN). The black line represents MAML, the red line represents Siamese network, and the green line represents traditional CNN. (Color figure online)

classify. They are all good research directions, but in experiments based on SVHN and MNIST datasets, MAML has better performance, both in terms of test accuracy and generalization performance. Meanwhile, from the experimental results of these two methods for SVHN dataset, the accuracy of the test still has a large space to improve.

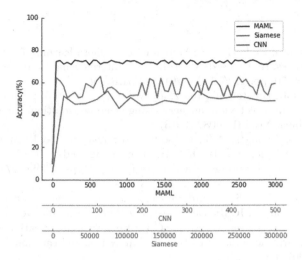

Fig. 17. Test accuracy of 5-way 5-shot of different methods (MNIST). The black line represents MAML, the red line represents Siamese network, and the green line represents traditional CNN. (Color figure online)

6   Conclusions and Future Works

In this paper, we introduce the algorithm of MAML and apply it to SVHN dataset based few shot learning. Our experiments include 2-way 1-shot, 2-way 5-shot and 5-way 5-shot, and the accuracy of these three experiments are about 70%, 80% and 50%, respectively. The accuracy will decrease with the increase of image category and the decrease of sample number. For 5-way 5-shot learning, we compared the accuracy of MAML application on different datasets: the accuracy based on simple datasets is significantly higher than that based on complex datasets. Also, we also verify that for SVHN and MNIST dataset, MAML has better performance than Siamese network.

In addition, from the experimental results, we find that the training accuracy of each experiment will eventually approach 100%, and the test accuracy will be stable at a specific value, which verifies that the datasets with fewer categories can also be applied to the few shot learning experiments, but in the process of training, the same kind of image data has a certain positive effect on the model parameters, and the training accuracy may be biased, and the type of test accuracy is different from the training part, so the test accuracy is credible.

For the future work, in order to prevent the above problem, SVHN dataset can be synthesized into images of multi digit numbers, and each number includes several images. Moreover, the influence of the value of the MAML hyper parameter on the experimental performance is worth further discussion.

References

1. Finn, C., Abbeel, P., Levine, S.: Model-agnostic meta-learning for fast adaptation of deep networks. In: Proceedings of the 34th International Conference on Machine Learning, vol. 70, pp. 1126–1135 (2017). JMLR.org
2. Goodfellow, I.J., Bulatov, Y., Ibarz, J., Arnoud, S., Shet, V.: Multi-digit number recognition from street view imagery using deep convolutional neural networks. arXiv preprint arXiv:1312.6082 (2013)
3. Hochreiter, S., Younger, A.S., Conwell, P.R.: Learning to learn using gradient descent. In: Dorffner, G., Bischof, H., Hornik, K. (eds.) ICANN 2001. LNCS, vol. 2130, pp. 87–94. Springer, Heidelberg (2001). https://doi.org/10.1007/3-540-44668-0_13
4. Koch, G., Zemel, R., Salakhutdinov, R.: Siamese neural networks for one-shot image recognition. In: ICML Deep Learning Workshop, Lille, vol. 2 (2015)
5. Krizhevsky, A., Sutskever, I., Hinton, G.E.: ImageNet classification with deep convolutional neural networks. In: Advances in Neural Information Processing Systems, pp. 1097–1105 (2012)
6. Nichol, A., Achiam, J., Schulman, J.: On first-order meta-learning algorithms. arXiv preprint arXiv:1803.02999 (2018)
7. Normalization, B.: Accelerating deep network training by reducing internal covariate shift. corr.-2015. Vol. abs/1502.03167. http://arxiv.org/abs/1502.03167 (2015)
8. Ravi, S., Larochelle, H.: Optimization as a model for few-shot learning (2016)
9. Santoro, A., Bartunov, S., Botvinick, M., Wierstra, D., Lillicrap, T.: One-shot learning with memory-augmented neural networks. arXiv preprint arXiv:1605.06065 (2016)
10. Snell, J., Swersky, K., Zemel, R.: Prototypical networks for few-shot learning. In: Advances in Neural Information Processing Systems, pp. 4077–4087 (2017)
11. Vinyals, O., Blundell, C., Lillicrap, T., Wierstra, D., et al.: Matching networks for one shot learning. In: Advances in Neural Information Processing Systems, pp. 3630–3638 (2016)
12. Xia, T.: Research on classification method of small sample image based on meta learning. Master's thesis, University of Electronic Science and technology (2019)
13. Zeiler, M.D., Fergus, R.: Visualizing and understanding convolutional networks. In: Fleet, D., Pajdla, T., Schiele, B., Tuytelaars, T. (eds.) ECCV 2014. LNCS, vol. 8689, pp. 818–833. Springer, Cham (2014). https://doi.org/10.1007/978-3-319-10590-1_53

Smart Sensing

TouchSense: Accurate and Transparent User Re-authentication via Finger Touching

Chong Zhang[ID], Songfan Li[ID], Yihang Song, Li Lu[✉], and Mengshu Hou

University of Electronic Science and Technology of China,
Chengdu 611731, Sichuan, China
{zhangchong,sfli,songyihang}@std.uestc.edu.cn
{luli2009,mshou}@uestc.edu.cn

Abstract. Re-authentication identifies the user during the whole usage to enhance the security of smartphones. To avoid frequent interrupts to users, user features should be imperceptibly collected for identification without user assistance. Conventionally, behavior habits (*e.g.* movement, trail) during the user operation are commonly considered as the most appropriate features for re-authentication. The behavior features, however, are often fluctuating and inevitably sacrifice the accuracy of re-authentication, which puts the phones at risk increasingly. In this paper, we propose *TouchSense*, an accurate and transparent scheme for user re-authentication. The basic idea is to leverage the combined information of human biometric capacitance and touching behavior for user identification. When the user touches capacitive-based sensors, both information can be automatically collected and applied in the authentication, which is transparent to the user. Based on the authentication results, we build up user-legitimate models to comprehensively evaluate the user's legitimacy, which reduces misjudgment and further improves accuracy. Moreover, we implement *TouchSense* on an SX9310 EVKA board and conduct comprehensive experiments to evaluate it. The results illustrate that *TouchSense* can identify 98% intruders within 10 s, but for legitimate users, the misjudgment is less than 0.9% in 2.6-hours-usage.

Keywords: User re-authentication · User-transparent · Touching behavior · Biometric capacitance · Continuous security

1 Introduction

Over the past decades, the dramatic outpouring of digital information has generated a mass of invaluable data stored in computer phones. One of the crucial concerns lies in the private data that is sensitive to be accessed by illegal users. To prevent this, user authentication schemes [3,35,41] are proposed to recognize who is operating the device at several critical operations (*e.g.* unlocking,

Supported by University of Electronic Science and Technology of China.

H. Jiang et al. (Eds.): ICECI 2020, LNICST 368, pp. 105–125, 2021.
https://doi.org/10.1007/978-3-030-73429-9_7

paying). These schemes, however, are vulnerable to attacks in that attackers can tamper with the private data between two authentications or even steal the keys (*e.g.* password, fingerprint) to pass the authentication [28,40]. Therefore, in order to enhance security, re-authentication schemes are desired to identify the user during the whole usage.

At first glance, user re-authentication may be a simple repeat of conventional authentications. However, many approaches for authentication are inadequate to re-authentication as they require user assistance and interrupt fluent operations. For instance, users may suffer from the bother of frequently checking their fingerprints for security. Therefore, we desire to find out a way to authenticate the user transparently from their operations. To this goal, a typical approach may exploit video streaming for continuous face recognition [4]. This approach, however, becomes insecure in that recent reports [24] have proofed that 3D face masks can fool facial recognition at airports.

To offer a guarantee to the privacy data, several works have been proposed for user-transparent re-authentication. Lingjun *et al.* [19] presents an on-screen gestures monitoring system to identify users according to screen operations including basic sliding and tapping. Further, the authors in [21,34] provide approaches for continuous authentication using movement data measured on smartphones. As a consequence, both gestures and movements belong to human habits built from individuals' daily life. Although habit features show potentials to be utilized in user authentication, they hardly achieve high accuracy in practice as the behaviors performed from habits are often fluctuating and mutable. Specifically, users cannot perform completely the same actions every time, even the same user repeats the same motion (*e.g.* tap) [10]. Besides, those works may also be affected by different Apps (Application software) and achieve lower accuracy in practice. For instance, some Apps require users to long-press the screen to copy text, which changes the user's behavior and may cause misjudgment in the authentication.

In this paper, we propose *TouchSense*, an accurate and transparent scheme for user re-authentication. Our basic idea originates an observation that past literature [23] has proofed that biometric capacitance of human bodies contains a unique feature for individuals recognition. Specifically, the biometric capacitance stands for the capability of the human body to store charges, which is proportional to the number of cells and size of cell mass in the body, thus different for everyone. Upon this, *TouchSense* collects the user's biometric capacitance via finger touching and imperceptibly authenticates users in the whole duration of human-machine interaction (HMI). Compared to habit features, biometric capacitance shows better accuracy for two reasons. First, the biometric feature is more stable than behaviors as it is determined by the user's physical characteristics and will not change in a short time [7,16,36]. Second, biometric features are not affected by different Apps as user use.

Although the basic idea seems effective, we have to address a fundamental challenge in *TouchSense*. Off-the-shelf capacitive touch screens [1,13,14,29,30] detects the touch by sensing the biometric capacitance during user touching, but

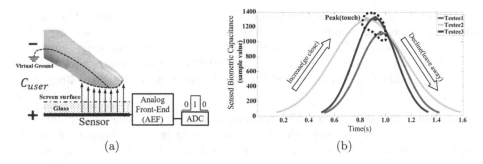

Fig. 1. Upon the capacitive sensors in a touchscreen, *TouchSense* continuously authenticates users according to their biometric capacitance during finger touching.

the accuracy is not adequate to achieve user authentication. The reason mainly stems from the fact that the accurate measurement of biometric capacitance requires the human standing with bare feet on a Styrofoam plate in a Faraday shield [11,18]. In practice, it is unrealistic to prepare such an experimental environment to measure the biometric capacitance.

We tackle this challenge by combining the biometric capacitance and touching behavior of the user to improve the accuracy. We show that both parameters can be obtained simultaneously by the touchscreen, as shown in Fig. 1. The peak value represents the biometric capacitance, while the rate of curve change is related to the user's operation habit (Fig. 1(b)). Specifically, when the user is going to touch the screen, the finger and the sensor will form a capacitor (C_{User}) in which the capacitance depends on both human biometric capacitance and the distance between the finger and the sensor under screen (Fig. 1(a)). Further, once the finger is touched on the screen surface, the distance can be treated as a constant value and thus the measurement result is only related to the biometric capacitance for different users. In addition, the finger movement speed results in the change to the distance and finally implies the user habits to touch the screen.

We also design an algorithm to avoid the impact of different Apps on user behaviors. The algorithm can distinguish and obtain the rising and falling edge of the sensed biometric capacitance which related to user behavior and exclude the holding period (finger keep on screen) which may be affected by different APPs. Finally, we build up a user-legitimate model to comprehensively evaluate the user's legitimacy in usage. This model accumulates the authentication results of each touching operation of the user and generates a legitimacy score, which increases with legal operations and decreases with illegal operations. Once the score drops below the threshold, the user will be considered an attacker and logged out to avoid further operations.

To show the feasibility of our design, we implement *TouchSense* on an SX9310 EVKA board [37] and evaluate it for 50 volunteers. To comprehensively evaluate the performance of *TouchSense*, we utilize the collected data set from 50 users and did mass simulations on 100,000 samples of the attackers and legitimate users. For each sample, the simulation is up to 50,000,000 times. The results show an interesting result that *TouchSense* can identify 98% attackers within 6 s (10 operations) and logout all of them within 11 s (18 operations). However, for legitimate users, the misjudgment is only 0.321% in 16-minutes-usage (1,000 touching operations), and only 0.895% in 2.6-hours-usage (10,000 touching operations).

Contributions. We propose *TouchSense*, a novel secure scheme for accurate and transparent user re-authentication. *TouchSense* leverages human biometric capacitance to achieve imperceptible user re-authentication. Further, we combine the biometric capacitance and touching habits to enhance accuracy. We also eliminate the impact of APPs on user behavior to ensure the robustness of *TouchSense* in practical. Finally, we build up a user-legitimate model to describe the user's legality much more accurately in using.

The remainder of the paper is organized as follows. Section 2 discusses the background. Section 3 introduces our scheme design. Next, Sect. 4 discusses the evaluation setup and test results. Section 5 discusses future works and ethical concerns of this paper. Finally, we make a summary in Sect. 6.

2   Background

The widespread use of smartphones has not only enriched our lives but also raise new issues of security and privacy concerns. For example, smartphones are no longer just communication tools, but become as powerful as computers, which may store many personal information (*e.g.* location, account, photos, shopping preferences) in it. Hence, smartphones become more and more private and build up a relationship with users. Having a victim's private information, the attacker can launch an impersonation attack [38]. Such attacks could threaten the owner's property and even reputation security. Therefore, protecting private information on smartphones is a key issue that has to be settled urgently.

To protect the user's privacy, most smartphones have deployed conventional authentications schemes to unlock the devices, such as passwords, fingerprints, facial recognition, palm textures [43] and signatures [2,26,27] which authenticate users when they are logging in. However, the device is still vulnerable to attackers for the remainder of the session. Specifically, an attacker can easily access the privacy information if the owner forgets to lock the device and loses it in public places. Even the device is locked, the attacker can also leverage system flaws to circumvent the lock screen, which is reported to exist in both IOS [5] and Android [17] systems. Hence, the continuous protection provided by re-authentication is necessary for smartphones, as it will repetitively verify the current user's legitimacy during the whole system execution.

As re-authentication schemes will keep running in the background as long as the user operating the phones, it should target not only accuracy but also to be user-transparent which can automatically run without user assistance. Previous re-authentication schemes are mainly base on the user's behavior or biometric information. However, none of them satisfies both aforementioned requirements simultaneously.

2.1 Behavior-Based User Re-authentication

Behavior information is the process of body motion, which contains the habit information of the user [25] and can be transparently sensed during it's process (*e.g.* gait [12] can be sensed when the user is walking). Hence, many re-authentication works are concentrate on it. Zijiang *et al.* made an efficient user re-authentication scheme which bases on keystrokes [15]. This scheme can verify the user's identity transparently by their typing behavior when the user is using the on-screen keyboard, but the accuracy is inadequate (90% at 20 typing operations) for high-security requirements, and it can only work when the user is typing. Lingjun *et al.* designed another scheme [19] to verify the user by the on-screen operation gestures. The same as Zijiang's work, it achieves the advantages of user-transparency but also not accurate enough. There are also some other works using other behavior information for user re-authentication. Such as gait-based schemes [8, 31, 33, 39, 44], which can work when the user is walking, but in practical, walking may not the most state of users.

2.2 Biometric-Based User Re-authentication

Biometric information is the reflection of our body characteristics, just like the internal passwords of us, which is good at stability and uniqueness [6]. However, biometric information doesn't contain any motion, which has to be sensed under user assistance (*e.g.* touching fingerprint panel). Hence, biometric-based schemes may interrupt user operations and bother users during the re-authentication process. There are relatively little works study on it.

David *et al.* designed an excellent work, which leverages the user's facial information for re-authentication [4]. This scheme uses the front camera to continuously verify the current user's legitimacy, which is accurate and easy to build on the existing phones. However, this work needs the user to keep facing the front camera when using, which constrains user-behavior in practical. Moreover, this scheme may be fooled by a 3D mask [24], which is insecure under such attacks. Feng *et al.* design another work that continuously authenticates the user by voice [9], but the user has to talk to assist the re-authentication, which influences user experience.

In summary, both existing biometric or behavior based re-authentication schemes can only satisfy either accuracy or transparency. To meet both requirements simultaneously, *TouchSense* should combine both biometric and behavior information in the authentication. As biometric information has to be sensed under user motion, the solution is to find a biometric whose necessary extraction step happens to be the user's device operation behavior. In this way, it can be extracted during the user's operation transparently without any additional auxiliary actions, thus avoid disturbing the user. In this paper, we start from the user's finger touching operation and combines the associated biometric

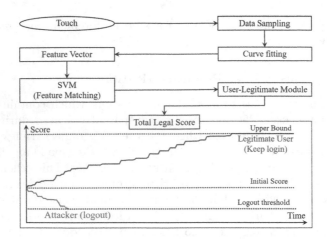

Fig. 2. *TouchSense* authenticates the user on every screen-touching operation and accumulates the results as the user's total legal score. If the score drops below the threshold, *TouchSense* will lock the device to protect private data on it.

information (biometric capacitance) and behavior information (touching behavior) to build up the re-authentication. Since the user needs to operate the device through finger touching, *TouchSense* can continuously work during the whole usage.

3   Scheme Design

The system design of *TouchSense* is shown in Fig. 2. When the user touches the screen, *TouchSense* scans the sensor and obtains the capacitance data. Then *TouchSense* fits the curve base on the sampled data and generate the user's feature vector according to the parameters of the curve function. After that, *TouchSense* compares the generated feature vector with the stored database to authenticate the user through Support Vector Machine (SVM). Finally, *TouchSense* builds up the user-legitimate module base on the authentication results during usage and generates the user's legal score. The score dynamically updates during user operation, which rises with legal operations or drops with illegal operations. If the score drops below the logout threshold, *TouchSense* logs out the user as an attacker, and locks the smartphones to avoid the user's further operation.

3.1   Data Sampling

The first step of *TouchSense* is data sampling. *TouchSense* periodically scanning the sensor during user operation to obtain data for the authentication. To eliminate the impact of different APPs on user behavior, we design a novel algorithm to combine the rising and falling edge together, and remove the holding period,

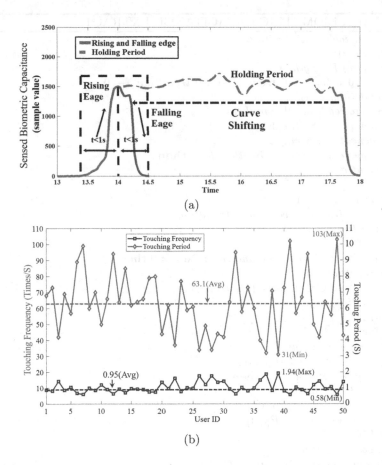

(a)

(b)

Fig. 3. (a) We only extract the rising and falling part of the sensed data and removing the holding period to avoid influence from different Apps. (b) Ignore the holding period, the touch frequency of 50 testers is 31–103 times per minute, and the period of each touch is 0.58–1.94 s.

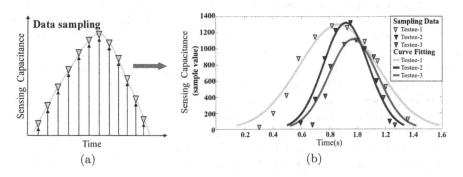

(a)   (b)

Fig. 4. Data sampling (a) and curve fitting (b) for 3 testers.

Algorithm 1. BIOMETRIC-CAPACITANCE-EXTRACT

1: ▷ *The variable initialization*
2: *New File String*
3: *New Array P[length][3]*
4: *time* ← 0, *value* ← 0, *trend* 50 ← 0, *trendflag* ← 0
5: ▷ *The data processing*
6: **for** *String.readLine()! = null* **do**
7:     *timenext* ← *String[0]*
8:     *valuenext* ← *String[1]*
9:     **if** |*timenext* − *time*| > *timethreshold* **then**
10:         *Continue*
11:     **else**
12:         *trendflag* ← 1
13:         *P* ← *timenext, valuenext, trendflag*
14:         *Continue*
15:     **end if**
16:     **if** *valuenext* − *value* > 0 *and trend* 50 == 0 **then**
17:         *trendflag* = 0
18:         *P* ← *timenext, valuenext, trendflag*
19:         *Continue*
20:     **end if**
21: **end for**
22: ▷ *Calculate the value*
23: **for** *for i* ← 0 *to length[P]* **do**
24:     **if** *flag* ← *P[i][3]* == 1 **then**
25:         *count* ← *count* + 1
26:         *time* ← *time* + *P[i][0]*
27:         *value* ← *value* + *P[i][1]*
28:     **end if**
29:     *timeavg* ← *P[i][0]/count*
30:     *valueavg* ← *P[i][1]/count*
31:     *Quick − Sort(P)*
32: **end for**

---

as shown in Fig. 3(a). Specifically, the holding period might be influenced by specific APPs (*e.g.* sliding, long pressing, have longer holding period than tapping), which may lead to misjudgment. This algorithm can identify the trend of the sensed biometric capacitance. If the value does not change significantly over a period of time, it will be defined as the holding period and deleted, and the portions that rise rapidly (finger go close to the screen) and fall (finger move away from the screen) will be recorded, as shown in Algorithm 1 (page 9). To set the appropriate length of the edge decision window, we analyzed the operating habits of 50 users, as shown in Fig. 3(b). Among 50 users, the operating frequency is 31–103 times, and the duration of each operation is 0.58–1.94 s. Hence, we set 1 s as the length of the decision widow to obtain the rising and falling edge of the curve (2 s in total).

3.2   Curve Fitting

After the data sampling, *TouchSense* gets the discrete capacitance value, shown in Fig. 4(a). These discrete points contain both biometric capacitance and touching behavior information of the user. The increasing or decreasing of the value depends on the user's touching behavior (*e.g.* finger moving speed, tapping frequency) and the peak value represents the biometric capacitance In this step, *TouchSense* uses the Gaussian function to fitting the curve base on these sampled data, and we can see the obvious differences between different users, shown in Fig. 4(b). The Gaussian function has three coefficients: (1) the peak value of the curve: a, (2) the abscissa value in the center of the curve: b, (3) the half-width of the curve: c. *TouchSense* utilizes these three coefficients and builds up a three-dimensional feature vector for the user, which represents the user's identity under the current finger touching. The formula of the Gaussian function is shown below.

$$f(x) = ae^{-\frac{(x-b)^2}{2c^2}} \tag{1}$$

3.3   Feature Vector Extraction

To obtain the accurate value for user feature vector, we need to solve Eq. (1) and get the optimal value of those three coefficients, which minimizes the variance between the fitted curve and sampled value.

We use logarithm and simplify it as follows:

$$ln(y_i) = \left\{ ln(a) - \frac{b^2}{2c^2} \right\} + \frac{2x_i b}{2c^2} - \frac{x_i^2}{2c^2} \tag{2}$$

Let $ln(y_i) = Z_i$, $ln(a) - \frac{b^2}{2c^2} = b_0$, $\frac{2b}{2c^2} = b_1$, $-\frac{1}{2c^2} = b_2$, and bring these equations into Eq. 2 to get the fitting function:

$$Z_i = b_0 + b_1 x_i + b_2 x_i^2 = \begin{pmatrix} 1 & x_i & x_i^2 \end{pmatrix} \begin{bmatrix} b_0 \\ b_1 \\ b_2 \end{bmatrix} \tag{3}$$

The sampled capacitance from the user's single operation is defined as

$$[X, Y] = [(x_1, y_1), (x_2, y_2) \cdots (x_i, y_i) \cdots] \tag{4}$$

Where x_i is the sampling time of the sensed biometric capacitance and y_i is the sampled value. We import all the sampled data into function (3) and get the following parameter matrix:

$$\begin{bmatrix} Z_1 \\ Z_2 \\ \vdots \\ Z_n \end{bmatrix} = \begin{bmatrix} 1 & x_1 & x_1^2 \\ 1 & x_2 & x_2^2 \\ \vdots & \vdots & \vdots \\ 1 & x_n & x_n^2 \end{bmatrix} \begin{bmatrix} b_0 \\ b_1 \\ b_2 \end{bmatrix} + \begin{bmatrix} \varepsilon_1 \\ \varepsilon_2 \\ \vdots \\ \varepsilon_n \end{bmatrix} \tag{5}$$

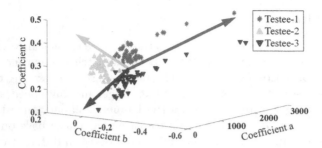

Fig. 5. Feature vector sets for three users. The coefficient a is the peak value of the Gaussian curve, b is the abscissa value at the center of the Gaussian curve, c is the half-width of the Gaussian curve.

Simplified as:

$$Z_{n \times 1} = X_{n \times 3} B_{3 \times 1} + E_{n \times 1} \tag{6}$$

To minimize the sum of squared errors of the calculation results, we can find the least squares solution of the B matrix according to the principle of least squares:

$$B = \left(X^T X\right)^{-1} X^T Z = \begin{bmatrix} b_0 \\ b_1 \\ b_2 \end{bmatrix} = \begin{bmatrix} ln(a) - \frac{b^2}{2c^2} \\ \frac{2b}{2c^2} \\ -\frac{1}{2c^2} \end{bmatrix} \tag{7}$$

By further solving the equation, we can get the optimal value of those three parameters (a, b, c), and define it as the user's three-dimensional feature vector for authentication.

To verify the rationality of feature vectors, we trained the data from 50 testers, and each tester has 80 groups of data tests to build their own feature vector set. Among them, the data sets of three users are shown in Fig. 5. We can see that the feature vectors for the different users are merged in different areas, which makes it possible to classify different users.

3.4   Feature Matching (Authentication)

In this step, *TouchSense* will compare the generated feature vector with the stored data to verify the current user's legality. To find a suitable algorithm for user authentication in *TouchSense*, we test common classification and matching algorithms, including curve distance difference, curve correlation and Support Vector Machine (SVM), and found that SVM results best, as shown in Fig. 6(a)

The SVM is a supervised learning model which has associated learning algorithms to analyze the data for classification. It needs a kernel function to work, and different kernel functions will bring different performance. We conduct many

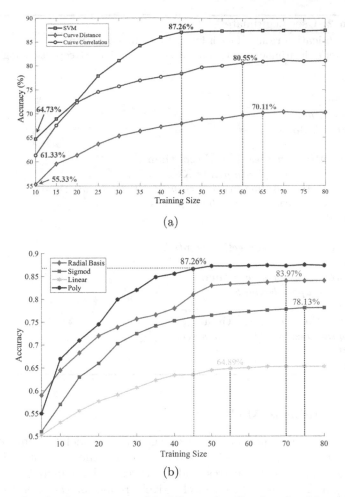

Fig. 6. The authentication accuracy with different classification algorithm (a) and SVM results best with polynomial kernel (Poly) (b)

experiments and finally find that the polynomial kernel achieves the best results, as shown in Fig. 6(b). The equation of polynomial kernel is shown below.

$$K\{x,y\} = \left(ax^T y + c\right)^d$$

x means the abscissa values, y means the ordinate value, T represents the matrix transpose, a, c and d is the artificial constants.

We can see that the performance of Polynomial Kernel gradually stable after 45 groups of data training. Hence, for better user experience, *TouchSense* only needs to collect 45 groups of data as the user's data set. By this configuration, *TouchSense* achieves 87.26% accuracy and provides 16.12% FAR (False Accept Rate) and 9.36% FRR (False Reject Rate) in a single finger touching.

Algorithm 2. User-Legitimate Module

Input : Authentication result of each finger touching operation.
Output : User's legitimacy score and system decision (Keep user login or lock screen).

1: *Start*
2: *Score* = 100
3: *Operation times* : $i = 0$
4: **for** *Score* ≥ 0 **do**
5:     $i++$
6:     **if** *Authentication result*[i] = *illegal* **then**
7:         *Score = Score− plenty points X*
8:         **if** (i≥2) **and** (*Authentication result*[$i-1$] = *illegal*) **then**
9:             *Score = Score − extra plenty points E*
10:        **end if**
11:    **else**
12:        *Score = Score + correction points Y*
13:    **end if**
14:    **if** *Score > upper bound S* **then**
15:        *Score = upper bound S*
16:    **end if**
17:    **if** *Score < 0 (Threshold)* **then**
18:        *Log the user out (Lock the screen)*
19:    **end if**
20: **end for**

3.5   User-Legitimate Model

Finally, *TouchSense* builds up the user-legitimate model to comprehensively evaluate the user's legitimacy. This model converts the authentication results of each finger touching into corresponding scores and accumulates it after the user logging in. The total score can effectively represent the user's legitimacy, and it increases if the result is legal, or decrease if the result is illegal. *TouchSense* works in the background without bothering the user until his score drops below the threshold. Then *TouchSense* regards the user as an attacker and locks the screen to ensure device security. Hence, we can set suitable parameters to quickly logout intruders while providing certain fault tolerance for legitimate users. By this, *TouchSense* can rapidly reduce misjudgment and improve accuracy, as shown in Algorithm 2.

This algorithm has four parameters: penalty points X for illegal operation, correction points Y for legal operation, extra penalty points E for continuously illegal operation, and upper bound S. When logging in, the user will get an initial score: 100, and the score will decrease by X points for illegal operation or increase by Y points for legal operation. For continuously illegal operation, the user will deduct extra penalty points E. After the user's i-th operation, the expectation of the legitimacy score can be expressed as

$$S(i) = MAX(100 - iPX + i(1 - P)Y - (i - 1)P^2E, S) \tag{8}$$

$S(i)$ is the expectation of user score after the i-th operation, and P is the average probability for the user to be judged illegal in each operation. If $S(i)$ drops below the threshold, *TouchSense* will lock the system and stop the user's $(i + 1)$ th operation. We did mass calculation and find the optimal values for those four parameters: $(X, Y, S, E) = (25, 67, 568, 40)$. By this configuration, 59% (calculated by $(1 - FAR)^3$) of the attackers will be logged out within three operations, and most legitimate users will increase their score to the upper bound within ten operations, which ensures the security while hardly bother the legitimate users.

4   Evaluation Results

To evaluate the feasibility of *TouchSense*, we built an experimental platform on the SX9310 evaluation board and did comprehensive experiments and simulations base on the data collected from 50 users.

4.1   Experimental Platform Setup

To ensure the validity of experiments, we need to choose the appropriate hardware to deploy *TouchSense*. Capacitive-screens are vital interfaces for users to interact with smartphones, which relying on biometric capacitance to detect the touch. However, we can not directly deploy *TouchSense* on existing capacitive-screens because the screen can not obtain the accurate value of the human body capacitance, which need for authentication. Specifically, capacitive-screens are aimed at the localization but not authentication. To precisely detect the touching coordinate, most capacitive screens are based on Projected Capacitive Touch (PCT) technologies[13, 22, 29], which comprised of millions of micro capacitors by the mixed array [1, 30, 42], but only use a single threshold ADC to sense the touch. When the user touches the screen, the finger forms an inductive

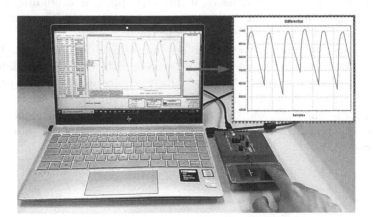

Fig. 7. The test platform for *TouchSense*. We use a laptop to observe the working states of our scheme. The sensed biometric capacitance is shown in the window real-timely.

capacitance with the touch sensor below the screen, which values proportional to the user's biometric capacitance and inversely proportional to the distance between the finger and the sensor. The touch takes effect if the value exceeds the threshold. So it can precisely detect the location where the user touches but fail to obtain the specific value of biometric capacitance. Hence, we need to find a suitable device embedded with a sensitive sensor and high-resolution ADC to deploy *TouchSense*.

We find the chip SX9310, which has up to $0.08fF$ ($1fF = 10^{-15}F$) resolution for capacitive sensing [37]. We use the evaluation board as the hardware to deploy *TouchSense*, and carry out experiments to verify the feasibility. This board has an SX9310 chip to gather the data and an MSP430F2132 chip to analyze the results. We can also use a laptop to monitor the working status of *TouchSense*, shown in Fig. 7.

Table 1. Biometric capacitance extract accuracy

UI	Gender	Temperature	Motion	Actual motions	Valid detection	Missed detection
1	Male	High (30 °C)	Tapping	48	48	0
9	Female	Low (10 °C)	Holding	50	50	0
12	Male	High (30 °C)	Holding	45	45	0
26	Female	Low (10 °C)	Tapping	48	46	2
39	Male	High (30 °C)	Tapping	44	44	0
42	Female	Low (10 °C)	Holding	46	46	0

Biometric capacitance detection accuracy of 50 users: 99.2%

Legend: UI = User ID

We test the platform for 50 users, including tapping and holding, and find that the extraction accuracy of the biometric capacitance is 99.2%; among them, the test results of 6 users are shown in Table 1.

Tapping and holding represent user operation for different Apps. Tapping fits most Apps in which the user tap the screen with negligible holding time. Holding represents some special APPs, which require users to long-press the screen, such as copy text or screenshots. Correspondingly, the finger stays on the screen for a long time, and the trend of the sensed biometric capacitance is completely different. The results show *TouchSense* achieves good robustness in different user APPs.

Table 2. Cross-validation for 50 users

UI	S												
	UI												
	1	2	3	4	5	6		45	46	47	48	49	50	FIR (%)
1	**0.38**	0.12	0.15	0.07	0.12	0.19	...	0.08	0.14	0.11	0.16	0.12	0.18	0
2	0.12	**0.41**	0.21	0.14	0.11	0.11	...	0.17	0.31	0.25	0.17	0.24	0.19	0
3	0.15	0.13	**0.44**	0.15	0.14	0.19	...	0.10	0.26	0.33	0.22	0.12	0.23	0
4	0.21	0.18	0.16	**0.42**	0.26	0.23	...	0.22	0.26	0.06	0.04	0.04	0.07	0
5	0.14	0.13	0.15	0.19	**0.35**	0.12	...	0.11	0.02	0.01	0.01	0.02	0.05	0
6	0.13	0.17	0.11	0.21	0.18	**0.36**	...	0.25	0.06	0.04	0.04	0.05	0.21	0
...	...	...	...	...	...	...	...	...	...	...	...	...	...	...
45	0.17	0.21	0.14	0.21	0.08	0.24	...	**0.41**	0.04	0.09	0.11	0.08	**0.42**	2
46	0.09	0.18	0.05	0.03	0.02	0.01	...	0.06	**0.47**	0.34	0.24	0.18	0.14	0
47	0.03	0.18	0.08	0.00	0.01	0.01	...	0.25	0.04	**0.45**	0.20	0.10	0.05	0
48	0.07	0.03	0.11	0.00	0.01	0.00	...	0.17	0.21	0.40	**0.42**	0.15	0.09	0
49	0.16	0.21	0.14	0.04	0.02	0.04	...	0.23	0.09	0.34	0.26	**0.44**	0.18	0
50	0.05	0.07	0.09	0.02	0.03	0.03	...	0.18	0.07	0.07	0.04	0.03	**0.42**	0

Average accuracy of 50 users: 99.6%, false identification rate of 50 users: 0.4%

Legend: S = Similarity; UI = User ID

4.2   Test Results

First, we cross-validated the data set of 50 users, as shown in Table 2. The first row and column show the ID of each user, and the value in the table means the similarity score between two users. The last column shows the FIR (False Identification Rate). In real experiments, we find that there is only one of 50 users who falsely identified. Hence the average FIR is 0.04%. From these results, we also observe that for correctly matched users, the similarity scores are ranged from 0.38–0.47 and which is below 0.37 for most false matched users. Hence, we can set 0.375 as the similarity threshold for *TouchSense* to identify legitimate users and attackers.

To further evaluate the performance of *TouchSense*. We did mass simulations on 100,000 samples of attackers and legitimate users based on the data set collected from 50 users. The FAR (False Accept Rate) and FRR (False Reject Rate) in different operation times are respectively shown in the Fig. 8 and 9.

The FAR curve (Fig. 8) shows the rate of attackers who falsely accepted by *TouchSense* in different operation times, represents the performance of security during usage. For 100,000 samples, the simulation result shows that only 2.19% of attackers will be left after 10 operations (9.5 s), and none of them will be left after 18 operations (17 s). Hence, *TouchSense* identify 97.8% attackers within 10 s, and locks all of them after 17 s. If an attacker stole a phone which deployed *TouchSense*, he knows the password, and he wants to steal 1 US dollar through E-bank payment, he has only 0.064% probability to succeed because he has to take at least 18 operations (Open software and find the payment function: at least 2 steps. Input the attackers account: at least 8 steps. Input the victim's password: at least 6 steps. Pay money: at least 2 steps).

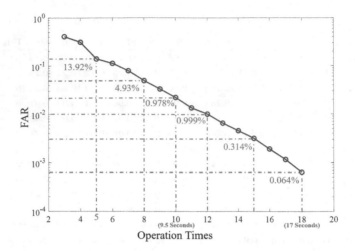

Fig. 8. The FAR (False Accept Rate) of attackers for different operation times. The FAR rapidly reduces with the increase of operations. For 10 operations the FAR is only 2.19%, and it goes to 0 after 18 operations.

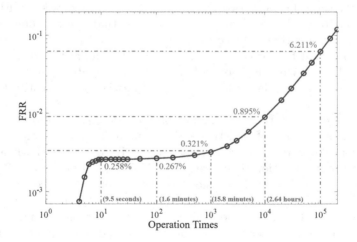

Fig. 9. The FRR (False Reject Rate) of legitimate users for different operation times. The FRR is very low in short usage, and it increases slowly with more operations as the legitimate users who misjudged by *TouchSense* will be accumulated during the usage. However, it hardly affects the majority of legitimate users, as even in 2.64-h of long-time continuous usage, the FRR keeps below 0.9%.

The FRR curve (Fig. 9) shows the rate of legitimate users which falsely rejected by *TouchSense*. The lower the FRR, the fewer legitimate users are misjudged and logged out by *TouchSense*. From the simulation results, we can see there are only 0.258% legitimate users falsely rejected by *TouchSense* for 10 operations (9.5 s), and for 100 operations (1.6 min), the FRR is only 0.267%. As user re-authentication is a repetitive process, despite in every operation, the legitimate users have very little chance to be logged out due to misjudging, the number will also be accumulated during usage. Hence the FRR increases slowly with more operations, for 1,000 operations (15.8 min), the FRR growth to 0.312%, and for 10,000 operations (2.64 h), the FRR is only 0.895%. Moreover, for the legitimate users who unfortunately be misjudged and excluded from the system, only need to re-login, and he can use the device freely like before. In summary, *TouchSense* can quickly identify and lock attackers but hardly affect legitimate users in daily use.

5   Discussion

The future works and ethical concerns of *TouchSense* are discussed below.

5.1   Feature Works

Due to the limitation of hardware, this paper only verifies the feasibility of *TouchSense* by one-finger touching, as the platform only deploys one sensor to sense the touch. In future works, we can use sensor arrays to authenticate users by more behaviors (*e.g.* multi-finger touches), and further improve accuracy by fusing the data collected from multi-sensors. The basic idea is to build sensing points which evenly distributed on the screen, shown in Fig. 10. The maxim interval to place sensing points (L_{Max}) can be defined as

$$L_{Max} = (2 \cdot L_2^2 - 2 \cdot L_1^2)^{\frac{1}{2}}$$

L_2 is the maximum sensing range of the sensing points, and L_1 is the maximum distance between the user's finger and the screen during the touching. In most cases, the user's fingers are close to the screen in using ($L_1 \approx 1$ cm by the test). Therefore, we only need to deploy a few sensing points to cover the whole screen. For SX9310 ($L_2 \approx 2$ cm by tested), the maximum deploy interval L_{Max} is 24.5 mm, and only 12 sensing points are required to cover a 6-inch screen (92×122 mm). Also, we can use low-power approaches to optimize power consumption of sensor array [20, 32].

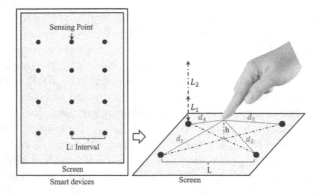

Fig. 10. The distribution schematic of sensing points. L_1: Maximum operation distance for most users ($h \leq L_1$). L_2: Maximum sensing range for the sensor. If the maximum distance from the finger to the sensing point $MAX(d_1, d_2, d_3, d_4) \leq L_2$, all the user motion trajectories can be captured.

5.2   Ethical Concerns

In this paper, the collected user features (*e.g.* biometric capacitance, finger touching behavior) will be only used and stored locally without appearing on Internet. Thus, we believe that our work does not involve ethical issues and user privacy leakage.

6   Conclusion

In this paper, we describe our approach towards *TouchSense*, a new method to re-authenticate the user accurately and transparently. *TouchSense* senses and authenticates the user by the combined information (touching behavior and biometric capacitance) as long as the user operates the smartphones. To complete our design, we build up User-Legitimate Module to comprehensively evaluate the user's legitimacy by stitch the authentication results of each finger touching. The experimental results show that *TouchSense* achieves 87.26% accuracy and offers 16.12% FAR and 9.36% FRR in a single touch. Further, the simulation result indicates that *TouchSense* identifies 98% attackers within 10 s (10 touching operations) and logs out all of them within 17 s (18 touching operations). However, for legitimate users, the misjudgment is only 0.321% in 16-minutes-usage (1,000 touching operations), and only 0.89% in 2.6-hours-usage (10,000 touching operations). Moreover, *TouchSense* is also designed in light-weight, which not require intensive computations and power. With the merits of high-security, user-transparency, low power consumption, and continuous security, we foresee that *TouchSense* can be wildly deployed on smartphones in the future.

Acknowledgments. The authors would like to thank the editors and anonymous reviewers for their comments and feedback, which is helpful to the publication of *Touch-*

Sense. This work is supported by the National Natural Science Foundation of China (61872061).

References

1. Barrett, G., Omote, R.: Projected-capacitive touch technology. Inf. Display **26**(3), 16–21 (2010)
2. Carrizo, C., Ochoa, C., Massuh, L.: Gesture-based signature authentication, 22 March 2016. US Patent 9,292,731
3. Clancy, T.C., Kiyavash, N., Lin, D.J.: Secure smartcard-based fingerprint authentication. In: Proceedings of the 2003 ACM SIGMM Workshop on Biometrics Methods and Applications, pp. 45–52. ACM (2003)
4. Crouse, D., Han, H., Chandra, D., Barbello, B., Jain, A.K.: Continuous authentication of mobile user: fusion of face image and inertial measurement unit data. In: 2015 International Conference on Biometrics (ICB), pp. 135–142. IEEE (2015)
5. Darlene, M.: Easy way to bypass passcode lock screens on iPhones, iPads running iOS 12 (2018). https://www.computerworld.com/article/3041302/4-new-ways-to-bypass-passcode-lock-screen-on-iphones-ipads-running-ios-9.html
6. Dascalescu, A.: Biometric authentication overview, advantages and disadvantages (2019). https://heimdalsecurity.com/blog/biometric-authentication/
7. Delač, K., Grgić M.: A survey of biometric recognition methods (2004)
8. Derawi, M.O., Nickel, C., Bours, P., Busch, C.: Unobtrusive user-authentication on mobile phones using biometric gait recognition. In: 2010 Sixth International Conference on Intelligent Information Hiding and Multimedia Signal Processing (IIH-MSP), pp. 306–311. IEEE (2010)
9. Feng, H., Fawaz, K., Shin, K.G.: Continuous authentication for voice assistants. In: Proceedings of the 23rd Annual International Conference on Mobile Computing and Networking, pp. 343–355. ACM (2017)
10. Frank, M., Biedert, R., Ma, E., Martinovic, I., Song, D.: Touchalytics: On the applicability of touchscreen input as a behavioral biometric for continuous authentication. IEEE Trans. Inf. Forensics Secur. **8**(1), 136–148 (2013)
11. Fujiwara, O., Ikawa, T.: Numerical calculation of human-body capacitance by surface charge method. Electron. Commun. Japan (Part I: Commun.) **85**(12), 38–44 (2002)
12. Gafurov, D.: A survey of biometric gait recognition: approaches, security and challenges. In: Annual Norwegian Computer Science Conference, pp. 19–21 (2007)
13. Gray, T.: Projected capacitive touch basics. Projected Capacitive Touch, pp. 5–17. Springer, Cham (2019). https://doi.org/10.1007/978-3-319-98392-9_2
14. Grivna, E.L.: Capacitance touch screen, 7 January 2014. US Patent 8,624,845
15. Hao, Z., Li, Q.: Towards user re-authentication on mobile devices via on-screen keyboard. In: 2016 Fourth IEEE Workshop on Hot Topics in Web Systems and Technologies (HotWeb), pp. 78–83. IEEE (2016)
16. Sampathkumar, K., Balaji Sr., P.: Biometric methods - a secure survey. SSRN Electron. J. (2009)
17. Jason: How to reset android lock screen password and pin (2019). https://www.lifewire.com/reset-android-lock-screen-password-2740708
18. Jonassen, N.: Human body capacitance: static or dynamic concept? [esd]. In: Electrical Overstress/Electrostatic Discharge Symposium Proceedings, 1998, pp. 111–117. IEEE (1998)

19. Li, L., Zhao, X., Xue, G.: Unobservable re-authentication for smartphones. In: NDSS, vol. 56, pp. 57–59 (2013)
20. Li, S., Lu, L., Hussain, M.J., Ye, Y., Zhu, H.: Sentinel: breaking the bottleneck of energy utilization efficiency in RF-powered devices. IEEE Internet Things J. **6**(1), 705–717 (2018)
21. Li, Y., Hu, H., Zhou, G.: Using data augmentation in continuous authentication on smartphones. IEEE Internet Things J. **6**(1), 628–640 (2019)
22. Liu, S.Y., Wang, Y.J., Lu, J.G., Shieh, H.P.D.: 38.3: one glass solution with a single layer of sensors for projected-capacitive touch panels. In: SID Symposium Digest of Technical Papers (2014)
23. Lorenzo, A.D., Andreoli, A., Battisti, P., Talluri, T., Yasumura, S.: Total body capacitance correlates with total body potassium. Ann. New York Acad. Sci. **904**, 259–262 (2010). (In vivo body composition studies)
24. Lovejoy, B.: 3D mask or photo fools airport and payment face-recognition, but not face id (2019). https://ww.9to5mac.com/2019/12/16/3d-mask/#aprd
25. Mahfouz, A., Mahmoud, T.M., Eldin, A.S.: A survey on behavioral biometric authentication on smartphones. Inf. Secur. Tech. Rep. **37**, 28–37 (2018)
26. Maiorana, E., Campisi, P., Neri, A.: Biometric signature authentication using radon transform-based watermarking techniques. In: Biometrics Symposium, 2007, pp. 1–6. IEEE (2007)
27. Maiorana, E., Campisi, P., Neri, A.: Template protection for dynamic time warping based biometric signature authentication. In: 2009 16th International Conference on Digital Signal Processing, pp. 1–6. IEEE (2009)
28. Matsumoto, T., Matsumoto, H., Yamada, K., Hoshino, S.: Impact of artificial "gummy" fingers on fingerprint systems. Electron. Imaging **4677**, 275–289 (2002)
29. Mi, D.: Single-layer projected capacitive touch panel and method of manufacturing the same (2017)
30. Mo, M., Li, H., Zhang, J.: Capacitance touch screen with mesh electrodes, 15 March 2012. uS Patent App. 13/226,902
31. Muaaz, M., Mayrhofer, R.: An analysis of different approaches to gait recognition using cell phone based accelerometers, pp. 293–300 (2013)
32. Nesa, N., Banerjee, I.: SensorRank: an energy efficient sensor activation algorithm for sensor data fusion in wireless networks. IEEE Internet Things J. **6**(2), 2532–2539 (2018)
33. Nickel, C., Busch, C., Rangarajan, S., Möbius, M.: Using hidden Markov models for accelerometer-based biometric gait recognition. In: Proceedings - 2011 IEEE 7th International Colloquium on Signal Processing and Its Applications, CSPA 2011, March 2011. https://doi.org/10.1109/CSPA.2011.5759842
34. Primo, A., Phoha, V.V., Kumar, R., Serwadda, A.: Context-aware active authentication using smartphone accelerometer measurements. In: Proceedings of the IEEE Conference on Computer Vision and Pattern Recognition Workshops, pp. 98–105 (2014)
35. Qi, M., Lu, Y., Li, J., Li, X., Kong, J.: User-specific iris authentication based on feature selection. In: 2008 International Conference on Computer Science and Software Engineering, vol. 1, pp. 1040–1043. IEEE (2008)
36. Rathgeb, C., Uhl, A.: A survey on biometric cryptosystems and cancelable biometrics. EURASIP J. Inf. Secur. **2011**(1), 3 (2011)
37. Semtech: Semtech sx9310, ultra-low power smart proximity sensor for SAR (2017). https://www.semtech.com/uploads/documents/sx9310.pdf
38. Sharma, K.: How dangerous are impersonation attacks? (2018). https://cybersecurity.att.com/blogs/security-essentials/how-dangerous-are-impersonation-attacks

39. Thang, H.M., Viet, V.Q., Thuc, N.D., Choi, D.: Gait identification using accelerometer on mobile phone, pp. 344–348 (2012)
40. TycoyokeI: How to fool a fingerprint security system as easy as ABC (2019). https://www.instructables.com/id/How-To-Fool-a-Fingerprint-Security-System-As-Easy-/
41. Yan, J., Blackwell, A.F., Anderson, R., Grant, A.M.: Password memorability and security: empirical results. In: IEEE Symposium on Security and Privacy, vol. 2, no. 5, pp. 25–31 (2004)
42. Zhang, S.: Main construction of capacitive touch screen (2019). https://www.vtouchscreen.com/news/main-construction-of-capacitive-touch-screen-28265581.html
43. Zhang, Y.-B., Li, Q., You, J., Bhattacharya, P.: Palm vein extraction and matching for personal authentication. In: Qiu, G., Leung, C., Xue, X., Laurini, R. (eds.) VISUAL 2007. LNCS, vol. 4781, pp. 154–164. Springer, Heidelberg (2007). https://doi.org/10.1007/978-3-540-76414-4_16
44. Zhong, Y., Deng, Y., Meltzner, G.S.: Pace independent mobile gait biometrics, pp. 1–8 (2015)

Android Malware Detection Using Ensemble Learning on Sensitive APIs

Junhui Yu[1,2]($\boxtimes$), Chunlei Zhao[1,2], Wenbai Zheng[1,2], Yunlong Li[1,2], Chunxiang Zhang[1,2], and Chao Chen[1,2]

[1] Key Laboratory of Computer Vision and System, Ministry of Education, Tianjin University of Technology, Tianjin 300384, China

[2] Tianjin Key Laboratory of Intelligence Computing and Novel Software Technology, Ministry of Education, Tianjin University of Technology, Tianjin 300384, China

Abstract. In recent years, with the quiet popularity of mobile payment methods, mobile terminal equipment also have potential security problems while facilitating people's lives. Behavior-based Android malware detection is mostly based on permission analysis and API calls. In this paper, we propose a static Android malicious detection scheme based on sensitive API calls. We extracted all APIs called in the experimental samples through decompilation, and then calculated and ranked the threats related to these APIs according to the mutual information model, selected the top 20 sensitive API calls, and generated a 20-dimensional feature vector for each application. In the classification process, an integrated learning model based on DT classifier, kNN classifier and SVM classifier is used to effectively detect unknown APK samples. We collected 516 benign samples and 528 malicious samples. Through a large number of experiments, the results show that the accuracy of our scheme can be up to 94%, and the precision is up to 95%.

Keywords: Android · Sensitive API · Mutual information · Malware detection

1 Introduction

The market share of smartphones running the Android operating system will rise from 85.1% in 2018 to 87% [1]. The strong compatibility of the Android system also attracts more and more developers. At the same time, due to the lack of strong detection mechanisms and processes in the Google [2], this provides a wide range of possibilities for the release and promotion of malicious applications.

The current behavior-based Android malware detection is mainly divided into two parts. One is dynamic malware detection technology that simulates running in sandboxes or virtual machines, and the other is static malware detection technology that extracts relevant features through reverse engineering. Static analysis matches specific characteristics of known malicious applications to detect

Supported by Tianjin Nature Science Youth Foundation (No.18JCQNJC69900).

whether the sample is malware. However, with the development and changes of malicious applications, the efficiency of a single static detection is not very high, and there are certain false positives and false negatives. At the same time, the dynamic analysis of Android malware can provide real-time and comprehensive detection when the application is running, but there are still higher requirements in terms of statistical information and the deployment of the detection environment. Moreover, the dynamic detection technology cannot simultaneously detect a large number of applications simultaneously.

However, there are obvious differences between malicious applications and normal applications in corresponding API function calls. This paper uses sensitive API functions as features to detect malicious application software.

This paper proposes a static Android malicious detection method based on integrated learning. The method is mainly divided into three parts: feature extraction stage, training stage and detection stage. For the feature extraction stage, the mutual information model is used to generate 20-dimensional API feature vectors ranked by sensitivity level; during the training stage, the feature vectors are input to the associated three basic classifiers (decision tree(DT)classifier, k nearest neighbor (kNN) classifier and support vector machine (SVM) classifier) to generate the final training results. In the detection phase, the main task is to quickly classify unknown APKs by using an integrated learning model. A large number of experimental results show that the accuracy of the scheme can reach 94%, and the precision is up to 95%.

The specific experimental content of this paper is as follows:

- We collect top20 sensitive API calls as detection features to improve detection accuracy.
- By comparing the detection performance of different combinations of various classification algorithms, we propose an integrated learning algorithm based on DT classifier, kNN classifier and SVM classifier as the basic classifier.
- Experiments show that this method can reduce the complexity of Android malware detection, and improve detection accuracy.

The rest of the paper is organized as follows: Sect. 2 introduces the related work, including the analysis of the research status of dynamic malware detection technology and static malware detection technology. Sections 3 and 4 introduce the experimental design of the feature extraction and detection process in this paper. Sections 5 and 6 give the results and conclusions of the experiment.

2   Related Work

2.1   Dynamic Detection Method

With the evolution and development of malicious applications, more and more malicious applications evade the corresponding static detection by obfuscating code or hardening protection. This led to a situation where the false detection rate of Android static detection was slightly higher under certain conditions.

Dynamic program behavior monitoring technology can record the behavior of the program during dynamic execution, so as to avoid the confusion of static code by malicious programs. Depending on the recording granularity, information such as instruction sequence, system call, API sequence, and API parameters can be recorded. According to the principle of program behavior monitoring technology, it can be divided into three categories: program behavior monitoring technology based on binary instrumentation, program behavior monitoring technology based on virtual machine and program behavior monitoring technology based on Hook.

Dynamic program behavior monitoring technology can record the behavior of the program during dynamic execution, so as to avoid the confusion of static code by malicious programs. TaintDroid [3] is an efficient system-level dynamic stain tracking and analysis system that can track multiple sensitive data sources at the same time, providing users with a view of the use and sharing of private data by third-party applications. TaintDroid is deployed on mobile phones, so its overhead cannot be ignored. Crowdroid [4] is a dynamic analysis method. It obtains the application behavior logs from the user's mobile phone through crowdsourcing. The specific data collected is the system call, and the data is uploaded to the remote server, and the data is clustered through K-means. In order to find malicious applications, it is difficult to apply them without incentives.

2.2   Static Detection Method

The most obvious feature of the static detection technology based on reverse engineering is that it does not need to execute the malicious application to obtain the relevant static features contained in the application by decompilation, including the permission information applied by the application, the API function calls, etc. Wu et al. [5] proposed an Android malware detection system, which uses a dataflow application program interfaces (APIs) as classification features to detect Android malware. This paper uses a thorough analysis, to extract dataflow-related API-level features, and to improve the kNN classification model, and uses machine learning to further optimize the API list dataflow-related and improve the detection efficiency. The accuracy of the system in detecting unknown Android malware is as high as 97.66%. Onwuzurike, L et al. [6] proposed a MAMADROID model based on a static analysis system is proposed, which uses the sequence obtained by the application's API call graph (such as Markov chain) to build the model to ensure that the model's changes to the API and the size of the feature set are convenient for management. The MAMADROID model has a high detection rate, but still has a certain FPR. Kim, T et al.[7] proposes A novel Android malware detection framework. The framework extracts multiple features such as permissions and API calls, and refines these features to achieve an effective feature representation for malware detection. In addition, a multi-modal deep learning method is proposed as a malware detection model. It was found that the detection method greatly improves the detection rate, but the complexity is high. Zhao et al.[8]propose a detection method that uses sensitive APIs as detection features. But they used two basic classifiers, the detection accuracy only to 92%.

3   Feature Extraction and Analysis

Based on the in-depth understanding of Android malware detection in this paper, you can extract the information of sensitive API calls and analyze based on this feature, which mainly includes the following 3 steps:

- Feature generation: decompilation of the application program of the experimental sample to extract all API call information.
- Generate a collection of sensitive API calls: use the mutual information model to calculate and rank the correlation between each API call and malware in the sample.
- Generate feature vectors: Select the top 20 sensitive API calls to generate a 20-dimensional feature vector for each application.

3.1   Preliminaries

In the early stage of this paper, a lot of information collection and data mining were carried out on the Android operating system, mainly including API features, sensitive API calls, and the selection of mutual information models.

API Features. The Android application is released in the form of an APK, which is essentially a compressed package file. The corresponding file obtained by decompressing APK is shown in Fig. 1.

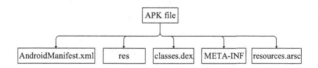

Fig. 1. APK file structure

Among them, the android manifest.xml file is used to store the package name of Android application, permissions, SDK version number, etc. It is the configuration file of Android application package (APK). The res file is a storage resource file in which the images, strings, layouts, etc. of Android APK are stored. The META-INF file is used to hold the signature information of APK to ensure the integrity of APK. The classes.dex is a Java bytecode file that can be directly run in a Dalvik virtual machine.

Due to the good adaptability of the APIs, the operating system can provide service interfaces for various types of applications. When the request of data access, network data connection, file read and write, or other important resources appear, the applications will invoke the APIs. Because of the important role of the APIs, malicious applications will call the target APIs to achieve some malicious behavior.

Sensitive API Call. In the Android platform, there is a correspondence between permissions and API calls to access specific resources of the system. The Android platform API list describes nearly 8000 calling methods. Among them, there is a specific correspondence between certain APIs and permissions. For example, when an application calls the SendMessage() API for sending short messages, the Android system process checks whether the application has applied for permission to send short messages: Android.permission.SEND_SMS. Only when the application has applied for the permission and the permission is declared in the manifest file $<Manifest>$ will the SendMessage() API be called when it is used. Android's official website lists all the permission information, mainly divided into four categories: normal, dangerous, signature, signature-orSystem. The permission risks they represent increase in turn, which means that the risk of the API corresponding to them also increases in turn.

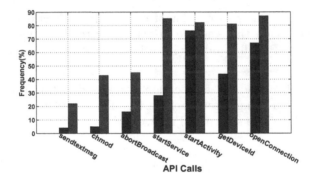

Fig. 2. Frequency of calling certain APIs in malware and benign applications

As shown in Fig. 2, we found that the frequency of calling certain APIs is quite different between malicious applications and normal applications through experiments. Therefore, these sensitive APIs can be used as one of the basis for identifying the maliciousness of the application. In this study, we focus on high-risk APIs that involve sensitive user data. Hanna [9] have studied the permission mechanism in depth and given the corresponding relationship between the permissions and APIs. According to the APIs corresponding to the sensitive permission list, the mutual information model is used to measure the relationship between API and application maliciousness.

Mutual Information Model. In machine learning, the correlation between measured features and class variables is called feature ranking, and its purpose is to select the features with the largest amount of information and improve the performance of the learning model [11]. In probability theory and information theory, Mutual Information (MI) [10] for two random variables is a measure of the interdependence between variables. Unlike correlation coefficients, mutual information is not limited to real-valued random variables. It is suitable for more general and common application scenarios and determines the product p(x) of the joint distribution p(X,Y) and the decomposed edge distribution. The similarity of p(y). Mutual information can be used to measure the mutual dependence between two sets of events. The mutual information calculation formula of two discrete random variables X and Y is shown as formula (1):

$$I(X,Y) = \sum_{x_i} \sum_{y_j} p(X = x_i, Y = y_j) \times log \frac{p(X = x_i, Y = y_j)}{p(X = x_i) \times p(Y = y_j)} \quad (1)$$

P(x, y) is the joint probability distribution function of X and Y, while p(x) and p(y) are marginal probability distribution functions of X and Y respectively. In formula (1), the variable X represents that the APIs exist in an Android application software (or not), variable Y on behalf of the application of categories (application belongs to malicious applications or benign applications). P(x) means the probability that the variable X is equal to x, p(y) means the probability that the variable Y is equal to y. P(x, y) is the value of x with respect to X, and the value of Y is the probability of y. In the case of continuous random variables, the summation formula is replaced by the double integral formula, which is shown in the following formula (2):

$$I(x,y) = \int_Y \int_X p(x,y) \times log(\frac{p(x,y)}{p(x) \times p(y)}) dx dy \quad (2)$$

Similar to formula (1), in Eq. (2), p(X, Y) still represents the joint probability distribution function of X and Y, while p(x) and p(y) are the marginal probability distribution functions of X and Y, respectively. Mutual information is the inherent dependence between the joint distribution of X and Y relative to the joint distribution under the assumption that X and Y are independent. So mutual information measures dependency in the following way: I(X,Y) = 0 if and only if X and Y are independent random variables. It is easy to see from one direction: when X and Y are independent, p(x,y) = p(x)·p(y), so we can draw the conclusion shown as formula (3):

$$log(\frac{p(x,y)}{p(x) \times p(y)}) = log1 = 0 \quad (3)$$

In addition, mutual information is non-negative ($I(X;Y) \geq 0$) and symmetrical (I(X,Y) = I(Y,X)).

3.2   Feature Generation

Feature Extraction. In this paper, we use the script file of the Androguard tool to statically analyze the experimental samples. Figure 3 shows the Android API call examples of some experimental samples obtained.

> java/lang/Long intValue()I
> java/lang/Long <init>(J)V
> java/lang/LongvalueOf(J)Ljava/lang/Long;
> android/util/StateSet stateSetMatches ([I[I)Z
> android/util/StateSet trimStateSet([I[I)[I
> android/view/ViewTreeObserver$InternalInsetsInfo <init>()V

Fig. 3. Android API call sequence

Generate a Collection of Sensitive API Calls. Mutual information can be used to measure the correlation between two sets of events. This paper uses an effective sorting method, that is, "mutual information" as shown in formula (1), to measure the correlation between Android applications and specific API calls, and based on the calculated correlation, a set of sensitive APIs is generated. And the sensitive value of each API is calculated separately.

The final calculation result is between 0 and 1. The larger the value of the result, the higher the correlation between the two. If the value is 1, it means that the two are necessarily related, and similarly, the value is 0 that the two are not related. Extract 20 API functions most relevant to malicious applications as a collection of sensitive API calls.

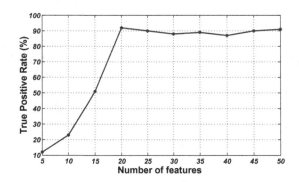

Fig. 4. The TPR of different number of features on detection results

As shown in Fig. 4, the reason why we choose the top 20 APIs for sensitivity calculation as the reference standard for selecting functional APIs is because if the number of selected APIs is too small, the detection accuracy will be low; if you choose a large number of APIs will cause redundancy of data, reduce detection efficiency, and increase detection time complexity. Through the final analysis of the experimental results, the top 20 APIs with the highest correlation coefficients with malicious applications were selected. The ranking of sensitivity calculation results is shown as Table 1.

Table 1. The 20 most sensitive API calls

Number	Score	API calls
1	0.467	sendMultipartTextMessage ( )
2	0.426	getNETWORKCountryIso ( )
3	0.402	openConnection( )
4	0.385	chmod ( )
5	0.343	abortBroadcast ( )
6	0.301	writeTextMessage ( )
7	0.279	writeExternalStorageState ( )
8	0.266	sendTextMessage ( )
9	0.257	getLine1Number ( )
10	0.252	getLastKnownLocation ( )
11	0.209	getSimOperator ( )
12	0.198	getAccountsByType ( )
13	0.194	getDisplayMessageBody ( )
14	0.193	com.android.contacts ( )
15	0.188	getOutputStream ( )
16	0.173	getDeviceId ( )
17	0.165	getInputStream ( )
18	0.161	startService ( )
19	0.157	getRunningTasks ( )
20	0.153	updateConfigurationLocked ( )

Generation of Eigenvectors. We create a 20-dimensional feature vector $[APIs]_{1*20}$ for each experimental sample, and unified the format of the feature vector as: $[X_1 : Y_1; X_2 : Y_2; X_3 : Y_3; \cdots X_i : Y_i; \cdots X_{20} : Y_{20}]$ (i = 1,2,3... 20). The X_i represents the i-th API calls in Table 1, and Y_i represents whether this API calls exists in the sample. If it exists, it is set to 1, otherwise it is set to 0. Then input the generated feature vector into kNN classifier, DT classifier and SVM classifier respectively. In this paper, we use 450 malicious samples and 450 benign samples to train, and then use 100 samples to detect.

4   Detection System Design

The malware detection flowchart is shown in Fig. 5. This section is the detection phase, which mainly uses the integrated learning model to detect unknown applications.

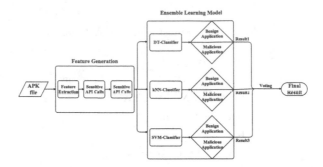

Fig. 5. Flow chart of malware detection

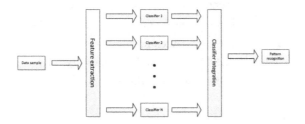

Fig. 6. Multi-classifier integrated learning model implementation diagram

4.1   Ensemble Learning Detection Model

Classification is a kind of supervised learning by training a classifier in the samples of the known category so that it can classify the unknown samples, as shown in Fig. 6. However, the detection accuracy of a single classification algorithm is not high, and it has a certain randomness. Therefore, this paper adopts the set learning method [12]. In this paper, we use DT, kNN and SVM as the basic classifier to classify the samples.

4.2   Base Classifiers

In this paper, kNN classifier, DT classifier and SVM classifier are used as the basic classifier of the integrated learning model.

KNN Classifier. The kNN algorithm is a classification algorithm. The idea of the algorithm is: A sample is most similar to the k samples in the data set. If most of the k samples belong to a certain category, the sample also belongs to this category. The choice of k value in this algorithm is critical. Too small k value will cause the model to be complicated and prone to over-fitting. Too large k value will reduce the accuracy of prediction. Sometimes benign and malicious applications call the same API, resulting in overlapping sample sets. For this, the classification performance of the kNN classifier is more advantageous than other classifiers.

In summary, the selection of k value is very important in the kNN algorithm. As shown in Fig. 7, according to the test data results, when the k value is 5, the classification accuracy of the kNN algorithm is the highest. Therefore, the value of k is 5 in this paper.

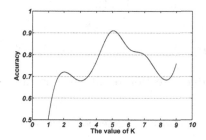

Fig. 7. The accuracy of different k value on detection results

DT Classifier. The algorithm of classification decision tree learning is a process of recursively selecting the optimal feature, and segmenting the training data according to the feature, so that each sub-data set has the best classification process. For the DT classifiers, the "information gain" is similar to the MI model used in feature extraction. Therefore, the DT classifier is very suitable as the basic classifier in the ensemble learning model.

SVM Classifier. Support vector machines are a two-class classification model (or called classifier). Its classification idea is to solve the separation hyperplane that can correctly divide the training data set and have the largest geometric interval for the sample set of positive and negative examples. Since the SVM algorithm was originally designed for binary classification problems, it has unique advantages and better performance in application scenarios to determine application maliciousness. This not only helps us to pay more attention to key samples and eliminate a large number of redundant samples, but also destined to have better robustness of SVM algorithms. Because of the advantages and good classification performance of the SVM algorithm, we also use the SVM classifier as a set of base classifiers in the experiments designed in this paper. Together with the kNN classifier and the DT classifier mentioned above, it forms the base classifier for integrated learning.

4.3 Weighting Combination Strategy

In this paper, we use [apkName, result-DT], [apkName, result-kNN] and [apkName, result-SVM] represent the detection results given by the DT classifier, kNN classifier and SVM classifier respectively. If the detected application is malware, result-DT, result-kNN, and result-SVM set the value to 0. Otherwise it will be set to 1.

The reason why the detection threshold is 0.5 is that the probability of the detection result of the detector on the sample is equal. In detail, we use the linear weighted sum method (LWSM) to calculate the final result. The linear weighted sum is calculated as formula (4):

$$Final - Result = P_1 * X_1 + P_2 * X_2 + \cdots + P_n * X_n = \sum (P_i * X_i) \qquad (4)$$

Based on this, the possible detection results are shown in the following Table 2:

Table 2. Detection results

Result	Classifier		
	DT	kNN	SVM
Benign	1	1	1
Benign	1	0	1
Benign	0	1	1
To be identified	0	0	1
To be identified	1	1	0
Malware	0	1	0
Malware	1	0	0
Malware	0	0	0

If the final result is greater than 0.5, the application will be classified as a benign application. If the final result is less than 0.5, the application is classified as a malicious application. If the result is equal to 0.5, then further manual recognition is required. However, the experimental results show that the probability of this situation is low, about 2–4%.

5   The Results of Experimental

5.1   Experimental Environment

In this experiment,we selected 1044 experimental samples as data sets. Among them, 528 malicious applications are download from the malicious sample set of the virusShare.com [13].And 516 normal Android applications are provided from third-party application market and Google Android Market [14] by using web crawler programs.The experimental environment is: operating system of Windows 10, processor: Intel Core i7, 16 GB of memory, Python 2.7 scripting languages.

5.2   Evaluation Indeces

Classification performance is commonly assessed by the accuracy, true positive rate (TPR), false positive rate (FPR) and precision.

$$Accuracy = \frac{TP + TN}{TP + TN + FP + FN} \tag{5}$$

$$TPR = \frac{TP}{TP + FN} \tag{6}$$

$$FPR = \frac{FP}{FP + TN} \tag{7}$$

$$Precision = \frac{TP}{FP + TP} \tag{8}$$

Here, TP and TN are the numbers of true and false samples that are correctly labeled by the classifier, respectively, and FN and FP are the numbers of true and false samplesthat are incorrectly labeled by the classifier, respectively.

5.3   Analysis of Experimental

In order to verify that the detection method proposed in this paper has good applicability, we conducted multiple classification tests on a large number of samples.

Detection Model Performance. This paper compares the experimental results of whether to use sensitive APIs. The results are shown in Fig. 8.

In Fig. 8, when a set of sensitive API calls are used, the effect of the detection model is significantly improved in terms of accuracy, TPR and accuracy. Among them, accuracy can reach 93% while the precision can reach 95%. In addition, our method proposed in this paper can achieve a TPR of 89%. All in all, our malicious application detection method based on sensitive API has better detection results.

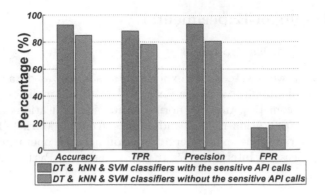

Fig. 8. Detection model performance

The Effect of Detection Model. Figure 9 and Fig. 10 respectively show that our ensemble learing model has a higher detection rate and a lower FPR in the six comparative experiments conducted. Among them, it can achieve the optimal accuracy of 94.8% and the average detection accuracy above 94%.

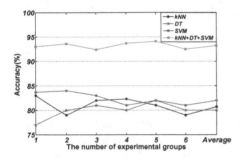

Fig. 9. Contrast of accuracy with different classifiers

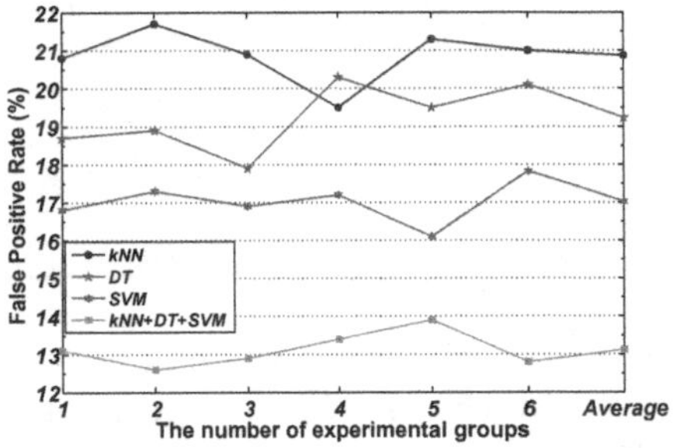

Fig. 10. Contrast of FPR with different classifiers

The Comparison of Different Classifiers. As shown in Fig. 11, we have selected five different classification algorithms to analyze our experimental results. It can be seen that combining the results of TPR and PRE, when the integrated learning model of DT + kNN + SVM algorithm is used, the entire system reaches the best performance. Therefore, they are used as basic classifiers.

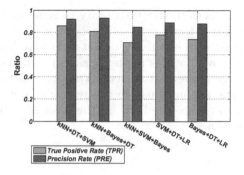

Fig. 11. The effect of different classifiers

The Comparison of Different Weights. We also conducted corresponding experiments on the different weights occupied by the kNN classifier, DT classifier and SVM classifier in the integrated learning module, and gave the classification results of the DT, kNN and SVM classifiers, respectively. Different weights, and the final test result is calculated according to the linear weighted sum. It can be seen from the calculation that there are different weight distribution combinations in total. In this paper, we conducted corresponding experiments on each combination of weights. As shown in Fig. 12, we selected nine representative weight combinations for drawing. It can be seen that the detection result of the whole system is the most optimal when the weight of the DT classifier is 0.2, the weight of kNN is 0.3 and the weight of SVM classifier is 0.5.

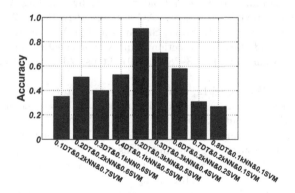

Fig. 12. The effect of different weights

6   Conclusion

This paper proposes an Android malicious application detection model based on integrated learning. By extracting API functions called by Android applications and combining MI models to generate a set of sensitive APIs. Then select the top

20 sensitive API functions as the feature library to generate 20-dimensional feature vectors. The integrated learning model based on kNN classifier, DT classifier and SVM classifier is used to effectively detect unknown Android applications. Experimental results show that this method has achieved good results in Precision, TPR and Accuracy. However, the method proposed in this paper has a high FPR due to the detection value of 0.5. In future research, we will conduct more experimental studies to reduce the FPR on the basis of ensuring the accuracy and accuracy of detection.

References

1. IDC new report: Android account for 87% market share in 2019, iPhone only accounts for 13%. https://baijiahao.baidu.com/s?id=16442723677103280528&wfr=spider&for=pc. Accessed 10 Sept 2019
2. Android. https://www.android.com/. Accessed 30 Nov 2016
3. Enck, W., Gilbert, P., Han, S., et al.: TaintDroid: an information-flow tracking system for realtime privacy monitoring on smartphones. ACM Trans. Comput. Syst. (TOCS) **32**(2), 5 (2014)
4. Burguera, I., Zurutuza, U., Nadjm-Tehrani, S.: Crowdroid: behavior-based malware detection system for android. In: Proceedings of the 1st ACM Workshop on Security and Privacy in Smartphones and Mobile Devices (2011), pp. 15–26. ACM (2011). https://doi.org/10.1145/2046614.2046619
5. Wu, S., Wang, P., Li, X., Zhang, Y.: Effective detection of android malware based on the usage of data flow APIs and machine learning. Inf. Softw. Technol. **75**, 17–25 (2016)
6. Onwuzurike, L., Mariconti, E., Andriotis, P., De Cristofaro, E., Ross, G., Stringhini, G.: MaMaDroid: detecting android malware by building Markov chains of behavioral models (extended version). ACM Trans. Priv. Secur. **22**(2), 1–34 (2019)
7. Kim, T., Kang, B., Rho, M., Sezer, S., Im, E.G.: A Multimodal Deep Learning Method for Android Malware Detection Using Various Features. IEEE Trans. Infor. Forensics and Secur. **14**(3), 773–788 (2019). https://doi.org/10.1109/TIFS.2018.2866-319
8. Zhao, C., Zheng, W., Gong, L., et al.: Quick and accurate android malware detection based on sensitive APIs. In: IEEE International Conference on Smart Internet of Things. IEEE Computer Society, pp. 143–148 (2018)
9. Felt, A.P., Chin, E., Hanna, S., et al.: Android permissions demystied. In: ACM Conference on Computer & Communications Security, vol. 10, p. 627 (2011)
10. Guyon, I., Elisseeff, A., et al.: An introduction to variable and feature selection. J. Mach. Learn. Res. **3**(6), 1157–1182 (2013)
11. Wang, X., Feng, D., Liu, J.: Exploring permission-induced risk in android applications for malicious application detection. IEEE Trans. Inf. Forensics Secur. **9**(11), 1869–1882 (2014)
12. Xiang, C., Yang, P., Tian, C., Liu, Y.: Calibrate without calibrating: an iterative approach in participatory sensing network. IEEE Trans. Parallel Distrib. Syst. **26**(2), 351–356 (2015)
13. Virusshare. http://virusshare.com. Accessed 30 Sept 2017
14. Google android market. https://play.google.com/store/apps?feature=corpusselector. Accessed 30 Jan 2017

Efficient Missing Tag Identification in Large High-Dynamic RFID Systems

Xinning Chen[1], Xuan Liu[1(✉)], Ying Xu[1], Jiangjin Yin[1], and Shigeng Zhang[2]

[1] Hunan University, Changsha 410082, China
{chenxinning,xuan_liu,xuyinghnu,jiangjinyin}@hnu.edu.cn
[2] Central South University, Changsha 410083, China
sgzhang@csu.edu.cn

Abstract. Missing tag detection is an important for many radio frequency identification (RFID) systems. Most existing methods can only work in relatively static systems, where there are no unknown tags entering the system. For highly dynamic RFID systems where tags move into and out from the system frequently, it is challenging to identify missing tags because of the interference from unknown tags. In this paper, we propose a new time efficient protocol called HDMI to identify missing tags in highly dynamic RFID systems. Our idea is to combine the index of the replying slot and the bits replied by the tag to efficiently filter out unknown tags and identify missing tags simultaneously. We theoretically analyze how to set optimal parameters (e.g., frame length and bit number replied by tags) to minimize the execution time while ensuring the recognition accuracy of missing tags. Extensive experimental results show that HDMI identify missing tags with a high accuracy rate, and achieving higher efficiency than state-of-art solutions.

Keywords: Radio frequency identification · Missing tag identification · Dynamic system · Time efficiency

1 Introduction

Radio frequency identification (RFID) has been extensively applied in warehouse management [16], inventory control [10] and supply chain management [3]. An RFID system usually consists of one or more readers and thousands of tags. The tags are small and inexpensive and can be attached to almost every object with a unique ID to identify the item. The reader is deployed with one or several antennas to scan tags in the monitoring area via wireless communications. With RFID technology, the tags can be monitored in nonline-of-sight manner and several tags can be read simultaneously.

Missing tag detection and identification plays an important role in the RFID applications. For example, consider a large storehouse in which there are tens of thousands of goods labeled by RFID tags. We might want to know whether some goods are lost and which good are lost because of thief or delivery. Thus how

© ICST Institute for Computer Sciences, Social Informatics and Telecommunications Engineering 2021
Published by Springer Nature Switzerland AG 2021. All Rights Reserved
H. Jiang et al. (Eds.): ICECI 2020, LNICST 368, pp. 141–156, 2021.
https://doi.org/10.1007/978-3-030-73429-9_9

to monitor these tagged items by identifying the missing tags is a challenging issue. A simple solution is to query all tags' IDs one by one and verify which one is missing. This method, while can find all the missing tags, is time-consuming because most tags are actually not missing. Another method is to broadcast tag ID one by one and identify missing tags by checking whether there are replies from tags matching the broadcasted IDs. This method is not suitable for large RFID systems that contains a large number of tags.

Existing solutions to missing tag identification always make each tag randomly select a slot to return a 1-bit response which shows the tag's existence in each frame. When the reader receives data transmitted from the slot selected by a tag, the reader knows that a tag is present and confirms that it is not missing. Otherwise, if the reader does not receive data as expected, the tag mapping to this slot is considered missing. However, existing missing tag identification protocols assume there are no unknown tags when performing missing tag identification. In practice, tags might enter the system and leave the system frequently. The newly entered tags will interfere with the identification process of missing tags and thus will decrease accuracy of missing tag identification.

Recently there are few works considering the scenario where unknown tags and missing tags co-exist in the RFID system [1, 14]. They generally consist of two phases. In the first phase, the reader deactivates the unknown tags. In the second phase, most existing protocols on missing tag identification can be used to solve the remaining issues. However, these protocols are time inefficient because they handle unknown tags and missing tags separately. Moreover, the interference between unknown tags and missing tags degrades accuracy in both phases.

In this paper, we propose a protocol to identify missing tags in a highly dynamic RFID system in which unknown tags exist. The protocol combines the tag's replying slot location in the frame along with the bits information to determine whether a tag is missing. The recognition and deactivation of unknown tags can be done simultaneously with the identification of missing tags, without the need of two phases as in previous works [1, 14]. The main contributions of this paper are as follows:

- We propose a novel method that can simultaneously recognize unknown tags and missing tags. The idea is to combine both the tag's replying slot location in the frame and the tag's replying bits to increase the ability to distinguish different types of tags. With this method, missing tags are identified with high accuracy and efficiency.
- We carry out theoretical analysis on how to optimize frame length and the reply bits length to minimize the execution time under the condition of ensuring the recognition accuracy of missing tags.
- We conduct extensive simulation experiments to evaluate the performance of the proposed algorithm and make comparison with existing algorithms.

The remainder of this paper is organized as follows. The related work is discussed in Sect. 2. The problem statement is introduced in Sect. 3, and we build the system model. In Sect. 4, we propose our protocol, and then calculate the optimal parameters in theoretical analyses in Sect. 5. Finally, our protocol is simulated to test the performance and summed up in Sect. 6 and Sect. 7 respectively.

2 Related Work

Tag identification, which is one of the most focus aspects in such areas as RFID, is divided into two categories: ALOHA-based protocols [6,7,12] and tree-based protocols [2,4,9]. Most existing missing or unknown tag identification methods are often designed on the basis of ALOHA protocol. In ALOHA protocol, a period of time few greater than sending a tag's echoes is defined as a slot. Several slots are combined into a frame. At the beginning of each frame, the reader first broadcasts the frame size f and a random seed r to all tags in its interrogating. Each tag computes $s = H(ID, r) \bmod f$ to "randomly" select only one slot to respond in a frame after it receives these parameter. If a tag successfully establishes communication with the reader, it will keep silence in the following frame. According to the listening condition of reader, the slots can be divided into three types. If no tag responds in this slot, we call it empty slot. If unique tag responds in this slot and communicates successfully, we call it single slot. If more than one tag reply in this slot, we call it collision slot.

As for the issue of missing tag problem, the study in the missing tag problem can be divided into two directions: missing tag detection and missing tag identification. When we just want to know if something is stolen, it is suitable to adopt the missing tag detection scheme. Luo et al. [13] used multiple random seeds, considering the balance between time-effectiveness and energy consumption, to increase the single-slot probability to detect the existence of missing tag. Yu et al. [15] used Bloom filters which have different lengths, considering the circumstance of multiple-group and multiple-region, to combine the responses from the tags receiving different parameters in each region as a Group filter. Compared with the pre-populated filter, the existence of missing tag can be detect.

If we try not only to judge the appearance of missing tag, but also to pick out which tag is missing, the missing tag identification scheme will go into operation. Li et al. [11] proposed a protocol to make the conflicting tags participate in the reply probabilistically. In this way, the probability of collision slots could be reduced. On the contrary, the chance of single slots increases. Liu et al. [5] applied hash function to adjust some predicted 2-collision and 3-collision slots into single slots in the additional vector, then the tags which are only precomputed on the single slots respond message to reader.

In recent years, most studies focus on solving the topics mentioned above, but these studies have a key limitation that the tag set always contains some unexpected tags whose IDs we never know in reality. In view of the actual situation, few protocol was designed. Shahzad et al. [8] only paid attention to the alteration of the predicted single slots to detect missing tag. Chen et al. [1] proposed a solution including two phases. In the first phase, the reader listened in the predicted empty slots to deactivate the unknown tags. In the second phase, the reader listened in the predicted single slots to identify the missing tag. Similarly, Yu et al. [14] utilized Bloom filter to complete the same tasks in two phases as well. However, with the increasing frequency of in and out warehousing, existing methods are inefficient or even cannot work. The missing tag identification interfered by unknown tags is still a valuable research issue.

3   System Model and Problem Statement

3.1   System Model

We consider an RFID system consisting of three parts: an RFID reader, a back-end server, and a large number of RFID tags. The background server is responsible for coordinating the processing and analyzing the information received by the reader. The reader broadcasts the parameters determined by the server to the tags, and transmits the tag replies back to the server. The readers communicate with tags by using the frame slotted ALOHA protocol [12]. Tag might move in and out from the system frequently. We assume that the background server knows all original tags in the system, and will update the tag list after each missing tag operation.

According to the states of tagged items, tags can be classified into three categories: present tag, unknown tag, and missing tag. In the monitoring field, the tag attached to the item that always exists in the system is called *present* tag. The tag attached to the strange item newly added into the system is called *unknown* tag. The tag attached to the item that has been taken out or lost from the system is called *missing* tag.

3.2   Problem Formulation

Definition 1 (The missing tag identification problem). *The current tags set in the system is N'. The original known tags set of the system is N_0. Referring to the system model mentioned above, there are present tags, missing tags and unknown tags in the RFID system. Given a specified probability α from 0 to 1, we need to identify the missing tag at least $\alpha * N_m$ under the influence of the appearance of an unknown tag, that is*

$$\frac{N_m - M}{N_m} \leq 1 - \alpha, \tag{1}$$

where N_m is the real number of missing tags in the system which is not known in advance but can be roughly estimated by some estimation algorithms. And M represents the number of missing tags actually identified by the reader. For example, if we set the specified probability α to 0.9, while 1000 tags were really lost in the system, only 100 missing tags are allowed to be misidentified on average.

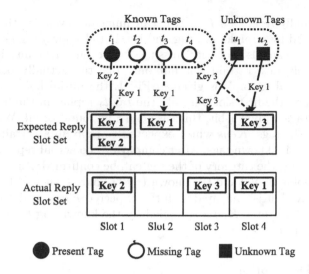

Fig. 1. Illustration of the solution.

4 Protocol Design

4.1 Design Overview

Our proposed protocol HDMI judges the category of a tag by means of slot position and reply Key together. Without divided into two phases, the missing tags can be quickly identified without the interference of unknown tags in a frame. If the tag should reply RN16, a hash function $P = H(id, r) \bmod 2^l$ is used to generate random bits which can be predicted. We define the random bits as the reply Key of the tag, whose total number is marked as L. The figure of random bits is called the reply Key length, which is marked as l. Hence $L = 2^l$. By the replied Key, some expected single slots and some expected collision slots can be able to participate in missing tag identification.

At the beginning, we predict the echoed slot and calculate the reply $Keys$ of the initial known tags. Then the reader starts to query the tags and collects the reply $Keys$ from all interrogated tag. First, some missing tags and unknown tags can be easily distinguish by comparison of pre-single slot and pre-empty slot like the previous works. Then, the remaining unidentified tags can be differentiated by contrasting the slot reply Key set. Finally, all tags are differentiated so that all the missing tags are identified. The details will be given in the next section.

For example, as shown in the Fig. 1, the known tag t_4 should have reply in the fourth slot but it has been lost. Unfortunately, an unknown tag u_2 responds actually in the fourth slot. As we all know, a 1-bit reply can not solve this case, but this situation can be solved easily when each tag has its own Key. It is evident from the Fig. 1 that the known tag t_4 holds the Key 3 while the unknown tag u_2 holds the distinct Key 1. When the reader expects to receive a

Key 3 but actually receives a *Key* 1, it can immediately judge that the actual reply *Key* replied by an unknown tag and the initial known tag t_4 is missing.

This method can also identify missing tags even when multiple tags are expected to reply in a certain slot but only one tag actually participates in the reply. A typical example is given in Fig. 1, the initial known tag t_1, t_2 all choose to reply in the first slot but only the tag t_1 replies in the first slot actually. If all the tags reply a 1-bit, this case can't be found at all. When each tag has a *Key*, all the tags' *Keys* which expected to reply in a certain slot can be known by the initial known tags. After comparing the actual reply *Key* with all the expected *Keys*, the category of the tag can be confirmed. As we can see, the known tag t_1 holds *Key* 2 and the known tag t_2 holds *Key* 1. When the *Key* 2 is actually received, it is compared with the expected *Key* 1 and *Key* 2. We can find that the actual reply *Key* 2 is replied by the known tag t_1 and the known tag t_2 has been lost.

4.2   Detail Description

In this section, we describe the details of the proposed protocol HDMI. And an example is given later.

Firstly, the system backend server generates the required parameters including the random seed r_1 which used to calculate the slot reply position in the frame of a round, and the random seed r_2 which used to calculate reply *Keys* held by the tags, combining the frame size f and the reply *Key* length l. Then the system server predicts the slot positions of all the known tags in a frame based on $S_i = H(id, r_1) \bmod f$, and infers the reply *Key* of each tag from $P_i = H(id, r_2) \bmod 2^l$. Associating with slot position and reply *Key*, the expected reply slot set E of a round is completed. If a expected reply slot selected by no tag, it is recorded as 0 in the expected reply slot set, i.e. $E[i] = \{0\}$.

Secondly, the reader broadcasts the same parameters r_1, r_2, f, l which was used to generate the expected reply slot set E to the known tags. At this moment, only the tags existing the coverage area can receive the parameters broadcast by the reader. With the parameters r_1, r_2, f, l, each tag performs $S_i = H(id, r_1) \bmod f$ as its reply slot position and $P_i = H(id, r_2) \bmod 2^l$ to determine its reply *Key*. Then the reader starts the slot signal at the beginning of each slot, and the tag determines whether replies in this slot according to the value of the counter where its slot position number is stored. If the counter value is not zero, the tag does not reply, storing the value subtracting 1 and waiting for the next slot signal. When the counter value of the tag is zero, the tag replies to the calculated reply *Key*. The reader receives reply *Key* in each slot. According to receive actual reply *Key* in each slot, the real reply slot set R can be formed. When no reply *Key* of the tag is received in a slot, the slot is an empty slot and we sign the reply slot set of this slot as 0, i.e. $R[i] = \{0\}$. When only one reply *Key* is received in a slot which is a single slot, the reply *Key* can be clearly read, i.e. $R[i] = \{Key\ L\}$. When multiple reply *Keys* are received in a slot which becomes a collision time slot, the reader cannot clearly distinguish several reply $Keys$ and we sign the reply slot set of this slot as X, i.e. $R[i] = \{X\}$.

Finally, by comparing every reply slot set of the actual reply slot set $R[i]$ and the expected reply slot set $E[i]$, the missing tags will be identified. The compared results between $E[i]$ and $R[i]$ are listed as follow:

- C1:$E[i] = \{0\}/E[i] = \{Key\ L_i\}/E[i] = \{Key\ 1, ...,$
  $Key\ L_i\}, R[i] = \{0\}$: There should be one or more known tags replying in this slot but no reply is received. Most previous works identify the missing tags through this situation, of course, our protocol HDMI can also identify the missing tags in this situation.
- C2:$E[i] = \{Key\ L_i\}/E[i] = \{Key\ 1, ..., Key\ L_i\}, R[i] = \{Key\ L_{ri}\}$: In this case, our proposed HDMI can use these slots to identify the missing tags. If $E[i] = \{Key\ L_i\}$, $R[i] = \{Key\ L_{ri}\}$, it means a known tag should reply in this slot and a reply is actually received in this slot. Then we compare the expected Key with the actual Key received by the reader. There will be two possible identification results. One is that the tag replying in this slot is a present tag while the expected $Key\ L_i$ is equal to the actual $Key\ L_{ri}$. The other is that the tag actually replying in this slot is a unknown tag and the tag which holds the expected $Key\ L_i$ in this slot is missing while the expected $Key\ L_i$ is not equal to the actual $Key\ L_{ri}$. If $E[i] = \{Key\ 1, ..., Key\ L_i\}$, $R[i] = \{Key\ L_{ri}\}$, it means more than one known tags should reply in this slot and a reply is actually received in this slot. There will also be two possible identification results. One is that the tag replying in this slot is a present tag while the actual $Key\ L_{ri}$ is equal to one of the expected $Key\ L_i$. The other is that the tag actually replying in this slot is a unknown tag and all the known tags which expected to reply in this slot are missing while there is no expected $Key\ L_i$ equaling to the actual $Key\ L_{ri}$.
- C3:$E[i] = \{Key\ L_i\}/E[i] = \{Key\ 1, ..., Key\ L_i\}, R[i] = \{X\}$: There should be one or more known tags replying in this slot but multiple tags actually reply in this slot so that no Key can be read. Therefore, the tags replying in this slot can not be identified and will continue to participate in reply in the next frame.
- C4:$E[i] = \{0\}, R[i] = \{Key\ L_{ri}\}/R[i] = \{X\}$: None of the known tags should reply in this slot but some $Keys$ are received in the slot actually. These must be the $Keys$ of the unknown tags. So, in this case, no missing tag will be identified. In contrast, the unknown tags can be easily distinguished in this slot.

5   Parameter Optimization

5.1   Setting the Key Length l

In this section, we discuss how to set Key length l for each round to achieve the required identification accuracy. For selecting the same slot, each known tag can be completely distinguished only if their $Keys$ are different. Assume that for the ith slot, k tags are expected to choose to reply l-length Key in this slot simultaneously. That being the case, $L = 2^l$ is all the kinds of $Keys$ which a tag may hold. Let $p_{n=k}$ be the probability that a reply Key is different from others. Then

$$p_{n=k} = \frac{L}{L} \cdot \frac{L-1}{L} \cdots \frac{L-k+1}{L} = \frac{A_L^k}{L^k} \tag{2}$$

For the ith slot, where a new tag replies in reality and one of expected tags is missing, the unknown tag can be successfully recognized with the different Key from all the other expected $Keys$ instead of being mistaken for the expected tag that has been lost. As a result, the missing tag can be correctly identified. So the probability p_{uk} that the missing tag can be recognized considering the presence of the unknown is

$$p_{uk} = p_{n=k} \cdot \frac{L-k}{L} = \frac{A_L^k}{L^k} \cdot \frac{L-k}{L}$$

$$= \frac{L}{L} \cdot \frac{L-1}{L} \cdots \frac{L-k+1}{L} \cdot \frac{L-k}{L} = \frac{A_L^{k+1}}{L^{k+1}} \tag{3}$$

which needs to be greater than the specified probability value α, i.e. $p_{uk} \geq \alpha$. With the Stirling Formula $n! \approx \sqrt{2\pi n}(\frac{n}{e})^n = \sqrt{2\pi n}e^{-n} \cdot n^n$, we can get

$$L \geq \frac{(2\ln\alpha - 1)N_0}{2\ln\alpha \cdot f} \tag{4}$$

where $L = 2^l$ is all the possible $Keys$ for a tag in this round. Furthermore, assume that the number of original known tags is N_0 and the frame size is f in this round, there are $k = \frac{N_0}{f}$ excepted tags responding in each slot on average.

5.2 Determining the Optimal Frame Size f

In this section, we discuss how to set frame length f for each round to achieve the best efficiency. For the sake of analysis, we assume that the number of present tags is denoted as N_s, with the number of missing tags is N_m and the number of unknown tags is N_u. Also, the number of original known tags is denoted as N_0, the frame size is f and the reply Key size is l, hence the possible $Keys$ are $L = 2^l$.

Firstly, we discuss the execution time of a round. Let $\rho = \frac{N_0}{f}$, the probability of the empty slot p_0, the single slot probability p_1, and the collision slot probability p_2 are respectively given by

$$p_0 = (1 - \frac{1}{f})^{N_0} = e^{-\rho} \tag{5}$$

$$p_1 = \frac{N_0}{f} \cdot (1 - \frac{1}{f})^{N_0-1} = \rho \cdot e^{-\rho} \tag{6}$$

$$p_2 = 1 - p_0 - p_1 = 1 - (1 + \rho) \cdot e^{-\rho} \tag{7}$$

When the transmission rate is 62.5 Kbps, referring to the EPC C1G2 specification, the time costs of empty slot, single slot and collision slot are

$$t_0 = 182.5\,\mu s, t_1 = t_c = (182.5 + 16l)\,\mu s \tag{8}$$

Therefore, the total execution time of a round t_{total} is:

$$
\begin{aligned}
t_{total} &= f \cdot p_0 \cdot t_0 + f \cdot p_1 \cdot t_1 + f \cdot p_2 \cdot t_c \\
&= f \cdot \{t_0 \cdot e^{-\rho} + (t_0 + 16l) \cdot \rho \cdot e^{-\rho} \\
&\quad + (t_0 + 16l) \cdot [1 - (1 + \rho) \cdot e^{-\rho}]\} \\
&= f \cdot (t_0 + 16l - 16l \cdot e^{-\rho})
\end{aligned} \tag{9}
$$

Secondly, we discuss the number of tags that can be identified in a round. According to the protocol, when the actual reply slot is a collision slot, all the corresponding tags in this slot can not be identified. Let event A be k excepted tags choosing a slot to reply their $Keys$ and event B be the number of tags which actually reply their $Keys$ in this slot. Thus the probability that tags in a slot are not identified is

$$
\begin{aligned}
P\{B \geq 2, A = k\} &= (1 - P\{B = 0|A = k\} \\
&\quad - P\{B = 1|A = k\}) \cdot P\{A = k\}
\end{aligned} \tag{10}
$$

Let the probability of losing a tag be $P_m^k = \frac{Nm}{N_0}$, k excepted tags in this slot are all missing, hence

$$
P\{B = 0|A = k\} = P_m^k \cdot (1 - \frac{1}{f})^{Nu} = (\frac{Nm}{N_0})^k \cdot (1 - \frac{1}{f})^{Nu} \tag{11}
$$

Let the probability of present tag in this slot be $P_s^k = \frac{Ns}{N_0}$, According to the protocol described above, when a reply Key is actually received from a tag, either an unknown tag appears with the k missing tags, or only one known tag exists with $k - 1$ missing tags. Hence

$$
\begin{aligned}
P\{B = 1|A = k\} &= P_m^k \cdot \frac{1}{f}(1 - \frac{1}{f})^{Nu-1} \cdot C_{Nu}^1 + C_k^{k-1} P_m^{k-1} P_s (1 - \frac{1}{f})^{Nu} \\
&= (\frac{Nm}{N_0})^k \cdot Nu \cdot \frac{1}{f}(1 - \frac{1}{f})^{Nu-1} + k \cdot (\frac{Nm}{N_0})^{k-1} \cdot \frac{Ns}{N_0} \cdot (1 - \frac{1}{f})^{Nu}
\end{aligned} \tag{12}
$$

And substituting $P\{A = k\} = C_{N_0}^k \cdot (\frac{1}{f})^k (1 - \frac{1}{f})^{N_0-k}$ with $Eq.$ (17) and (18) into $Eq.$ (16), the probability that the missing tag can not be identified in this slot p_k is:

$$
\begin{aligned}
p_k &= P\{B \geq 2, A = k\} = (1 - P\{B = 0|A = k\} \\
&\quad - P\{B = 1|A = k\}) \cdot P\{A = k\} \\
&= C_{N_0}^k \cdot (\frac{1}{f})^k (1 - \frac{1}{f})^{N_0-k} \cdot \{1 - (\frac{Nm}{N_0})^k (1 - \frac{1}{f})^{Nu} \cdot [1 + k \cdot \frac{Ns}{Nm} - \frac{Nu}{1-f}]\}
\end{aligned} \tag{13}
$$

Since the quantity of tags mapped to this slot k is between 1 and N_0. Therefore, the expected unidentified tags in this slot become $\sum_{k=1}^{N_0} k \cdot p_k$, the expected number of unidentified tags in this round is:

$$
\begin{aligned}
E(Q) = f \cdot \sum_{k=1}^{N_0} k \cdot p_k &= f \cdot \sum_{k=1}^{N_0} k \cdot C_{N_0}^k (\frac{1}{f})^k (1 - \frac{1}{f})^{N_0-k} \\
&\cdot \{1 - (\frac{Nm}{N_0})^k (1 - \frac{1}{f})^{Nu} \cdot [1 + k \cdot \frac{Ns}{Nm} - \frac{Nu}{1-f}]\}
\end{aligned}
\tag{14}
$$

Because $f \gg 1$, the $Eq.$ 20 can be turned into

$$
\begin{aligned}
E(Q) = f \cdot \sum_{k=1}^{N_0} k \cdot p_k &= f \cdot \sum_{k=1}^{N_0} k \cdot C_{N_0}^k (\frac{1}{f})^k (1 - \frac{1}{f})^{N_0-k} \\
&\cdot \{1 - (\frac{Nm}{N_0})^k (1 - \frac{1}{f})^{Nu} \cdot [1 + k \cdot \frac{Ns}{Nm} + \frac{Nu}{f}]\}
\end{aligned}
\tag{15}
$$

Then the number of identified tags is $N_0 - E(Q)$.

Finally, by the total time and the identified tags number in a round, the time average identifying one tag η is give by:

$$
\begin{aligned}
\eta &= \frac{t_{total}}{N_0 - E(Q)} = \frac{t_{total}}{N_0 - f \cdot \sum_{k=1}^{N_0} k \cdot p_k} \\
&= \frac{f \cdot (t_0 + 16l - 16l \cdot e^{-\rho})}{N_0 - f \cdot \sum_{k=1}^{N_0} k \cdot p_k} = \frac{t_0 + 16l - 16l \cdot e^{-\rho}}{\rho - \sum_{k=1}^{N_0} k \cdot p_k}
\end{aligned}
\tag{16}
$$

Substituting $Eq.$ (21) into $Eq.$ (22) gives:

$$
\eta = \frac{(t_0 + 16l) \cdot e^{(\frac{Nu+Ns}{N_0} - 2\frac{Ns}{N_0^2})\rho} - 16l \cdot e^{(\frac{Nu+Ns-N_0}{N_0} - 2\frac{Ns}{N_0^2})\rho}}{\rho + \frac{Nm}{N_0^2} \left[(Nu+Ns) - \frac{2Ns}{N_0} - \frac{N_s^2}{NmN_0} \right] \cdot \rho^2 - \frac{NuNsNm}{N_0^4} \cdot \rho^3}
\tag{17}
$$

In order to minimize the execution time to achieve the best efficiency, we want to get the average time of identifying one tag η as short as possible. In addition, the high efficiency not only to be met in the process of the missing tag identification, but it is also necessary to ensure the accuracy of the identification. To achieve the required accuracy, we refer to $Eq.$ (7) and an equation is used for subsequent analysis as follows:

$$
2^l = \frac{(2 \ln \alpha - 1)N_0}{2 \ln \alpha \cdot f}
\tag{18}
$$

Due to $\rho = \frac{N_0}{f}$, the length of reply Key in this round is given by

$$
l = \log_2 \left(\frac{(2 \ln \alpha - 1) \cdot \rho}{2 \ln \alpha} \right)
\tag{19}
$$

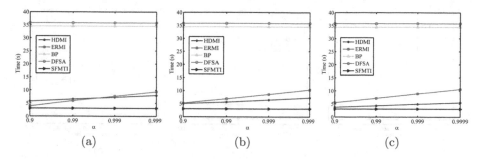

Fig. 2. Impact of the required identification accuracy on the performance of total execution time, where $N_0 = 10000$ and the number of missing tags and unknown tags are set to (a) $N_m = N_u = 1000$, (b) $N_m = N_u = 5000$, (c) $N_m = N_u = 9000$.

Therefore, by substituting *Eq.* (25) into *Eq.* (23), a linear equation with one unknown equation for ρ, η can be obtained. Then, we just need to find out the minimal value of η to get the optimal frame size f.

6   Performance Evaluation

We evaluate the performance of the proposed HDMI algorithm and compare it with state-of-the-art solutions, including ERMI [1] and SFMTI [5]. Meanwhile, we also compare HDMI with two straightforward solutions: the first collects all the tags' ID by using the DFSA protocol and the second broadcasts all tag IDs one by one. We call the former DFSA and the latter one BP.

When evaluating the performance of different algorithms, we consider the following parameters: (1) the missing tag identification accuracy α; (2) the ratio of missing tags and unknown tags in the system; (3) the total number of tags in the system. For each parameter setting, we repeat the simulation experiment 20 times and report the averaged data over the 20 experiments.

6.1   The Impact of Required Identification Accuracy α

In this subsection, we investigate the performance of total execution time under different required identification accuracy α. We set the number of the initially known tags as 10000, i.e. $N_0 = 10000$. We consider three scenarios: (a) the low-dynamic scenario where $N_m = N_u = 1000$; (b) the median-dynamic scenario where $N_m = N_u = 5000$; (c) the highly-dynamic scenario where $N_m = N_u = 9000$. In these tag dynamic case, we obtain the total execution time with different required identification accuracy α, i.e., when $\alpha = 0.9, \alpha = 0.99, \alpha = 0.999, \alpha = 0.9999$ respectively.

Figure 2 shows the identification time in three different scenarios for different α. It can be observed that HDMI consumes less time than all other algorithms except SFMTI when α becomes larger. Actually, HDMI significantly outperforms

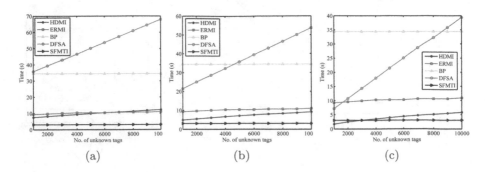

Fig. 3. Impact of the number of unknown tags on the performance of total execution time, where $N_0 = 10000$, $\alpha = 0.9999$ and the number of missing tags are set to (a) $N_m = 1000$, (b) $N_m = 5000$, (c) $N_m = 9000$.

ERMI by reducing total time nearly 50%. SFMTI uses least time and its execution time is not affected by α. However, as to be discussed in the next section, SFMTI cannot satisfy the required identification accuracy. A large portion of missing tags cannot be detected by SFMTI.

6.2   The Impact of the Number of Unknown Tags

In this subsection, we investigate the total execution time under different unknown tag ratios. We set the number of initially known tags to 10000, i.e. $N_0 = 10000$. We also set required identification accuracy to 0.9999, i.e. $\alpha = 0.9999$. First, for the low-dynamic case, we set the missing tag ratios to 10

Figure 3 shows the total execution time in the three different number of missing tags for changing number of unknown tags. In three cases, with the increase of unknown tags, the execution time of most protocols is gradually increasing. Only the total execution time of BP and SFMTI is still unchanged. This is because the execution time of the BP is only related to the number of initial known tags as described in the previous section. The number of initial known tags remains unchanged, so does the execution time. As for the SFMTI protocol, since it does not consider the existence of unknown tags, the change of unknown tags' number has little effect on its execution time. What's more, Fig. 3(c) illustrates that our proposed protocol HDMI is able to better identify the missing tags in the case of higher and higher tag dynamic environment. Compared with the latest method ERMI, our method has shortened the execution time by more than half in this case.

What needs to be explained here is that more and more tags are missing, fewer and fewer tags are actually in the coverage of the reader within the same number of unknown tags. So it takes the less time for DFSA to identify the tags in the current reader range, which is why the execution time of DFSA in the highly-dynamic case is getting shorter and shorter. As can be seen in Fig. 3(c), the execution time is even less than ERMI when the number of unknown tags is 0.

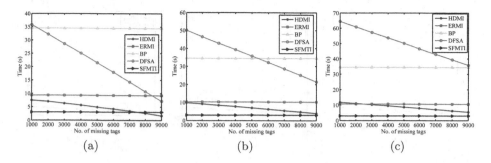

Fig. 4. Impact of the number of missing tags on the performance of total execution time, where $N_0 = 10000$, $\alpha = 0.9999$ and the number of unknown tags are set to (a) $N_u = 1000$, (b) $N_u = 5000$, (c) $N_u = 9000$.

Similarly, the SFMTI silences or identifies tags based on the 1-bit reply from without distinguishing the unknown tags. Many unknown tags are silenced as the identified present tags, which causes the missing tags can not be found out accurately. Thus, its identification accuracy is far from the required identification accuracy α, which will be proved in the following section.

6.3 The Impact of the Number of Missing Tags

In this subsection, we investigate the performance of total execution time under different missing tag ratios. The number of initially known tags is set to 10000 as before, i.e. $N_0 = 10000$. The required identification accuracy is still 0.9999, i.e. $\alpha = 0.9999$. In the three tag dynamic cases, we set the unknown tag ratios to three ratios of the initial known tags, which is 0.1, 0.5, 0.9 respectively, hence $N_u = 1000$, $N_u = 5000$, $N_u = 9000$. Then we vary the number of missing tags N_u from 1000 to 9000 to get the total execution time.

Figure 4 shows the total execution time in the three cases of unknown tags with changing number of missing tags. With the increase of missing tags, the execution time of HDMI, ERMI, DFSA are gradually declining. The DFSA needs to identify all tags in the coverage of the reader currently. The more tags are missing, the fewer tags exist in the area, so the execution time of DFSA varies greatly. Moreover, with the increasing number of missing tags, HDMI can achieve better efficiency than ERMI and DFSA. Even our HDMI's total execution time is less than all the other protocols when N_m is 9000 and N_u is 1000.

What's more, the total execution time of BP and SFMTI are still unchange. The number of initial known tags remains unchanged, so the execution time of the BP remains unchanged. In SFMTI protocol, it identifies the missing tags by the slot position of each known tags, so its execution time almost remains unchanged with the fixed number of initial known tags. Similarly, the SFMTI's identification accuracy does not meet the required identification accuracy α, even if it often has the least time.

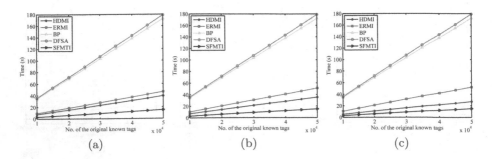

Fig. 5. Impact of the initial known tags N_0 on the performance of total execution time, where $\alpha = 0.9999$ and the number of missing tags and unknown tags are set to (a) $N_m = N_u = 0.1 * N_0$, (b) $N_m = N_u = 0.5 * N_0$, (c) $N_m = N_u = 0.9 * N_0$.

6.4   The Impact of the Number of Initial Known Tags

In this subsection, we investigate the performance of total execution time under different number of initial known tags. We set the number of missing tags N_m equal the number of unknown tags N_u, which is $N_m = N_u = 0.1N_0$, $N_m = N_u = 0.5N_0$, $N_m = N_u = 0.9N_0$ respectively. And the number of initially known tags N_0 varies from 10000 to 50000. The required identification accuracy α is 0.9999.

Figure 5 shows the total execution time of all protocols when $N_m = N_u = 0.1N_0$, $N_m = N_u = 0.5N_0$, $N_m = N_u = 0.9N_0$ respectively. With the increasing number of initially known tags, the execution time of all the protocols is gradually increasing. In these case, both the total number of initial tags N_0 and the total number of current tags N' are increasing, so the execution time of BP and DFSA is getting longer. In particular, our HDMI protocol is more efficient than ERMI, BP and DFSA in the low-dynamic case, the higher-dynamic case and the highly-dynamic case. Especially, the efficiency of HDMI has obvious advantages in the highly-dynamic case. Although SFMTI consumes little time, its identification accuracy does not satisfy α,which will be explained in the next section.

6.5   False Positive Tags

In this subsection, we investigate the performance of the number of false positive tags to study the identification accuracy of the protocols. The BP and DFSA can identify the missing tags by the ID, so their identification accuracy can reach 100%. Next, we will not study the accuracy of these two protocols, but discuss the accuracy of the other three protocols.

Figure 6 shows the number of false positive tags which is identified incorrectly when $\alpha = 0.9999$, $N_m = N_u = 0.1N_0$, $N_m = N_u = 0.5N_0$ and $N_m = N_u = 0.9N_0$ respectively. It can be clearly seen that the SFMTI identifies a large number of false positive tags in the three dynamic cases. From 6(a) and (b), the HDMI and ERMI can meet the identification accuracy α in the low-dynamic case and the higher-dynamic case. However, as can be seen in 6(c), the false positive tags

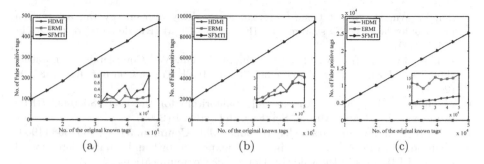

Fig. 6. Impact of the initial known tags N_0 on the performance of the number of false positive tags, where $\alpha = 0.9999$ and the number of missing tags and unknown tags are set to $(a)\, N_m = N_u = 0.1 * N_0, (b)\, N_m = N_u = 0.5 * N_0, (c)\, N_m = N_u = 0.9 * N_0$.

of ERMI can not meet the requirements in the highly-dynamic case. Only our HDMI can identify the missing tags under the identification accuracy in the highly-dynamic case.

7   Conclusion

In this paper, based on the high-dynamic RFID system, where missing tags, unknown tags, and present tags coexist, we propose a protocol HDMI to identify missing tags with high accuracy and efficiency, which maximizes the use of tag reply slot information without the interference of the unknown tags. The core is identifying a tag by the slot reply position with the reply Key. This paper also discuss the optimal frame length f and reply Key length l. Furthermore, we implemented our HDMI to evaluate its performance. Our proposed protocol HDMI can make a great contribution to the convenience of logistics monitoring in practical high-dynamic RFID scenarios.

Acknowledgements. This work is partially supported by the National Natural Science Foundation of China (Grant Nos. 61602167 and 61972140), the Natural Science Foundation of Hunan Province under grant No. 2020JJ3016, and the National Defense Basic Research Plan under Grant JCKY2018110C145.

References

1. Chen, H., Xue, G., Wang, Z.: Efficient and reliable missing tag identification for large-scale RFID systems with unknown tags. IEEE Internet Things J. **PP**(99), 1 (2017)
2. Hou, Y., Zheng, Y.: PHY assisted tree-based RFID identification. In: IEEE Infocom -IEEE Conference on Computer Communications (2017)
3. Jia, L., Xiao, B., Kai, B., Chen, L.: Efficient distributed query processing in large RFID-enabled supply chains. In: Infocom. IEEE (2014)

4. Lei, P., Wu, H.: Smart trend-traversal: a low delay and energy tag arbitration protocol for large RFID systems. In: IEEE INFOCOM (Rio de Janeiro, pp. 2571–2579 (2009)
5. Liu, X., Li, K., Min, G., Shen, Y., Liu, A.X., Qu, W.: Completely pinpointing the missing RFID tags in a time-efficient way. IEEE Trans. Comput. **64**(1), 87–96 (2014)
6. Maguire, Y., Pappu, R.: An optimal Q-algorithm for the ISO 18000-6C RFID protocol. IEEE Trans. Autom. Sci. Eng. **6**(1), 16–24 (2009)
7. Schoute, F.C.: Dynamic frame length aloha. Mob. Commun. **31**(4), 565–568 (1983)
8. Shahzad, M., Liu, A.X.: Expecting the unexpected: fast and reliable detection of missing RFID tags in the wild. In: Computer Communications (2015)
9. Shahzad, M., Liu, A.X.: Probabilistic optimal tree hopping for RFID identification. IEEE/ACM Trans. Netw. **23**(3), 796–809 (2015)
10. Smith, A.D., Smith, A.A., Baker, D.L.: Inventory management shrinkage and employee anti-theft approaches. Int. J. Electron. Finan. **5**(3), 209–234 (2011)
11. Tao, L., Chen, S., Ling, Y.: Identifying the missing tags in a large RFID system. In: Eleventh ACM International Symposium on Mobile Ad Hoc Networking and Computing (2010)
12. Wang, J., Hassanieh, H., Katabi, D., Indyk, P.: Efficient and reliable low-power backscatter networks. In: ACM Sigcomm Conference on Applications (2012)
13. Wen, L., Chen, S., Yan, Q., Tao, L.: Missing-tag detection and energy time tradeoff in large-scale RFID systems with unreliable channels. IEEE/ACM Trans. Netw. **22**(4), 1079–1091 (2014)
14. Yu, J., Lin, C.: Finding needles in a haystack: missing tag detection in large RFID systems. IEEE Trans. Commun. **65**(5), 2036–2047 (2019)
15. Yu, J., Lin, C.: On missing tag detection in multiple-group multiple-region RFID systems. IEEE Trans. Mob. Comput. **PP**(99), 1 (2019)
16. Zheng, Y., Li, M.: Fast tag searching protocol for large-scale RFID systems. IEEE/ACM Trans. Netw. **21**(3), 924–934 (2013)

Internet of Things

Self-secure Communication for Internet of Things

Bin Hao[1,2(✉)] 🆔 and Sheng Xiao[1,2] 🆔

[1] College of Computer Science and Electronic Engineering, Hunan University, Changsha, China
{binhao,xiaosheng}@hnu.edu.cn
[2] National 2011 Collaborative Innovation Center for High Performance Computing, Changsha, China

Abstract. Cryptographic key management is a challenge for the large scale deployment of Internet of Things (IoT) devices. It is difficult to properly setup and constantly update keys for numerous IoT devices, especially when these devices are restricted by size and lack of the key input interface. This paper proposes a lightweight key management scheme which embeds the key distribution and update process into the communication process. The keys are constantly changing as the communication data flowing back and forth between IoT devices. Therefore even if a key is stolen by the attacker, it will quickly become invalid as the communication goes on. The proposed scheme also contains a key initialization protocol which generates independent keys for multiple IoT devices simultaneously. This paper describes the protocols in detail and analyzes its security properties. The practicality of the protocol is verified by experiments.

Keywords: Wireless randomness · Key agreement · Secure communication · Internet of Things

1 Introduction

The Internet of Things (IoT) technology allows the ordinary objects that perform independent functions to achieve interconnection [1]. With the communication ability, IoT devices provide great convenience to people's lives such as to create a smart home, to help monitoring the patients, and to allow a vehicle to sense its surroundings [2].

Since the communication among IoT devices carries the sensitive data which closely associates with the people's private lives, it becomes a prominent target for the malicious attackers [3]. Moreover, IoT devices are often restricted by the form factor and the power supply, the Internet security solutions are not entirely suitable for the IoT environment [4]. One particular challenge for the IoT communication security is the key management. It is difficult to preset cryptographic keys in the IoT devices as they are great in numbers and the IoT device manufacturers have no information about when these devices would be installed and what would be the network topology. It is even more difficult to update the keys in IoT devices as they are often scattered in the fields. It would be desirable

H. Jiang et al. (Eds.): ICECI 2020, LNICST 368, pp. 159–173, 2021.
https://doi.org/10.1007/978-3-030-73429-9_10

to have a key management scheme that allows the IoT devices to negotiate and update the keys by themselves, in the field, with negligible performance penalty. The paper responses to the challenge and proposes a key management scheme that enables self-secure communication for Internet of Things.

Self-secure communication does not rely on the PKI infrastructure or any pre-shared key material. It collects the physical layer randomness in wireless transmissions and converts the randomness into symmetric keys. Unlike traditional physical layer security methods such as [5–8], our scheme does not go deep into the physical channel status or coding schemes. Our scheme embeds the key management in the communication process and takes advantages of the error re-transmission mechanism, therefore minimizes the security overhead on communication bandwidth or delay. The main idea of self-secure communication is to utilize the inevitable packet loss phenomenon in wireless communications. Particularly for the IoT devices, because the transmission power limit, such packet loss phenomenon occurs for both the benign user IoT devices and for any attacker who attempts to eavesdrop the IoT communication.

The main contributions of this paper are:

1. This paper proposes a lightweight key management scheme which allows IoT devices to autonomously establish and update keys without pre-shared key materials or pre-installed public key certificates.
2. The proposed key management scheme supports the secure one-to-many communications and the secure relay communications. These communication modes are essential for IoT applications.
3. The proposed key management scheme considers the abnormal situations such as node failures, power outages, and connection losses. It could be easily implemented into engineering solutions.
4. This paper verified the practicality of the proposed scheme using experiments.

The rest of the paper is organized as follows: Sect. 2 briefs the previous works related to our research. Section 3 describes the proposed self-secure communication scheme. Section 4 verifies the feasibility and robustness of our protocol by experiments. Section 5 summarizes the paper.

2   Related Work

Since the concept of "Internet of Things" was proposed, researchers have been searching for effective key management protocols with the constraint of the limited resources of IoT nodes. The previous works could be roughly divided into three categories: trusted third parties, proxy-based encryption calculations, and batch processing. The key management protocol proposed in [9–11] is based on the public key system of a trusted third party and requires a trusted certification authority to issue a certificate for it or generate and distribute keys. J. Shen et al. [12–14] describe agent-based end-to-end key management protocols. The core idea of these three protocols is to delegate the complex key calculation operations in the public key encryption system to multiple adjacent unrestricted or less-constrained nodes for execution. These nodes are called agents. Each agent participates in the calculation and transfer of a sender's public DH (Diffie-helloman) key, and also participates in the derivation of the public DH key before the sender is constructed. This approach reduces the computational pressure on the communication nodes. References [15, 16] proposed a group key management protocol based on batch processing. The group key is distributed securely to all group members through a key distribution center (KDC). If a node joins or leaves, the KDC will establish the new group key and send it to all group members again.

The above-mentioned protocols are basically aimed at the problem of limited node resources in the Internet of Things, focusing on how to design lightweight key management protocols. However, the Internet of Things has some characteristics that are different from the traditional Internet. First, the nodes cannot be specially monitored and inspected [17, 18]. Some nodes in the IoT system are deployed in some complex geographical environment [20, 21], and it is difficult to achieve real-time monitoring and inspection of each node by a dedicated administrator. This may cause the keys to be lost for a long time without being discovered, leading to a leak. Second, some scenarios lack human-computer interaction interface [22–24]. Some terminal nodes of the IoT system lack the means to interact with key managers, and many devices still need to manually enter the keys regularly to update them. For example, if the smart home requires workers to come to the home to update the keys regularly, and leave an interface for external devices to connect, this is neither convenient nor secure.

3 Self-secure Communication

The main challenge to secure IoT communication is that the IoT devices need to operate in a fully autonomous manner. Therefore, it is necessary to have the IoT devices to negotiate and establish the initial keys *after* the physical deployment of the IoT network and frequently update keys by themselves. Some may argue that to have a public key infrastructure (PKI) with a unified root certificate authority (CA) would help solve the key management problem. However, to have PKI reachable for all IoT devices is over demanding in many application scenarios. To have an interoperable root CA mechanism is even more impractical since IoT devices could come from many independent vendors around the world. In this paper, we propose the self-secure communication scheme that allows IoT devices to autonomously establish and update keys, without the need of pre-shared key materials or public key certificates. Moreover, the self-secure communication is resistant to the key theft attacks. The attacker may obtain the key and compromise the communication security for a short period of time. The communication security could automatically recover as the communication goes on. All these security features are based on the inevitable, random packet losses in the wireless communications among IoT devices.

The self-secure communication involves two phases: key establishment and key updates. In both phases, only symmetric key cryptography is needed. Without loss of generality, this paper uses Alice-Bob-Eve model to illustrate the self-secure communication protocols. As shown in Fig. 1, the attacker Eve is allowed to eavesdropping and injecting the communication between Alice and Bob.

Fig. 1. Secure communication with the eavesdropping attacker

3.1 Notations

Table 1 summarizes the symbols used for the rest of the paper.

Table 1. Point to multipoint key negotiation situation

Symbol	Definition
P_p	The constructed plaintext packet
P_m	The constructed temporary packet
P_c	The constructed ciphertext packet
N	Minimum number of random messages sent by the sender to negotiate the key
M	Minimum number of random messages the receiver uses to negotiate the key
K_0	Initial communication key
K_D	Derived key
K_i	Communication encryption key
α	Communication times parameter
W	Number of communication rounds where the sender stores the key to the hard disk during the communication phase
K_{j*w}	The jth W round key
Ω	Maximum number of retransmissions of the sender during the communication phase

Figure 2 shows the packet format used in the self-secure communication protocols. A data packet contains the following fields: phase identification (Phase), sequence number (Seq), retransmission information (Retran), message length (Len), random data (Rand), communication message (Message) and message authentication code (HMAC), as shown in Fig. 2.

Phase	Retran	Len	Seq	Rand	Message	HMAC

Fig. 2. Packet format

3.2   Key Establishment Stage

It is assumed that Alice and Bob are two IoT devices without any pre-shared secret information, nor do they have any public key certificates installed. Figure 3 illustrates the key establishment process.

– The sender Alice sends a request negotiation packet

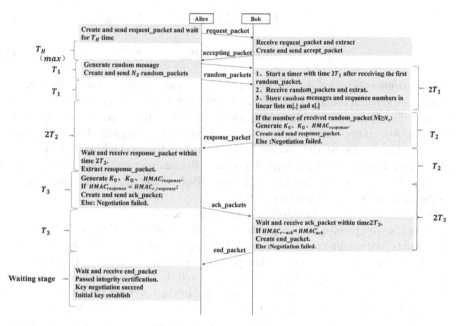

Fig. 3. Key negotiation process

Alice wants to communicate with Bob, so construct a request packet named req_pkt, and fills in the value of each field according to the format of the packet specified by the protocol. At this time, the value of Phase(P) is set to 0; the Retran(R) field is set to 0; The Message(M) field is set to Alice's identification information, such as the MAC address; the Len(L) field is set according to the length of the value of the Message field; the Seq(S) field is set from 0.
Then concatenate these fields to get the Plaintext(P_p):

$$P_p = (P\|S\|T\|L\|R) \tag{1}$$

Next, the P_p is filled by OAEP function to get a temporary data packet Mediantext(P_m), to prevent short message attacks. As shown in formula (2):

$$P_m = f_{OAEP}(P_p, a) \tag{2}$$

A is a one-time random number generated by Alice.
Then calculate the hash value $Hash_A$ according to formula (3).

$$Hash_A = f_{Hash}(P_m) \tag{3}$$

The req_pkt is constructed by connecting P_m and $Hash_A$.

Finally, Alice sends it to the receiver and starts a wait timer with the time set to T_H.

– Receiver sends rcv_pkt

Bob receives and extracts the req-pkt to get Mediantext$_r$($P_{m\cdot r}$) and Hash$_r$. Then the plaintext data packet $P_p \cdot r$ are calculated by the OAEP solution function whose parameter is $P_m \cdot r$. and the Hash$_r^l$ is calculated according to formula (5), which is used to compare with the received HMAC$_r$ to verify the completeness.

$$P_{p\cdot r} = f_{OAEP}^{-1}(P_{m\cdot r}) \tag{4}$$

$$Hash_r^l = f_{Hash}(P_{m\cdot r}) \tag{5}$$

Bob determines whether the equation Hash$_r^l$ = Hash$_r$ is true. If it is true, he will extract the value of the Message field and verify that it conforms to the MAC address format. If so, Bob will consider whether to agree to negotiate a key with Alice. When Bob is unwilling to communication with Alice, he will remain silent. If Bob frequently receives Alice's request packets later, he will reject each packet within T_d time. If Bob also wants to negotiate a key with Alice, he will construct an accept packet named accept_pkt, set the value of the Message field to Bob's identification information, such as the MAC address, and send it to Alice.

– The sender sends a random message to negotiate the key.

If Alice does not receive the accept_pkt sent by Bob within T_H time, she will wait for T_W time before sending the next request. If Alice receives the accept_pkt and passes verification, she will send random data packets as the key negotiation material. Alice sends N_S random message packets rand_pkt$_i$ (i = 0, 1, 2 ..., N_S) within T_1 time. The Phase field of these packets is set to 0; the value of the Seq field are set from 0 to N_S in sequence according to the sending order, which are represented by Seq$_i$ (i = 0, 1, 2 ..., N_S); the value of the Message field are set by information randomly generated by Alice, expressed in Randmsg$_i$ (i = 0, 1, 2 ..., N_S). After sending all the data packets, a timer T_1 is started to wait for Bob's reply, so that Bob has enough time to receive the data packets. The sender saves all random messages that have been sent and the corresponding sequence numbers in memory and hard disk.

– Receiver sends serial number set and generates initial key

After receiving the first rand_pkt, Bob starts a timer with a time of $2T_1$. During this period, each time Bob receives a rand_pkt, he extracts the content of each field and performs integrity and sequence number check. During the period of verification, if there are two packets that have the same sequence number, the two packets will be directly discarded and the sequence number is added to the blacklist; If the random message data packet passes the integrity and the sequence number check, the values of Message field and Seq field will be stored in the memory. Bob keeps two linear lists, m[.] and s[.], m[.] is used to store the value of the Message field, and s[.] is used to store the value of the Seq field in the same order as m[.].

When the $2T_1$ timer expires, Bob starts a $2T_2$ timer and checks whether the number of received packets M exceeds a preset threshold N_r. If M ≥ N_r is not true, Bob reports to the upper layer: the negotiation fails and the initial key cannot be generated; If M ≥ N_r holds, Bob generates an initial key K_0. Assume that all completely received random data is represented as m[i] ($i = 0,1,2, ..., M$), Bob uses the hash function, such as sha256(.), to process m[i] to get the message digest $m_h[i]$ ($i = 0, 1, 2, ..., M$). As shown in formula (6):

$$m_h[i] = f_{Hash}(m[i]) \tag{6}$$

After obtaining the list $m_h[i]$, Bob calculates the Key_0.

$$K_0 = f_{Hash}(m_h[0] + ... + m_h[i] + ... + m_h[M]) \tag{7}$$

In order to ensure the security of the initial key K_0, the derived function is used to encrypt the information to be transmitted, he uses the key derivation function kdf(.) to generates the derived key K_D:

$$K_D = kdf(K_0, 0, 1) \tag{8}$$

Among them, the first parameter in kdf(.) is the initial key K_0 obtained earlier; the second parameter is the encryption salt, which is a random number and is set to 0 in this protocol; the third parameter is the iteration the number of times, which is set to 1 in this formula.

Next, Bob uses digital compression technology, such as Zigzag, to compress the set s[.] to obtain Cpr_s, and then uses the K_D to generate the corresponding message authentication code, which is calculated as shown in formula (9):

$$HMAC_{rsp} = hmac_{md5}(K_D, Cpr_s) \tag{9}$$

Finally, Bob fills Cpr_s into the Message field, and fills the message authentication code $HMAC_{rsp}$ into the HMAC field. After building the rsp_pkt, Bob sends it to Alice.

- The sender receives the serial number set and generates the initial key.

Alice starts a $2T_2$ timer after the T_1 timer ends. Within $2T_2$, if Alice does not receive the rsp_pkt sent by Bob, she abandons the negotiation and reports to the upper layer: the key was not successfully established and the negotiation failed. During this period of time, if Alice receives the rsp_pkt from Bob, she will extract the content of each field. Alice extracts and decompresses the $Cpr_{s \cdot r}$ to get the set $s[.]_r$ received by Bob. Then, she takes the corresponding random message from the memory according to $s[.]_r$, and calculates the initial key K_0, the derived key K_D, and the message authentication digest $HMAC_{rsp}^l$ according to formulas (6), (7), (8), and (9).

Next, Alice compares whether the calculated $HMAC_{rsp}^l$ is the same as the $HMAC_{r \cdot rsp}$ extracted from the rsp_pkt. If not the same, it means that the rsp_pkt was damaged or attacked during transmission, Alice will report to the upper layer: Negotiation failed; If same, it means that the calculated initial key K_0 is also correct.

After the timer of $2T_2$ is over, Alice starts a timer with the time of T_3 again. During this time period, Alice constructs an acknowledgement packet ack_pkt indicating that the initial key K_0 has been generated, and then uses the derived key K_D to calculate the $HMAC_{ack}$ according to the formula (10) and form the ack_pkt and sends it to Bob.

$$HMAC_{ack} = f_{HMAC}(K_D, RandData) \tag{10}$$

Then Alice needs to wait for T_3 time again. After the T_3 time ends, Alice enters the waiting phase. At this stage, Alice cannot leave the effective communication range to avoid missing the data packet sent by Bob indicating that the negotiation is over. If during the waiting phase, Alice does not receive the end-of-negotiation packet, even if both parties have established the initial password, the negotiation still fails. The length of the waiting phase is the maximum time that Alice promises Bob, and it can also be set according to the channel conditions, but the premise is that the length of the waiting phase needs to be guaranteed to the maximum.

– Receiver sends negotiation end packet after the $2T_2$ timer expires, Bob starts another timer with a time of $2T_3$. During this period, if Bob receives the ack_pkt, he will extract the $HMAC_{r \cdot ack}$, $RandData_r$, and the values of other fields. Then, Bob calculates the $HMAC_{ack}^{l}$ according to formula (10) based on the K_D and the $RandData_r$. Determine whether $HMAC_{acl}^{l} = HMAC_{r \cdot ack}$ is true. If it is true, it indicates that Alice has successfully generated the initial key K_0. After the $2T_3$ timer expires, Bob constructs the end packet and sends it to Alice, indicating that the initial key K_0 was successfully generated. If the HMAC verification equation does not hold or Bob does not receive the confirmation message packet within T_3, the key negotiation fails.

– Negotiation successful

In the waiting phase, if Alice receives the end_pkt and passes the integrity authentication, both communicating parties know that the other party has successfully generated the initial key and the negotiation is successful. Next, both parties can enter the secure communication phase.

3.3 Secure Communication Stage

After obtaining the initial key, Alice and Bob could begin their secure communication. Without loss of generality, we assume that Alice sends messages to Bob. A fully duplex secure communication scheme could be naturally extended from the unidirectional protocol.

This section will introduce the stop and wait mode for self-secure communication. In this mode, each time Alice sends a data packet, she will not send the next data packet until she have received the response packet from Bob. The receiver only needs to process and respond to the received data packets. In order to ensure communication efficiency, the protocol stipulates that Alice and Bob store some information needed for communication in the hard disk and memory, respectively. Meanwhile, during the communication process, Alice will retransmit the data packets which Bob did not receive completely.

For the sender Alice, the content stored in memory contains the following information:

– Sequence number of the packet to be sent Seq_s;
– The latest communication key K_i;
– the latest data Msg_i that have been sent and the corresponding $ACK_{s \cdot i}$;
– Communication times α_s;
– The value of the Retran field of the current latest packet; The contents stored on the hard disk include the following:

- The latest key obtained after each W round of communication ends normally is called the W-round key. Store the last two W-round keys $K_{(j-1)*W}$, K_{j*W};
- All data and corresponding serial numbers have been sent.

For receiver Bob, the content stored in memory includes the following information:

- The latest communication key K_i;
- The previous round communication key K_{i-1};
- The sequence number of the next expected received packet Seq_r;
- Communication times α_r;
- The latest data Msg_{i-1} currently received and the corresponding $ACK_{r \cdot (i-1)}$

The contents stored on the hard disk include the following:

- The latest communication key K_i;
- The latest key obtained after each W round of communication ends normally is called the W-round key. Store the last two W-round keys $K_{(j-1)*W}$, K_{j*W};
- All message and serial numbers that have been completely received;

The communication flow between the two communicating parties is shown in Fig. 4:

First, the communication parties Alice and Bob need to initialize the parameters required for communication. If they are communicating for the first time after negotiating the key, the Seq_s of packets that Alice wants to sent and the Seq_r of packets that Bob wants to receive will be initialized to 0; both parties use the key K_0 established during the negotiation phase as the key K_i for this communication.

$$Seq_s = Seq_r = 0$$
$$K_i = K_0$$

If this is not the first communication, they will take out the latest packet sequence numbers Seq_s and Seq_r and the communication key K_i stored in memory to initialize the information parameters of this communication. At the beginning of each communication, Alice and Bob set the parameters for recording the number of communication times to 0, that is, $\alpha_s = \alpha_r = 0$.

Next, the two parties began formal communication. First, Alice needs to create a communication packet, The packet construction process is shown in Fig. 5.

She fills the contents of each field in the packet to get the packet $P_{p \cdot s \cdot i}$. According to formula (2), the $P_{p \cdot s \cdot i}$ is filled by the OAEP function to obtain the mediantext packet $P_{m \cdot s \cdot i}$. Then, the key K_i is divided into three parts K_H, K_E, K_A using a key splitting function, to be used to calculate $HMAC_{s \cdot i}$, $P_{c \cdot s \cdot i}$ and $ACK_{s \cdot i}$ respectively.

$$P_{c \cdot s \cdot i} = encrypted_{AES}(K_E, P_{m \cdot s \cdot i}) \tag{11}$$

$$HMAC_{s \cdot i} = f_{HMAC(K_H, P_{m \cdot s \cdot i})} \tag{12}$$

$$ACK_{s \cdot i} = f_{HMAC((K_A, \, exchange(P_{m \cdot s \cdot i}))} \tag{13}$$

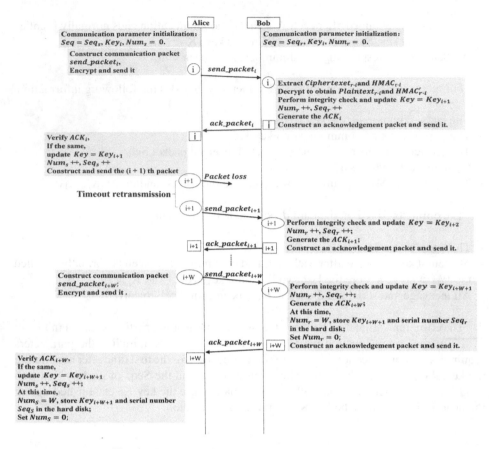

Fig. 4. Stop and wait protocol communication process

Then, the $P_{c \cdot s \cdot i}$ and $HMAC_{s \cdot i}$ are connected to get the send packet sent_pkt, and the $ACK_{s \cdot i}$ is stored to the specified location in memory. Finally, Alice sends send_pkt$_i$ over the wireless channel and starts the timer at the same time.

For the receiver Bob, he extracts communication messages according to the process shown in Fig. 6.

He extracts $P_{c \cdot r \cdot i}$ and $HMAC_{r \cdot i}$ from the data packet according to the length specified by the protocol. Samely, K_i is divided into three parts K_H, K_E, K_A. Next, according to formulas (6) and (7), Bob uses K_E to decrypt the $P_{c \cdot r \cdot i}$ to obtain the $P_{p \cdot r \cdot i}$, and then further extracts the content of each field according to the length of each field. According to formula (12), the message authentication code $HMAC_{r \cdot i}^l$ is obtained.

Next, Bob performs error checking. If $HMAC_{r \cdot i}^l = HMAC_{r \cdot i}$ Bob can consider that the received data packet is complete. Then, Bob checks whether the Seq_{temp} in the Seq field of the received data packet is not greater than the sequence number Seq_r stored in memory. Bob will perform a parameter update operation. If the equation $Seq_{temp} = Seq_r$ holds, Bob will perform the parameter update operation as follow:

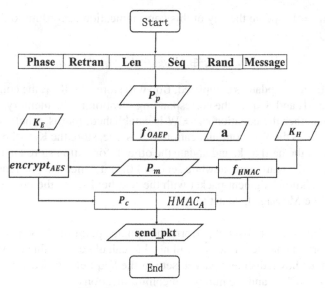

Fig. 5. Packet construction process

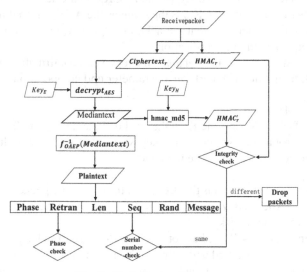

Fig. 6. Packet extraction process

- $Seq_r = Seq_r + 1$;
- According to the formula (13), calculate the acknowledgement message ACK_r based on $P_{m \cdot r \cdot i}$;
- According to the different values of the Retran field, Bob updates the key differently. When Retran = 0, update the key of this communication according to the following formula (14):

$$K_{i+1} = sha256(K_i \oplus (Msg_i \oplus Rand_i)) \tag{14}$$

When Retran $= 1$, update the key of this communication according to the following formula (15):

$$K_{i+1} = sha256(K_i \oplus (Msg_i \oplus Rand_i) \oplus (seq_r - 1)) \tag{15}$$

After the parameter update is completed, Bob will stores the K_{i+1}, the communication data, the Seq_r-1, and Seq_r to the corresponding location in the memory.

- Determine whether the equation $\alpha_r = W$ is established, that is, whether the current communication is the Wth communication. If it is true, store the K_i to the corresponding location on the hard disk, and update the other information stored in the hard disk to the current information, meanwhile set α_r to 0. If it is not true, increase α_r by 1.
- Bob sends a acknowledgment packet with the Seq field set to the updated Seq_r, and the value of the Message field set to $ACK_{r \cdot i}$.

If $Seq_r > Seq_{temp}$, Bob will not perform the update operation, leaving the parameter values in memory unchanged. But Bob still need to calculate the value of $ACK_{r \cdot i}$ meanwhile sends an acknowledgement packet, setting the Seq field to Seq_r, the value of the Message field to $ACK_{r \cdot i}$ and the number of communications α_r.

For the sender Alice, if Alice receives the acknowledgment packet from Bob before the timer expires, she will extract the Seq_{ACK} and $ACK_{r \cdot i}$ in the acknowledgment packet, and check whether the received $ACK_{r \cdot i}$ is the same as the $ACK_{s \cdot i}$ stored in the memory. If the same, Alice can determine that the acknowledgement packet was sent by Bob. Then perform sequence number verification.

If $Seq_{ACK} = Seq_S + 1$, it means that this is the receiver's confirmation of the currently sent data packet, then Alice will perform a parameter update operation:

- $Seq_S = Seq_S + 1$;
- $\alpha_s = \alpha_s + 1$; if $\alpha_s = W$, save the K_i in the hard disk, and set α_s to 0.
- Calculate a new round of communication key K_{i+1} according to formulas (14) or (15), and update the corresponding value in memory;

If $Seq_{ACK} > Seq_S + 1$, it means that Bob went to receive the packet whose sequence number is Seq_{ACK}. Alice sets $\alpha_s = \alpha_r$, $Seq_S = Seq_{ACK}$, and store Seq_S in memory and Seq_S-1 is stored in the hard disk.

If after the timer expires, Alice has not received Bob's acknowledgement packet, the send packet will be retransmitted and retimed. During the retransmission, the value of the Retran field needs to be set to 1, and the random data is regenerated and filled in the Rand field. Connect α_s to the communication data, and recalculate HMAC and ACK. The values of other fields remain unchanged. If the number of data packet retransmissions exceeds Ω, this communication will end, and Alice reports a communication failure to the upper layer.

4 Experiment

To verify that the proposed protocol is feasible and stable in practical application environments, we use Raspberry 3 to design experiments based on Bluetooth channels, and use wireshark software installed in a laptop to simulate an attacker to capture packets. The experiment is divided into two parts: verifying the feasibility and the robustness of the protocol. Next, the experimental content and results will be introduced.

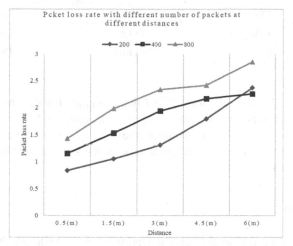

Fig. 7. Pcket loss rate with different number of packets at different distances

– Feasibility experiment
  The key agreement algorithm of this protocol uses the characteristics of unavoidable packet loss and error of the wireless channel. Therefore, to verify the feasibility of the protocol, it is necessary to prove that random events such as packet loss and error will occur in the wireless channel. First, we set up a wireless Bluetooth channel between two raspberry 3 s and transfer packets between them. We set the amount of data packets sent by the sender to 200 each time, and the length of the data packet is 64 bytes. The distance between the two parties of the communication is set to 0.5 m, 1.5 m, 3 m, 4.5 m, and 6 m, respectively. Observe the number of correctly and completely received packets by the receiver to calculate the corresponding packet loss rate. Each experiment was repeated 10 times, and the average value were calculated. The sender sends a packet every 10 ms and sends it continuously. Then we changed the number of packets sent again: 400 and 800. The Fig. 7 shows the relationship between the packet loss rate of the wireless Bluetooth channel, the number of packets sent, and the distance. From the Fig. 7 we can observe that as the distance increases, the packet loss rate increases; meanwhile,as the number of sent data packets increases, the packet loss rate also increases to a certain extent. This proves that packet loss events exist in each case. Thus we proved that our protocol is feasible in practical application scenarios.
– Overhead compare
  This article also compares the overhead with three key update protocols that have been proposed in the reference. The experimental scenario is that one node in the network is compromised and the key needs to be updated to ensure communication security. We compared the transmission overhead, calculation overhead, and space overhead,

Table 2. Overhead comparison

Update algorithm	Transmission overhead	Calculation overhead	Space overhead
[2]	$O(n)$	$O(n)$	$O(n)$
[4]	$O(n)$	$O(1)$	$O(\log n)$
[19]	$O(\log n)$	$O(n)$	$O(\log n)$
Propose	0	$O(n)$	$O(n)$

as shown in the Table 2. We have found that, compared with other protocols, the computational and space overheads of this protocol are relatively large, but because no key or key material needs to be transmitted, the transmission overhead is 0. Compared with other protocols, it has a great advantage in the limited bandwidth and highly dynamic IoT scenarios.

5   Conclusion

This paper proposed a self-secure communication scheme to address the challenges in IoT secure communications. The scheme contributes new ides in the key distribution and the key update processes, so that IoT device nodes could establish secure communication without relying on the pre-shared key materials or the inter-operable public key infrastructure. More importantly, the proposed scheme is resilient to the key theft attacks. The scheme would force the stolen key to become invalid as the communication goes on. The IoT device nodes do not need to intervene and the communication security is recovered. This paper further illustrates a fail-safe implementation strategy for the propose scheme that allows the scheme to be readily converted into an engineering solution.

References

1. Ashton, K.: That 'Internet of Things' thing. RFID J. 101-1 (2009)
2. Xia, F., Yang, L.T., et al.: Internet of Things. Int. J. Commun. Syst. 25, 1101–1102 (2012)
3. Alabaa, F.A., Othmana, M., et al.: Internet of Things security: a survey. J. Netw. Comput. Appl. 88, 10–28 (2017)
4. Romana, R., Alcaraza, C., et al.: Key management systems for sensor networks in the context of the Internet of Things. Comput. Electr. Eng. 37, 147–159 (2011)
5. Jie, C., Liang, Y.-C., et al.: Intelligent reflecting surface: a programmable wireless environment for physical layer security. IEEE Access 7, 82599–82612 (2019)
6. Pinto, T., Gomes, M., et al.: Polar coding for physical-layer security without knowledge of the eavesdropper's channel. In: 2019 IEEE 89th Vehicular Technology Conference (VTC 2019-Spring), pp. 1–5, IEEE, Kuala Lumpur (2019)
7. Xiang, Z., Yang, W., et al.: Physical layer security in cognitive radio inspired NOMA network. IEEE J. Sel. Top. Sig. Process. 13(3), 700–714 (2019)
8. Melki, R., et al.: A survey on OFDM physical layer security. Phys. Commun. 32, 1–30 (2019)
9. Shen, J., Moh, S., et al.: A novel key management protocol in body area networks. In: ICNS 2011: The Seventh International Conference on Networking and Services, pp. 246–251 (2011)

10. Li, Y.: Design of a key establishment protocol for smart home energy management system. In: 2013 Fifth International Conference on Computational Intelligence, Communication Systems and Networks, pp. 88–93. IEEE, Madrid (2013)
11. Sciancalepore, S., Capossele, A., et al.: Key management protocol with implicit certificates for IoT systems. In: IoT-Sys 2015, Proceedings of the 2015 Workshop on IoT Challenges in Mobile and Industrial Systems, pp. 37–42. Association for Computing Machinery, New York (2015)
12. Saied, Y.B., Olivereau, A.,: D-HIP: a distributed key exchange scheme for HIP-based Internet of Things. In: 2012 IEEE International Symposium on a World of Wireless, Mobile and Multimedia Networks (WoWMoM), pp. 1–7. IEEE, San Francisco (2012)
13. Riyadh, M., Affiliated, A., Djamel, T.: A cooperative end to end key management scheme for e-health applications in the context of Internet of Things. Ad-hoc Netw. Wirel. **8629**, 35–46 (2015)
14. Porambage, P., Braeken, A., et al.: Proxy-based end-to-end key establishment protocol for the Internet of Things. In: 2015 IEEE International Conference on Communication Workshop (ICCW), pp. 2677–2682. IEEE, London (2015)
15. Veltri, L., Cirani, S., et al.: A novel batch-based group key management protocol applied to the Internet of Things. Ad Hoc Netw. **11**(8), 2724–2737 (2013)
16. Abdmeziem, M.R., Tandjaoui, D., et al.: A decentralized batch-based group key management protocol for mobile Internet of Things (DBGK). In: 2015 IEEE International Conference on Computer and Information Technology; Ubiquitous Computing and Communications; Dependable, Autonomic and Secure Computing; Pervasive Intelligence and Computing, pp. 1109–1117. IEEE, Liverpool (2015)
17. Jing, Q., Vasilakos, A.V., Wan, J., Lu, J., Qiu, D.: Security of the Internet of Things: perspectives and challenges. Wirel. Netw. **20**(8), 2481–2501 (2014). https://doi.org/10.1007/s11276-014-0761-7
18. He, X., Niedermeie, M., et al.: Dynamic key management in wireless sensor networks: a survey. J. Netw. Comput. Appl. **36**(2), 611–622 (2013)
19. Varalakshmi, R., Uthariaraj, V.R.: Huddle hierarchy based group key management protocol using gray code. Wirel. Netw. **20**(4), 695–704 (2013). https://doi.org/10.1007/s11276-013-0631-8
20. Conti, M., Dehghantanha, A., et al.: Internet of Things security and forensics: challenges and opportunities. Future Gener. Comput. Syst. **78**, 544–546 (2018)
21. Al-Sarawi, S., Anbar, M., et al.: Internet of Things (IoT) communication protocols: review. In: 2017 8th International Conference on Information Technology (ICIT), pp. 685–690. IEEE, Amman (2017)
22. Li, Y.: Design of a key establishment protocol for smart home energy management system. In: 2013 Fifth International Conference on Computational Intelligence, Communication Systems and Networks, Madrid, , pp. 88–93 (2013)
23. Nguyen, K.T., Laurent, M., et al.: Survey on secure communication protocols for the Internet of Things. Ad Hoc Netw. **32**, 17–31 (2015)
24. Abdmeziem, M.R., Tandjaoui, D.: An end-to-end secure key management protocol for e-health applications. Comput. Electr. Eng. **44**, 184–197 (2015)

Characterization of OFDM Based Free Space Optical (FSO) Transmission System Under Heavy Rain Weather

Drissa Kamissoko[1], Jing He[1(⊠)], Macki Tall[1], and Hassana Ganamé[2]

[1] College of Computer Science and Electronic Engineering, Hunan University,
Changsha 410082, China
{idkamis2020,jhe}@hnu.edu.cn
[2] School of Electronics and Information Engineering, Huazhong University of Science and Technology, Wuhan 430074, China
hganame@hust.edu.cn

Abstract. We investigate the performance of OFDM-based FSO transmission link under heavy rain weather conditions in Ségou region, Mali. The proposed system is consisted of a single MZM modulator and a PIN photodiode that performs the optical direct detection. By selecting the convenient values for beam divergence angle and lunch power, the simulation results prove that the generated 42 Gbps OFDM data could be sent up to 1.90 km, using the Carbonneau rain attenuation Model under the worst rain conditions for the considered location.

Keywords: FSO · OFDM · Rain attenuation

1 Introduction

Nowadays, the wireless transmission links that can handle multi gigabit-per-second capacities in both back and front haul links are getting much more attention from researchers and network operators. To satisfy the increasing demand for bandwidth-hungry applications, optical communication systems are an adequate solution. The radio over fiber (RoF) system is widely utilized as a strong and low-cost solution to enhance wireless links capacity and the mobility of users [1–3]. As part of 5G mobile networks, RoF systems are sought to deliver information data from a central station (CS) to a base station (BS). Unfortunately, due to some constraints such as highways crossing or accidental regions, fiber deployment becomes expensive and impracticable. In that case, free-space optical (FSO) can be an ideal alternative to supply the equivalent capacity and quality of the fiber [4]. FSO is a wireless line-of-sight (LOS) technology that provide optical bandwidth connections through invisible light beams. Severe atmospheric attenuation such as rain can degrade the performance of the FSO link. OFDM is a high spectrally efficient modulation technique that can resist strong turbulence and achieve very high-speed transmission as the data is spread over a massive number of orthogonal

H. Jiang et al. (Eds.): ICECI 2020, LNICST 368, pp. 174–183, 2021.
https://doi.org/10.1007/978-3-030-73429-9_11

sub-carriers. OFDM-FSO system is currently being positioned as a possible 5G backhaul and fronthaul solution because it can deliver huge volumes of data at super-fast speeds, without wires.

In [2], a heterogeneous radio access network (RAN) architecture based on a hybrid RoF/FSO front hauling scenario is demonstrated to provide a resilient integration path for currently deployed 4G long term evolution (LTE) systems and the novel 5G technologies. A major drawback of FSO transmission is that bad weather conditions like fog and rain can seriously affect the FSO transmission link. Adjusting some internal parameters such as input power and beam divergence can significantly improve the transmission performance of FSO during bad weather. In [5], an FSO link was designed to transmit 20 Gbps OFDM data through 260 km in clear weather conditions. That link range was reduced to no more than 4-km due to the effects of heavy fog weather. In the paper [6], a hybrid radio over multi-mode/single-mode fiber (RoMMF/SMF)-FSO system was proposed to boost the performance of the 4G-LTE signal for the radio over indoor MMF system in the local area access networks (LAN). Similar to the optical fiber, the FSO can provide hundreds of Gigabit data rates for the broadband transmission links over short distances. In [7], a 200 Gbit/s transmission has been achieved over a 55-m outdoor FSO link by using a single 35 GHz photodiode to deliver a 32QAM dual-carrier signal; a Kramers-Kronig (KK) receiver was applied to achieve the high-capacity transmission. The performance of these systems is severely affected by the signal-signal beat interference (SSBI) caused by the square-law detection of the photodiode. In the paper [8], based on the Marshal-Palmer model and the Carbonneau model, a 16QAM-OFDM FSO communication system was proposed and investigated under heavy-rain weather in Changsha, China. During the worst rain case for a considered location that has a humid subtropical climate, a maximum bit rate of 4 Gbps could be transmitted over 6.3-km transmission distance at a bit-error-rate (BER) performance of 1.0E–3. The reference [9] investigated the impact of beam divergence using binary phase-shift keying (BPSK) and On-Off Keying (OOK) modulation schemes. The adaptive data rate method was used to reduce the BER of the proposed system. Using a narrow beam in the FSO system can generate much higher data rates and increase the link distance. Beam diverging is an indispensable phenomenon on the quality of the FSO communication system. OFDM modulation technique can mitigate the combined effect of beam diverging and atmospheric attenuation. Therefore, the effects of beam divergence on OFDM-FSO system during bad meteorological season remains an important issue to be further explored. By balancing the beam divergence and the input power adequately, the transmission range can be significantly extended without any more additional complexity.

In this paper, based on the heavy-rain weather in Ségou, Mali, a 64 QAM-OFDM baseband data is simulated to establish an FSO link to cover a distance up to 1.9 km at the data rate of 42 Gbps during the heavy rain of 79.9 mm/h. The simulation is carried out to analyze the error vector magnitude (EVM) for different beam divergence angle, the transmitting distance, and the launching power for constant rain rate and data rate. In addition, the proposed OFDM modulation format is assessed by comparing the system performance when using different rain rates as calculated based on the Carbonneau rain attenuation model.

2 Characterization of the FSO Channel Model

To design a transmission link that can resist to the atmospheric turbulence, it is of great importance to characterize the channel with proper model. We study here the impact of the beam divergence on the proposed channel model. The maximum achievable link distance is determined considering the rain attenuation model and the receive power level.

2.1 Receive Optical Power

We consider the situation of optical propagation between points in line of sight (LOS) path. Consider a single mode Gaussian beam of beam divergence angle θ and, a laser emitting a total power P_{TX}, the received power P_{RX} at an aperture of area A at range L equals [4]:

$$P_{RX} = P_{TX} * \frac{A_{RX}}{(\theta L)^2} * \tau * 10^{-\frac{\alpha L}{10}} \tag{1}$$

where α is the atmospheric attenuation coefficient along the LOS path, A_{RX} is receiver aperture size, $\tau = \tau_{TX} * \tau_{RX}$ is the combined transmitter and receiver optical efficiency. As shown in the Eq. (1), the power at the receiver is directly proportional to the transmit power and receiver aperture area, and inversely proportional to the link length and the deviation angle. Exponential part of the equation is related to atmospheric attenuation and it has the strongest influence on the link quality.

2.2 Beam Divergence Impact Analysis

Another factor that sub-serves attenuation of the signal is beam divergence. The received power can be upraised by increasing the transmitter power, the receiver area, or by diminishing the beam divergence of the transmitter beam, which is diffraction limited. The laser beam divergence is directly related to the link range as shown in (2):

$$\theta = \sqrt{\frac{P_{TX}.A_{RX}}{P_{RX}.L} * \tau * 10^{\frac{-\alpha L}{10}}} \tag{2}$$

θ can directly alter the additional noise, provoking the optical signal attenuation. The impact factor of the beam angle can be measured by taking out following term from (2) [8].

$$D_{ivg} = \frac{P_{TX}}{10^{\frac{\alpha L}{10}}\theta L^2} \tag{3}$$

In (3), we can notice that the influence of link length is more than the beam angle. A small increase in link length can introduce high additional noise. On the other hand, we can reduce the effect of increasing distance by adjusting θ, which leads us to a tradeoff between distance and beam divergence of FSO link.

2.3 Rain-Attenuation Models

Rain has pronounced impacts on electromagnetic wave propagation and one of the well-known effects is attenuation of the transmitted wave. Similarly, rain contributes to the degradation of the FSO transmission channel. In general, the rain consists of water droplets whose dimensions can vary from 100 μm to few millimeters. It is measured in attenuation per unit length [10]. The rain-attenuation is caused by geometric scattering due to raindrops. This attenuation $Att_{rain}(dB/km)$ is independent of the wavelength, but theoretically related to the raindrop size distribution, f_I, [11–16] by the following:

$$Att_{rain} = 27.29 \times 10^5 . \int_0^\infty r^2 . f_I dr \qquad (4)$$

where:

r is the diameter of the rain drops (m).

Theoretical prediction of attenuation as a function of rainfall rate (in many cases one hour rate $R(mm/h)$) is determined using the raindrop size distribution and the International Telecommunications Union Radio communication Sector (ITU-R) recommendation [11]. For a certain location and a link distance, f_I can be given by the statistical data of rainfall rate as follows:

$$f_I = N_0 \times e^{(-8,2R^{-0,21}*r)} \qquad (5)$$

with $N_0 = 8000 \, mm^{-1}/m^3$, R is the rainfall rate in (mm/h). In practice, $0.1 \, mm < 2r < 5 \, mm$, which implies that, for the visible light and the infrared windows, the raindrop sizes are very large compared to the wavelength. This means a very large scattering cross section (effective section close to 2). The thickness of the drops, the duration of rain and the climatic zone such as tropical, temperate or equatorial climate may influence attenuation [13]. Then, the effect of Att_{rain} can be generally derived as a function of the rainfall rate using Eqs. (4) and (5).

$$Att_{rain} = \alpha * R^\beta \qquad (6)$$

where α and β are power-law parameters. These parameters depend on the wave length, the rain drop size distribution and the rain temperature. To calculate the attenuation, it is important to make assumption that raindrops have spherical shape. This assumption makes α & β independent of polarization [15, 16]. The rain effect on the FSO link can be analyzed by knowing the rain attenuation on FSO links and corresponding rainfall intensity. Rain intensity is the fundamental parameter used to describe the rain in a given climate zone.

In this paper, the rainfall data of Ségou weather from 2012 to 2016 is studied. Ségou is the 4th administrative region of Mali, a West African country. The city is situated in the middle of the country, and it has a hot semi-arid climate. Two seasons compose the year, the rainy season (from June to September) and the dry season from October to May). Using the rainfall data reported as recorded in the climate and weather information system [18], the maximum rainfall rate within the selected period is shown in Table 1.

The Carbonneau rain-attenuation model is adopted to analyze the performance of FSO link based on the OFDM technique with 64 QAM modulation format. For this model values assigned to the parameters α and β are 1.076 and 0.67, respectively. According to the given parameters in Table 1, based on the rain Carbonneau attenuation model applied to the FSO channel, it can be seen that the rain attenuation is 21 dB/km.

Table 1. Climatic data of Ségou, Mali Latitude: 13°25′54″ longitude: 6°12′56″ latitude above sea level: 288 m

Observation period of the studied rain data	Observation date of the maximum rain intensity	Value of the maximum rain intensity observed (mm/h)	Corresponding attenuation (dB/km)
From 2012 to 2016	2016, July, 20	79.99	21

3 Simulation Setup

In the simulation, we have evaluated the system performance, considering the maximum rain attenuation level calculated from the data collected in the selected location. First, we analyze the impact of the beam divergence on the FSO link in terms of Q-factor and OSNR. Then, we have plotted the variation of the FSO link length and the EVM with respect to laser beam divergence in terms of lunch power. Finally, the constellation diagram of the received 64 QAM-OFDM formats after transmission over the FSO link considering different BD values are shown. Constant data rates of 42 Gbps is maintained during the whole simulation. The proposed OFDM–FSO system is modeled using OptiSystemTM from Optiwave Corp. As shown in Fig. 1, a 64-QAM OFDM baseband signal is used to modulate continuous wave (CW) laser using a single electrode-MZM Modulator (SD-MZM). The MZM modulator has nonlinear properties that can be exploited to eliminate the intermodulation distortion (IMD) and other nonlinear factors inherent to the modulation process [22]. A 20 dB gain optical pre-amplifier (OA) is used to boost the modulated optical signal before it is sent to the receiver through the air. In order to improve the signal strength for direct detection, an optical gain amplifier is inserted at the end of the FSO channel and before the PD.

At the receiver side, the ODD is performed using a single PIN PD. The PD delivers the electrical equivalent of the received optical signal. The low pass filter (LPF) to eliminate the unwanted signal components from the high frequency. Then, the received signal is down-converted to retrieve the original baseband data with the help of the OFDM demodulator and QAM demapper. A constellation visualizer is used to display the scatter plot of the output data. A set of parameters is given in Table 2; these parameters are optimized and used to carry the generated signal to a maximum distance. For the generation of the 42 Gbps baseband OFDM signal, the basic parameters are to be chosen according to the desired data rates [19].

Therefore, a 64 FFT block is used to map the pseudorandom- bit-sequence (PRBS) data, the central subcarrier is loaded with zero, 48 subcarriers are filled with the 64 QAM

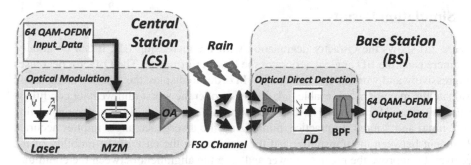

Fig. 1. Principle of FSO communication system

Table 2. System main parameters

System block	Parameters	Values
OFDM	FFT/IFFT size	64
	Number of subcarriers	52
	Data number	48
	Symbol number	80
	CP length	16
	Pilot number	4
FSO link	Max link range	1.9 km
	Beam divergence	2–4 mrad
	Transmitted power	0–30 dBm
	Transmitter aperture	10 cm
	Receiver aperture	30 cm
PIN photodiode	Receiver sensitivity	20 dBm
	Responsivity	1 A/M
	Dark current	10 nA

data shape, and 4 subcarriers are committed for pilot symbols. A CP of 16 samples is used to set a guard interval between OFDM symbols, and two OFDM symbols in the preamble are used for training.

A total of 502 OFDM symbols, including two OFDM training symbols, are used for the transmission simulation. Before the 64-point IFFT operation, the block of 52 QAM and 4 pilot symbols are converted into a block of 64 complex numbers such that zeros are put at positions that correspond to higher frequency subcarriers. Once this block of 64 complex numbers is ready, the last 16 complex numbers of each block are copied to the beginning of the block to constitute the CP. Then, this block of 80 complex numbers is serialized and split into I and Q components before converting to analog waveforms using digital-to-analog converters (DACs). A symbol-rate/subcarrier of 146 Mbaud is chosen in our system that results in a useful bit rate of 42 Gbps using 64-QAM (48 × 146 × 6).

4 Simulation Results

Figure 2a) shows the Q-factor degradation with the increasing BD. It can be noticed that increasing the BD angle deteriorates the link performance. The Q-factor decreases progressively and worsens the link quality. In order to display the OSNR variation and evaluate the maximum achievable link distance under the worst rain weather conditions in the considered location, we have chosen two different values of beam divergence that are 2 mrad and 4 mrad. In practice, minimizing the divergence angle implies accurate alignment between the transmitter and the receiver. In the case of the mobility of the receiver, to improve the received power and ease the alignment between the communicating terminals, an adaptive beam technique is generally implemented [23]. It consists of adapting the divergence angle according to the receiver aperture diameter and the communication distance. In Fig. 2b), we explain the change in the Q-factor vs. optical signal to noise ratio (OSNR) characteristic considering BD values of 2mrad and 4mrad. We assess the performance of the proposed system by adding a certain amount of noise using the Set OSNR block of Optisystem software; then, we measure the corresponding received Q-factor values. It can be noted that a global increase of the OSNR from 5 dB to 60 dB improves the Q value from 15.52 dB to 17.01 dB. It means that a great variation in OSNR has only a slight influence on the Q-factor. The obtained graphs prove that the link can tolerate more attenuation by decreasing the divergence angle. The maximum achievable link distance for 2 mrad and 4 mrad beam divergence is displayed in Fig. 3a). In Fig. 3b), the FSO range and the EVM level are evaluated, varying the input power. At 0 dBm lunch power, a range of 0.8 km with receive power of −14.760 dBm was achieved for 2 mrad; and 0.63 km, −14.947 dBm link range and optical power were achieved for 4 mrad. Upgrading the lunch power to 30 dBm, the link range linearly increases up to 1.90 km for −15.108 dBm received and 1.60 km for −14.557 dBm respectively for 2 mrad and 4 mrad divergence angles. Observing the EVM variation in Fig. 3b), albeit the significant deterioration of the EVM with the increasing power, 30 dBm lunch power can be supported in our proposed system for both selected angle values. It can be observed that after 1.9 km in the heavy and 2 mrad divergence angle, the EVM is less than 8%. It proves that the 64 QAM-OFDM formats are less affected in the FSO channel regardless of the raindrop size. The EVM is 7.8% and the performance is less when transmitting 42 Gbps data rate within an FSO channel using a beam divergence of 4 mrad.

Figure 4 shows the constellation of the 64 QAM-OFDM formats after different transmission distances over the FSO channel. From Fig. 4a), the clear constellation of the received signal after 1.90 km with 2 mrad divergence angle can be seen. The receive constellation after 1.60 km with 4 mrad is less clear and acceptable, as shown in Fig. 4b).

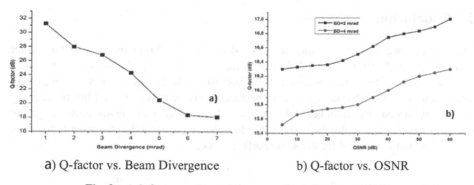

a) Q-factor vs. Beam Divergence   b) Q-factor vs. OSNR

Fig. 2. a) Q-factor vs. Beam Divergence b) Q-factor vs. OSNR

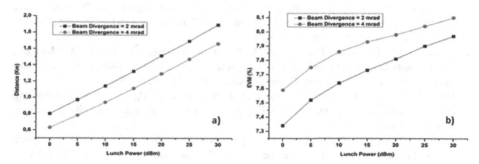

Fig. 3. a) the maximum achievable distance depending on the lunch power b) the EVM values depending on the lunch power.

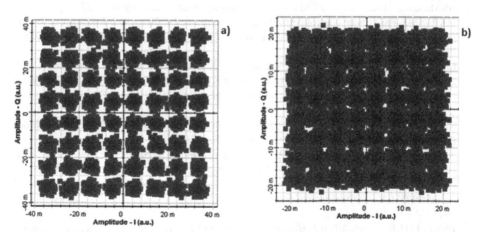

Fig. 4. The constellation of 64 QAM-OFDM format after transmission over FSO link a) with beam divergence angle of 2 mrad, b) with beam divergence angle of 4 mrad.

5 Conclusion

In the paper, we have investigated a 64 QAM-OFDM FSO transmission system under heavy-rain weather in Ségou, Mali. The performance of the OFDM-FSO system based on the Carbonneau Model was assessed. The effect of beam divergence was also analyzed, and results revealed that the quality of the reception decreases on the high broadening of the FSO transmitter light beam. It is evident that raising the transmit power augment the performance and make the system able to achieve prolonged transmission distance. Up to 1.90 km is reached for the same performance.

References

1. Chang, G., Peng, P.: Grand challenges of fiber wireless convergence for 5G mobile data communications. In: 2018 23rd Opto-Electronics and Communications Conference (OECC), Jeju Island, Korea (South), pp. 1–2 (2018)
2. Mufutau, A.O., Guiomar, F.P., Fernandes, M.A., Lorences-Riesgo, A., Oliveira, A., Monteiro, P.P.: Demonstration of a hybrid optical fiber–wireless 5G fronthaul coexisting with end-to-end 4G networks. IEEE/OSA J. Opt. Commun. Netw. **12**(3), 72–78 (2020)
3. Dat, P.T., Kanno, A., Kawanishi, T.: Low-latency fiber-wireless bridge for flexible fronthauling in future mobile networks. In: 2015 10th European Microwave Integrated Circuits Conference (EuMIC), Paris, pp. 305–308 (2015)
4. Pham, A.T., Trinh, P.V., Mai, V.V., Dang, N.T., Truong, C.T.: Hybrid free-space optics/millimeter-wave architecture for 5G cellular backhaul networks. In: 2015 Opto-Electronics and Communications Conference (OECC), Shanghai, pp. 1–3 (2015)
5. Singh, R., Soni, G.: Realization of OFDM based free space optics. In: 2015 International Conference on Green Computing and Internet of Things (ICGCIoT), Noida, pp. 32–35 (2015)
6. Al-Musawi, H.K., et al.: Fundamental investigation of extending 4G-LTE signal over MMF/SMF-FSO under controlled turbulence conditions. In: 2016 10th International Symposium on Communication Systems, Networks and Digital Signal Processing (CSNDSP), Prague, pp. 1–6 (2016)
7. Lorences-Riesgo, A., Guiomar, F.P., Sousa, A.N., Teixeira, A.N., Muga, N.J., Monteiro, P.P.: 200 Gbit/s free-space optics transmission using a Kramers-Kronig receiver. In: 2019 Optical Fiber Communications Conference and Exhibition (OFC), San Diego, CA, USA, pp. 1–3 (2019)
8. Rashidi, F., et al.: Performance investigation of FSO–OFDM communication systems under the heavy rain weather. J. Opt. Commun. **39**, 37–42 (2016)
9. Awan, M.B., Mohan, S.: Analysis of beam divergence and input bit rate for free space optical communication link. In: 2016 IEEE 37th Sarnoff Symposium, Newark, NJ, pp. 83–87 (2016)
10. Grover, A., Sheetal, A.: Improved performance investigation of 10 Gb/s–10 GHz 4-QAM based OFDM-Ro-FSO transmission link. J. Opt. Commun. eISSN 2191–6322, ISSN 0173-4911
11. Report ITU-R F.2106–1 (11/2010), Fixed service applications using free-space optical links. https://www.itu.int/pub/R-REP-F.2106-2007
12. Norouzian, F., et al.: Rain attenuation at millimeter wave and low-THz frequencies. IEEE Trans. Antennas Propag. **68**(1), 421–431 (2020). https://doi.org/10.1109/TAP.2019.2938735
13. Dath, C.A.B., Faye, N.A.B.: Resilience of long range free space optical link under a tropical weather effects. Sci. Afr. **7**, e00243 (2020). www.elsevier.com/locate/sciaf. Accessed 13 Nov 2019

14. Benestad, R.E., Parding, K.M., Erlandsen, H.B., Mezghani, A.: A simple equation to study changes in rainfall statistics. Environ. Res. Lett. **14**, (2019)
15. Shrestha, S., Choi, D.Y.: Characterization of rain specific attenuation and frequency scaling method for satellite communication in South Korea. Int. J. Antennas Propag, Article ID 8694748, 16 (2017)
16. Shrestha, Sujan, Choi, Dong-You: Rain attenuation statistics over millimeter wave bands in South Korea. J. Atmos. Solar-Terrestrial Phys. Volumes **152–153**, 1–10 (2017)
17. Adirosi, E., Volpi, E., Lombardo, F., Baldini, L.: Raindrop size distribution: fitting performance of common theoretical models. Adv. Water Res. **96**, 290–305 (2016)
18. Agence Nationale de la Météorologie (MALI-METEO) Copyright © 2020. Sise Zone Aéroportuaire de Bamako-Sénou I BP: 237 Tél. (223) 20 20 62 04 - Fax: 223) 20 20 21 10 site web: http://www.malimeteo.ml/
19. Li, C.X., Shao, Y.F., Wang, Z.F., Zhou, J.Y., Zhou, Y., Ma, W.Z.: Optical 64QAM-OFDM transmission systems with different sub-carriers. Opt. Photonics J. **6**, 196–200 (2016)
20. Liu, X., et al.: 128 Gbit/s free-space laser transmission performance in a simulated atmosphere channel with adjusted turbulence. IEEE Photonics J. **10**(2), 1–10 (2018)
21. Chen, H., Chi, Y., Lin, C., Lin, G.: Adjacent channel beating with recombined dual-mode colorless FPLD for MMW-PON. IEEE J. Sel. Topics Quantum Electron. **23**(6), 1–9 (2017)
22. Sun, J., Yu, L., Zhong, Y.: A single sideband radio-over-fiber system with improved dynamic range incorporating a dual-electrode dual-parallel Mach-Zehnder modulator. Opt. Commun. **336**(1), 315–318 (2015)
23. Kaymak, Y., et al.: Beam with adaptive divergence angle in free-space optical communications for high-speed trains. http://arxiv.org/arXiv:1812.11233, 28 December 2018

Author Index

Printed in the United States
by Baker & Taylor Publisher Services